Nick Thorner
Louis Rogers

Foundation
IELTS
MASTERCLASS

Student's Book

OXFORD
UNIVERSITY PRESS

2   CONTENTS

CONTENTS 3

GUIDE TO THE IELTS EXAM

IELTS is divided into four modules, taken in the order below

Listening (30 minutes)

The recording for each of the four sections is played once only. The sections become progressively more difficult. In each section you need to answer a series of questions of one type.

Section	Number of items	Text type	Task types
1	10	Conversation in a social context (2 speakers)	completing notes, table, sentences, diagram, flow chart or summary
2	10	Talk or speech in a social context (1 speaker)	short-answer questions
3	10	Conversation in an educational context (2–4 speakers)	multiple-choice questions labelling parts of a diagram matching lists
4	10	Talk or lecture on an academic topic (1 speaker)	sentence completion

Academic Reading (60 minutes)

The three passages contain 2,000-2,750 words in total and become progressively more difficult. The texts are suitable for non-specialist readers. If technical terms are used, they are explained in a glossary.

Passage	Number of items	Text type	Task types
1	11-15	topics of general interest	multiple-choice questions
2	11-15	authentic articles or extracts from books, journals, magazines and newspapers	short-answer questions
3	11-15	at least one has detailed logical argument	sentence completion
			classification
			matching headings
			completing notes, table, sentences, diagram, flow chart
			summary completion
			matching lists / phrases
			locating information in paragraphs
			true / false / not given
			yes / no / not given

Academic Writing (60 minutes)

There is no choice of task, either in Part 1 or Part 2. You must be prepared to write about any topic. The topics will be of general interest and they do not require expert knowledge.

Task	Time	Format	Task types
1	20 minutes	150-word report describing or explaining a table or diagram	Presenting information based on: data, e.g. bar chart, line graph, table a process / procedure in various stages an object, event or series of events
2	40 minutes	250-word essay responding to a written opinion / problem	Presenting and/or discussing: your opinions solutions to problems evidence, opinions and implications ideas or arguments

Speaking (11-14 minutes)

You will be interviewed on your own by one examiner. The conversation will be recorded. The three-part structure of the exam is always the same but the topics will vary from candidate to candidate.

Part	Time	Format	Task types
1	4–5 minutes	introduction and ID check answer questions on familiar topics, e.g. your home, studies, etc.	familiar discussion
2	3–4 minutes	you are given a task verbally and a card with prompts you have a minute to prepare your talk speak for 1–2 minutes answer 1 or 2 follow-up questions	extended speaking
3	4–5 minutes	answer verbal questions about more abstract ideas relating to the topic in Part 2	topic discussion

GUIDE TO THE STUDENT'S BOOK

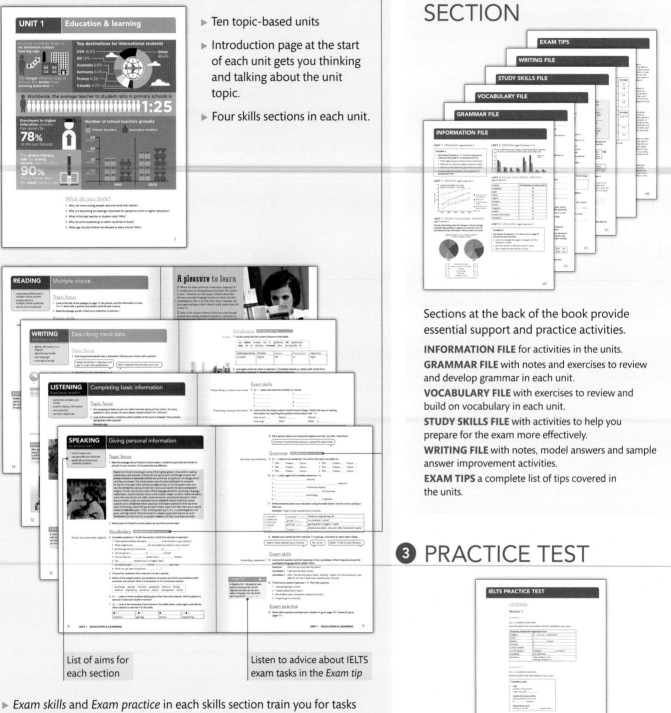

❶ UNITS

▶ Ten topic-based units

▶ Introduction page at the start of each unit gets you thinking and talking about the unit topic.

▶ Four skills sections in each unit.

List of aims for each section

Listen to advice about IELTS exam tasks in the *Exam tip*

▶ *Exam skills* and *Exam practice* in each skills section train you for tasks in the IELTS exam.

▶ Exam challenge activities at the end of each unit get you to put your exam training into practice with corresponding task types in the IELTS Practice test.

❷ SUPPLEMENTARY SECTION

Sections at the back of the book provide essential support and practice activities.

INFORMATION FILE for activities in the units.

GRAMMAR FILE with notes and exercises to review and develop grammar in each unit.

VOCABULARY FILE with exercises to review and build on vocabulary in each unit.

STUDY SKILLS FILE with activities to help you prepare for the exam more effectively.

WRITING FILE with notes, model answers and sample answer improvement activities.

EXAM TIPS a complete list of tips covered in the units.

❸ PRACTICE TEST

Full IELTS Practice test on pages 149–163.

UNIT 1 — Education & learning

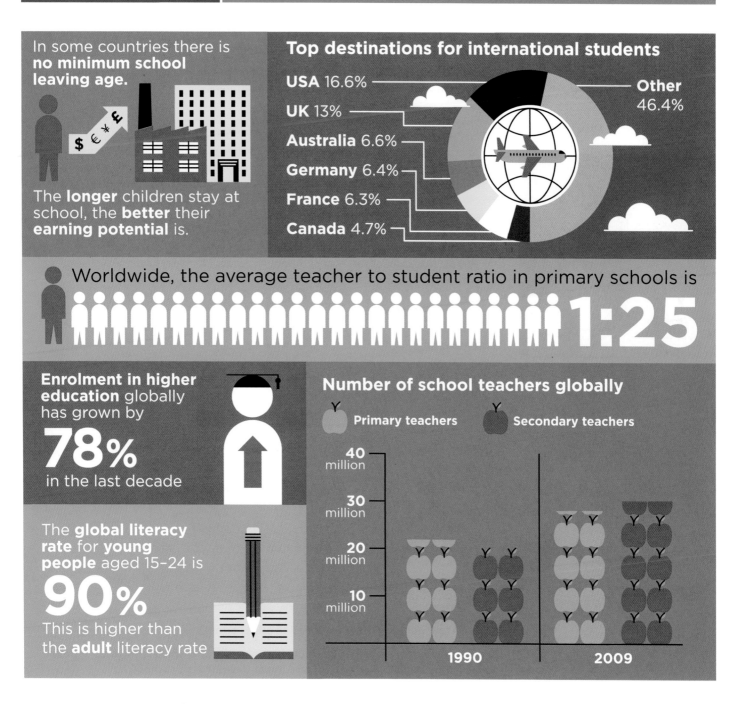

In some countries there is **no minimum school leaving age.**

The **longer** children stay at school, the **better** their **earning potential** is.

Top destinations for international students

- USA 16.6%
- UK 13%
- Australia 6.6%
- Germany 6.4%
- France 6.3%
- Canada 4.7%
- Other 46.4%

Worldwide, the average teacher to student ratio in primary schools is **1:25**

Enrolment in higher education globally has grown by **78%** in the last decade

The **global literacy rate** for **young people** aged 15–24 is **90%** This is higher than the **adult** literacy rate

Number of school teachers globally

- Primary teachers
- Secondary teachers

40 million
30 million
20 million
10 million

1990   2009

What do you think?

1 Why can more young people read and write than adults?

2 Why is it becoming increasingly important for people to enrol in higher education?

3 What is the best teacher to student ratio? Why?

4 Why do some students go to other countries to study?

5 What age should children be allowed to leave school? Why?

▶ extend responses
▶ use gerunds and infinitives
▶ speak about school and university subjects

Topic focus

1 Read the passage about Finland's school system. Underline parts that are similar to schools in your country. Circle parts that are different.

Pupils from Finnish schools gain some of the highest grades in the world in reading, mathematics, and sciences. Children do not start school until the age of seven and **primary school** and **secondary school** are combined, so pupils do not change school until they are sixteen. The school system uses the same **curriculum** for everyone for the first nine years. Most schools are **state** schools, run by the government, and very few **private** fee-paying schools exist. Every pupil studies the same **compulsory** subjects: Finnish, the country's other official language (Swedish), one foreign language, mathematics, natural sciences, history, social studies, religion or ethics, health education, music; they also do arts and crafts, home economics, and physical education. When they are sixteen, pupils are separated into an **academic** stream (traditional school subjects) and a **vocational** stream (practical work-based subjects) for their last three years of schooling. About 50% go into each stream. Apart from that, there are no special classes for **talented** pupils. In fact, formal grades (e.g. A, B, C, or percentages) are not given until high school. The environment is relaxed: pupils don't have to do much **homework** and they don't do compulsory **exams** until they are at least seventeen.

2 Which parts of Finland's school system do you think are the best?

Vocabulary   VOCABULARY FILE » page 121

School and university subjects

3 Complete questions 1–8 with the words in bold from the text in exercise 1.

1 Does everyone follow the same _____ in all schools in your country?
2 What subjects are _____ for all students at school in your country?
3 At what age do you move from _____ to _____ ?
4 Did you go to a _____ or _____ school?
5 Do you have an _____ stream and a _____ stream?
6 Are _____ students put in a higher class?
7 Do teachers give _____ a lot of _____ each day?
8 When do you take compulsory _____ ?

4 Choose four questions from exercise 3 to ask a partner.

5 Which of the subjects below are studied at university and which are studied at both university and school? Write *U* (university) or *U/S* (university/school).

> *psychology geology chemistry geography literature biology medicine engineering economics physics management history*

6 🔊 1.1 Listen to three students talking about their favourite subjects. Which subjects in exercise 5 does each student mention?

7 🔊 1.2 Look at the examples of word stress in the table below. Listen again and add the other subjects in exercise 5 to the table.

● · ·	· ● · ·	● ·	· · ● ·
literature	geology	physics	engineering

8 Tell a partner about your favourite subjects and why you like / liked them.

> At school I loved chemistry because I enjoyed the experiments.

Grammar GRAMMAR FILE » page 116

Gerunds and infinitives

9 🔊 1.3 Listen to six sentences. Tick which time each one refers to.

1 Past .... Present .... Future ....   4 Past .... Present .... Future ....
2 Past .... Present .... Future ....   5 Past .... Present .... Future ....
3 Past .... Present .... Future ....   6 Past .... Present .... Future ....

10 🔊 1.4 Listen again and complete sentences 1–6.

1 I .... sciences.
2 I .... medicine.
3 I .... vocational subjects.
4 I .... into business.
5 I .... psychology.
6 I .... in general.

11 Write sentences about your education using the table below. Use the colour coding to help you.

Example: *I hope to study engineering at university.*

I enjoy(ed) I prefer(red) I didn't like I hate(d) I'd like I hope	studying / to study	literature, engineering, etc.
	going / to go	to university / school
	getting / to get	good grades in English / maths
	doing / to do	physical education, arts and crafts, homework, exams

12 Repeat your sentences from exercise 11 in groups. Comment on each other's ideas.

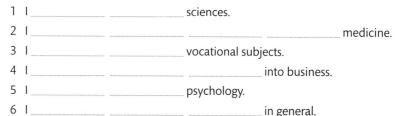

> I hope to study engineering at university.

> Yes, me too.

> Really? I'd like to study literature.

Exam skills

Extending responses 1

13 Look at the question and the responses of two candidates. Which response shows the candidate's language ability better? Why?

Examiner *What do you enjoy learning about?*

Candidate 1 *I like learning about history.*

Candidate 2 *Well, I like learning about history. Actually, I hated it at school because it was difficult, but now I really enjoy reading about the past.*

14 Think how to extend responses 1–4. Then tell a partner.

1 I enjoyed going to school …
2 I hated preparing for exams …
3 We studied many compulsory subjects at school …
4 I hope to go to university …

EXAM TIP 🔊 1.5

In Speaking Part 1, the examiner asks questions about your life. Give full responses and show you can use a variety of language. How long should each response be? » page 145

Exam practice

15 Work with a partner and take turns. Student A, go to page 107. Student B, go to page 111.

LISTENING
EXAM FOCUS: SECTION 1

Completing basic information

- ▸ transcribe numbers and names
- ▸ predict missing information
- ▸ use synonyms
- ▸ set exam objectives

Topic focus

1 You are going to listen to part of a radio interview about *private tuition*. Do many students in your country do extra classes outside school? Do / Did you?

2 Look at the numbers. Underline which syllable of the word is stressed. Then practise saying them with a partner.

Example: *six*ty

60 (sixty)	65 (sixty-five)	21 (twenty-one)	17 (seventeen)	71 (seventy-one)
16 (sixteen)	20 (twenty)	25 (twenty-five)	70 (seventy)	75 (seventy-five)

3 ◖◗ 1.6 **Listen to the information. Circle the numbers in exercise 2 that you hear. Do you hear any *ranges* (e.g. 20–25)?**

4 ◖◗ 1.7 **Listen again. Complete the information with the correct numbers or ranges.**

a students attending additional courses outside school globally: .... %

b students in Colombia, Latvia, the Slovak Republic, the Philippines, and South Africa receiving private tuition in mathematics: more than .... %

c students in Japan and South Korea receiving private tuition: .... % and .... % respectively.

d students in the UK attending extra courses: .... %

e students in East Asian countries receiving private tuition at some point in their school careers: over .... %

f students in Germany receiving private tuition, usually in mathematics: .... %

5 Which piece of information in exercise 4 was the most surprising? Why?

Vocabulary VOCABULARY FILE » page 121

Synonyms 6 Tick the statements you agree with.

1 Learning English requires a lot of **hard work** – skill isn't enough.

2 The **standard** of the education system in my country is very high.

3 My parents' **ambitions for** me are too high.

4 People who have private tuition place too much **importance** on **success**.

5 You only need private tuition when you're really **stressed**, for example during exams.

7 Replace the words and phrases in bold in exercise 6 with the synonyms below.

under pressure	effort	value	expectations of	quality	achievement

8 Ask a partner if they agree with the statements in exercise 6. Use the synonyms from exercise 7 in your discussion.

> *Do you agree learning English requires a lot of hard work?*

> *Yes, I think **effort** is very important ...*

EXAM TIP 🔊 1.8

In Listening Section 1, you often have to write down details such as numbers and names. What's the main thing you can do to avoid making mistakes?

» page 146

Exam skills

Transcribing numbers and names 9 ◀◗ 1.9 Listen and write the numbers or names.

a ....   e ....

b ....   f ....

c ....   g ....

d ....   h ....

Predicting missing information 10 Look at the information about Foxhill House College. Predict the type of missing information by matching the question words below with 1–9.

How much? ....   When? ....   Where? ....

How long? ....   Who? ....   What? O ....

FOXHILL HOUSE
C O L E G E

COURSES AVAILABLE

⁰Introduction to international law

`TIME` 7 p.m.–9 p.m.

`LENGTH` ¹ ....

`COST` £500

`CONTENT` International law and how it works

`NEAREST LOCATION` Nottingham

`NEXT COURSE DATE` ² ....

Intercultural ³ ....

`LENGTH` 12 weeks

`TIME` ⁴ .... –8 p.m.

`COST` ⁵£ ....

`CONTENT` Month one: Language and culture
Month two: Cultural training methods
Month three: ⁶ ....

`NEAREST LOCATION` Derby

`NEXT COURSE DATE` 25th April or 2nd September

Caller's details
Name: ⁷ ....
Address: 20 ⁸ ....,
Oxford, OX1 5NP
Email: ⁹ ....

Exam practice

11 ◀◗ 1.10 Listen and complete the information in exercise 10. Write no more than three words and/or a number for each answer.

What do you think?

12 Read the students' comments. Who do you agree with? Why?

> I go to study clubs after school until 10 p.m. every night. You have to if you want to get into a good university. (Ji Min – South Korea)

> I have extra tuition before exams, but it's more important to do a range of activities after school, like music. (Anders – Sweden)

Study skills

Setting exam objectives Tell your partner your objectives for IELTS. Include information about:

- the score you need / want to achieve
- any score(s) you may already have
- your strengths and weaknesses in each skill
- how many hours a week you plan to spend practising and studying to reach your goal
- what you plan to do outside class to improve your level.

Are your objectives realistic? How do you know?

WRITING

EXAM FOCUS: TASK 1

Describing trend data

- ▸ define information in a diagram
- ▸ describe key trends
- ▸ vary language
- ▸ write about trends

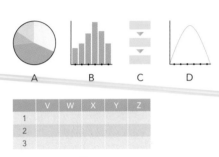

A   B   C   D

	V	W	X	Y	Z
1					
2					
3					

E

Topic focus

1 **How long should people stay in education? Discuss your choice with a partner.**

> *People should stay in education until age 21 to get more qualifications.*

> *Well, it depends what job they want to do ...*

2 **Match the words with diagrams A–E.**

> bar chart ....   line graph ....   pie chart ....   table ....   flow chart ....

3 **Look at the bar chart on the right. Which sentences 1–4 are true or false? Write *T* (true) or *F* (false).**

1 The data covers a period of about 40 years. ....
2 The number of people attending school went down. ....
3 Fewer people went to university than to primary school. ....
4 There were about 400 people in primary education in 1970. ....

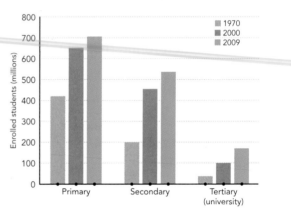

Exam skills

Defining information in a diagram

4 **Write sentences based on diagram titles 1–5 below. Change as much of the language as you can. The first one is done for you.**

1 Visitor numbers to Qatar (Jan–Dec)
   The diagram shows the number of people who visited Qatar from January to December.
2 Hours of television viewing (9 a.m.–9 p.m.)
3 Average length of holiday in days (2000–2012)
4 Average annual distance per person travelled in miles (age 18–80)
5 Females in university education (1900–2000)

EXAM TIP   ⚙   🔊 1.11

When you write a report about a trend diagram like a chart or graph, start by defining what the diagram shows. What's the next thing you should do?
» page 147

Describing key trends

5 **Look at the cartoon. What important information is the man missing?**

6 **Read the two descriptions below of the bar chart in exercise 3. Which one provides a description of the key trend, A or B?**

Description A

> The bar chart shows the number of people in education globally. In all sectors, numbers increased dramatically in the 40 years from 1970 to 2009. Growth was particularly strong in the tertiary sector ...

Description B

> The bar chart shows the number of people in education globally. In 1970 there were 400 million children in primary school. This figure grew to 650 million in 1990. Then in 2009 the number reached 700 million ...

STATISTICS

CHRIS MADDEN

12   **UNIT 1   EDUCATION & LEARNING**

Vocabulary VOCABULARY FILE » page 121

Trends 7 Put the words into the correct columns of the table.

> rose ~~slightly~~ increase rise in significant ~~fall~~ significantly slight fell by dramatic ~~increased~~ from dramatically ~~to~~

Verbs (past tense)	Adverbs	Nouns	Prepositions	Adjectives
increased	slightly	fall	to	slight

8 Look again at the bar chart in exercise 3. Complete extracts a–c below with words from the table in exercise 7. Use the colour coding to help you.

    a in the secondary sector, there was a particularly [1]................. [2]................. in numbers, [3]................. 200 million students in 1970 [4]................. 520 million students in 2009

    b the number of people [5]................. [6]................. in all sectors

    c the [7]................. [8]................. student numbers was smaller in the primary sector, and numbers rose [9]................. just under 300 million overall; while between 2000 and 2009 they only [10]................. [11]................. from 650 million to 700 million

9 Complete the description below with extracts a–c from exercise 8.

> The bar chart shows the number of people who were in education from 1970 to 2009. In general, we can see that [1]......... . Looking in more detail, the bar chart illustrates that the number of students who attended tertiary education rose most dramatically, from just 30 million in 1970 to around 160 million in 2009. The other sectors showed similar trends. We can see that [2]......... . In comparison, [3]......... .
>
> To summarize, there were still more students in primary education in 2009 than in other sectors. However, the ratio between the number of people who attended primary education and the number who attended tertiary education became smaller during the period shown.

Exam skills

Varying language 1 10 Look at the sentences. How are the phrases in bold different?

    1 The number of students that attended tertiary education **rose dramatically**.

    2 There was a **dramatic rise** in the number of students that attended tertiary education.

11 Vary the language of sentences 1–4 by changing the phrases in bold.

    1 The number of female students in Eastern Europe **declined steadily**.

    2 The number of female students in Asia **increased significantly**.

    3 There was a **slight fall** in the number of people studying maths.

    4 There was a **dramatic fall** in the number of people studying law.

12 Why is it useful to be able to vary language in your writing?

Exam practice

13 Describe the key trends of the line graph on page 107. Use the completed text in exercise 9 as a model. Change words where necessary.

READING | Multiple choice

- understand differences in multiple-choice options
- analyse stems in multiple-choice questions
- use the first conditional

Topic focus

1 Look at the title of the passage on page 15, the picture, and the information in lines 15–17. Work with a partner and predict what the text is about.

2 Read the passage quickly. Check your prediction in exercise 1.

Exam skills

Understanding differences in multiple-choice options

3 Read sentences 1–4. Choose which option (a or b) has a similar meaning.

1 Online learning is very important for some schoolchildren.
   a Online learning is more useful than going to school.
   b Using the internet can be an essential part of a child's education.

2 There are more internet connections than there are teachers and classrooms.
   a Some teachers don't use the internet in their classrooms.
   b It is not easy to find schools with internet access.

3 Learning is a result of children's natural curiosity.
   a Learning is a very natural process for children.
   b Learning naturally makes children curious to discover more.

4 Young people enjoy online learning more than traditional lessons.
   a For many school-age people, learning via the internet is better than 'older' methods.
   b Young people are now used to learning with computers and rarely do traditional lessons.

4 Look again at the incorrect options in exercise 3. Underline the words that have different meanings from sentences 1–4.

Using stems in multiple-choice questions

5 Look at the stems in questions 1–5 below and on page 15. Underline the word(s) that will help you to find the information you need in the passage.

1 Research shows that reading
   A is more useful than other types of media.
   B could help you write very well.
   C is only useful when you read romantic stories.
   D isn't effective if your teacher chooses the book.

2 Sugata Mitra's research showed that
   A children from poor countries are more motivated than others.
   B it is not necessary to have a teacher to learn.
   C children from poor countries prefer using computers to attending schools.
   D children can use the internet better than a teacher.

3 Playing computer games probably *won't* help you learn a language
   A as much as using English in other ways.
   B if you watch your friends play them.
   C if you don't play for a long time.
   D if they have too much language content.

4 Doing a language course to help you prepare for an exam
   A will not help you pass.
   B is not as useful as reading if you want to do well.
   C can help you pass as much as reading a book can.
   D works if you read at the same time.

EXAM TIP   ◀))1.12

Multiple-choice questions with four options often feature in the Reading test. How are the stems useful in answering the questions? » page 148

A pleasure to learn

A What's the most useful way of learning a language? Is it writing essays or doing grammar exercises? The answer is clear – whatever you like doing. Evidence shows that the most successful language learners are those who find
5 something they like to do with their chosen language and do it again and again. And it doesn't really matter what the activity is.

B Some of the clearest evidence of this has come through research into reading. Stephen D. Krashen, a professor at
10 the University of California, decided to look at how well language learners who read for fun did in grammar tests. He discovered that they did better than people who went on courses and it wasn't important what books they read.

Factors affecting success in grammar tests	
15	Regular reading	51.6%
Formal study	7.2%
Time in place where language is spoken	5.2%

To prove this, he gave students books from a series called *Sweet Valley High*. These are popular books about teenage
20 life. Although the books' literary quality may not have been high, the readers made good progress in vocabulary, reading, and speaking tests. In a separate case study, a girl improved her writing so much that her angry teacher accused her of copying. The only explanation she had was that she'd
25 started reading regularly.

C It's not just reading stories that can help. Studying online may have a similar effect. Sugata Mitra, a professor at the University of Newcastle, proved that in parts of the world where there are no schools, children will learn to navigate
30 the web in foreign languages and also teach themselves academic subjects if they have access to the internet. Not only that, but the children in his experiments learnt to speak new languages with good accents. Newspapers have also reported a growing group of 'polyglots' (people who
35 speak many languages) who are using the internet to learn unusual languages. One of this group, Timothy Doner, aged 16, now speaks over 20 languages and is currently learning

Hindi through a diet of Bollywood soap operas, pop music, and regular chats with Hindi speakers.

40 **D** Though any contact with a language is useful, some kinds of contact may be more useful than others. For example, studies on computer-gaming in a foreign language have shown that watching people play computer games may help more than actually playing them because you
45 have time to listen to or read the language in the games. This shows that being exposed to a language is not enough; it's necessary to focus on it. Researchers are still unsure about exactly how such casual contact helps learning. But almost certainly, using language repeatedly is essential and
50 enjoyment encourages us to do this. This does not mean that language courses are a waste of time. Krashen also discovered that if you want to take an exam in English, doing a course will be as useful as reading for fun. But doing both is clearly best.

5 The main idea of the passage is that
  A you shouldn't go to school to learn a language.
  B you can learn a language through self-study.
  C it's best to have fun to learn a language well.
  D some learning activities are much more useful than others.

Exam practice

6 **Choose the correct option (A–D) for questions 1–5 in exercise 5.**

Grammar   **GRAMMAR FILE** » page 117

First conditional   7   Underline the sentences with a first conditional structure in the passage on page 15.

8   Complete the sentences in your own words. Use ideas from the passage to help you.

   1   If you do something you enjoy using English, ...

   2   If you choose your own reading materials, ...

   3   If you give children access to a computer, ...

What do you think?

9   Number the factors in order of importance for learning (1 = most important, 6 = least important). Give reasons using sentences with a first conditional structure.

> school buildings   teachers   classmates   money   internet access   a library

> *I think money is an important factor because if you have money, you will ...*

10   Repeat your sentences from exercise 9 in groups. Give each student a point if they give a good reason. Give each student an extra point if they use a first conditional structure.

EXAM CHALLENGE

SPEAKING

1   Look at questions 1-3. Speak for 15 seconds about each one. Ask a partner to listen to you or record your responses.

   1   What did you enjoy about school?

   2   Who was your favourite teacher at school?

   3   Describe a typical day in your education at the moment.

2   Ask your partner or yourself the questions.

   1   Did you give a full answer of 15 seconds?

   2   Did you use gerunds and infinitives correctly?

   3   Did you stress the correct syllables of vocabulary for school and university subjects?

LISTENING

1   Do questions 1-7 in Practice test: Listening on page 149. Try to get at least five answers correct.

2   Did you write down the numbers accurately and spell the names correctly?

READING

1   Do questions 5-7 in Practice test: Reading on page 154. Try to get at least two answers correct in 6 minutes.

2   Did you make notes to help you answer the questions?

WRITING

1   Read the question on page 107. Work alone and write your description. Finish it in 20 minutes.

2   Compare your description with the model answer on page 111-112. Then answer the questions.

   1   Did you rewrite the diagram title for your opening sentence?

   2   Did you give general information at the start of your description?

   3   Did you describe only the key trend(s)?

UNIT 2   Health & medicine

Jiroemon Kimura 🇯🇵

Read the newspaper every day. Ate small portions of food.

116 years
+54 days
(WORLD'S OLDEST MAN)

Christian Mortensen ✚

Had many friends and a positive attitude.

115 years
+252 days

Sarah Knauss 🇺🇸

Lived a quiet life with little stress.

119 years
+97 days

Walter Breuning 🇺🇸

Ate 2 meals a day. Worked until he was 99.

114 years
+205 days

Emiliano Mercado del Toro 🇵🇷

Had a good sense of humour.

115 years
+156 days

Marie-Louise Meilleur 🇨🇦

Worked hard all her life.

117 years
+230 days

Jeanne Calment ⬛

Rode a bicycle until she was 100. Ate a lot of chocolate.

122 years
+164 days
(WORLD'S OLDEST WOMAN)

What do you think?

1 According to the infographic, what is the secret to a long, healthy life?

2 Why do women usually live longer than men?

3 Why do people in rich countries usually live longer than people in poorer countries?

4 How important is diet (what you eat and drink) for staying healthy?

5 How healthy do you think *you* are?

Extended speaking

- ▶ prepare for Speaking Part 2
- ▶ use time clauses
- ▶ use adjectives with a positive or negative meaning
- ▶ improve intonation

Topic focus

1 Tell a partner how you keep fit. Do you use any sports equipment?

2 🔊 1.13 Listen and match descriptions 1–4 with pictures A–D.

A

B

C

D

Vocabulary   VOCABULARY FILE » page 122

Adjectives

3 Which adjectives have a positive meaning (+) or a negative meaning (-)? Write + or -.

convenient .... demanding .... repetitive .... effective ....
dull .... expensive .... beneficial .... ideal .... simple ....

4 Complete the sentences with adjectives from exercise 3.

1 Sitting on a Swiss ball is a / an _____ way of building your muscles.

2 They're also _____ for doing yoga and Pilates.

3 It's a/an _____ way of exercising because you can use it whenever you're at home.

4 It's also _____ to use because it actually remembers your exercise programmes for you.

5 You need a Wii and the *Wii Fit* game to use the Balance Board, which are all quite _____ .

6 They're really _____ as they encourage people to be as active as possible.

7 For some people, jogging can be a bit _____ .

8 They have a variety of programmes to make the exercise as easy or as _____ as you want.

9 Some people find doing the same exercise programmes a little _____ .

5 🔊 1.14 Listen and check your answers.

6 Work with a partner and take turns. Student A: Ask Student B if they have tried any of the fitness activities in exercise 4. Student B: Use adjectives from exercise 3 in your response.

Have you ever tried Pilates?   Yes, it's very **demanding** ...

Grammar GRAMMAR FILE » page 117

Time clauses

7 Match 1–5 with a–e to make complete sentences.

1 A lot of people go running **as soon as**
2 I like to go for a walk **when**
3 **Every time** you take a step,
4 You can see people on exercise bikes **whenever**
5 Some people watch TV **while**

a you go to the gym.
b they get up.
c they're using exercise bikes.
d I've eaten too much.
e the watch counts it.

8 Choose the correct alternative to complete the sentences.

1 I listen to music *while / as soon as* I'm running.
2 I go to the gym after 9 a.m. *when / whenever* it's less crowded.
3 *Whenever / Every time* I can, I try to do yoga.
4 I have a shower *while / as soon as* I finish running.
5 I don't exercise indoors *when / whenever* it's warm and sunny.

9 🔊 1.15 Listen to the sentences in exercise 8. Which speaker communicates more effectively, A or B? Give reasons.

10 Ask and answer questions 1–3 using time clauses. Use appropriate intonation.

> *When do you do exercise?*

> *I go to the gym **whenever** I can.*

1 When do you do exercise?
2 How often do you go running?
3 When do you go to the park?

Exam skills

Preparing for Speaking Part 2

11 Look at the topic on the card. How many *prompts* (things to speak about) are there? How is the last prompt different?

> Describe a person that you know who is very healthy.
> You should say:
> – who they are
> – what activities they do
> – what equipment they use
> and explain what you think about their lifestyle.

12 🔊 1.17 Listen to a student speaking about the topic in exercise 11. Answer the questions below. Then compare with a partner.

1 What words does the student use to begin?
2 Does she speak in a formal or informal style? How do you know?
3 Does she pause between prompts on the card?

Exam practice

13 Speak for 1–2 minutes about the topic on the card.

> Describe an activity you do that can help you keep fit.
> You should say:
> – what it is
> – when and where you do it
> – what equipment or clothing you use for it
> and explain the benefits you get from this activity.

Completing tables

▸ complete tables with information
▸ understand word formation
▸ record word knowledge

Topic focus

1 Match the activities with pictures A–H. Tell a partner which activities you have done and which you think are the healthiest.

| riding a motorbike _____ | playing the drums _____ | scuba-diving _____ | doing karate _____ |
| running _____ | swimming _____ | walking the dog _____ | chopping wood _____ |

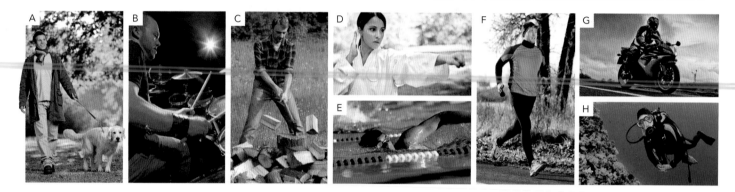

Exam skills

Completing tables

2 Look at the table below. What type of word or number is required in each space? Write question numbers next to the following items.

Gerund (e.g. *running*) ....

Plural / uncountable noun (e.g. *joints* / *exercise*) ....

Singular noun (e.g. *dog*) ....

Third-person verb ....

Number ....

EXAM TIP 🔊 1.18

In Listening Section 2, you may have to complete a table with information. What can help you to decide the type of word or number you need? » page 146

Activity	Benefits	Calories per hour (Based on energy burnt by a 70kg person)
Running (at [1] _____ kph)	Strengthens joints	1,267
Chopping [2] _____	Builds [3] _____	1,196
Swimming (on your front)	Provides low impact exercise	[4] _____
Martial arts	Builds leg strength	704
[5] _____	Reduces stress	844
Playing the drums	[6] _____ tension	281
Walking the dog or playing with [7] _____	Exposes you to fresh air	[8] _____
Riding a [9] _____	Strengthens [10] _____ and thighs	176

3 🔊 1.19 Listen to part of a radio programme about healthy activities. Complete the table in exercise 2.

4 What information in the table was the most interesting or surprising?

Vocabulary   VOCABULARY FILE » page 122

Word formation

5 Complete the questions with the correct form of the word in brackets.

1 What's the best way to _____ stress levels? (reduction)

2 Which activity do you find most _____? (relax)

3 What activity do you think _____ your legs the most? (strength)

4 How do you _____ yourself to do exercise? (motivating)

5 What _____ people's confidence more: team or individual sports? (increase)

6 Ask and answer the questions in exercise 5 with a partner.

Exam practice

7 🔊 1.20 Listen and complete the table. Write no more than three words and/or a number for each answer.

		MONDAY–FRIDAY	SATURDAY	SUNDAY
TIMETABLE OF CLASSES —— **EVENINGS ONLY**	7 p.m.	SPINNING Deborah *45 mins*	3 _____ Paul *45 mins*	6 _____ Moira *45 mins*
	7.45 p.m.	ABS BLAST Paul *30 mins*	AEROBICS Moira *45 mins*	KARATE FOR BEGINNERS Visiting instructor *45 mins*
	8.30 p.m.	CORE BLAST Paul 1 _____	BOXERCISE 4 _____ *45 mins*	ZUMBA Moira *45 mins*
	2 _____	AEROBICS Deborah *1 hour*	5 _____ Moira *1 hour*	PILATES Paul *1 hour*

8 🔊 1.21 Listen and complete the sentences. Write no more than three words and/or a number for each answer.

1 You can't come into the main room without your _____.

2 Spray and _____ have been provided to clean the equipment.

3 As well as clean shoes and loose clothing, you should bring _____.

4 From reception you can buy a _____.

What do you think?

9 Discuss with a partner whether you agree or disagree with the statements. Give reasons.

1 If people don't do exercise, they become stressed.

2 Most people don't have enough time to take exercise.

---

different (adj) = not the same
(don't forget + from)
noun = difference(s)
verb = differ,
e.g. My sister and I differ in that she's lazy!

pron = 'dɪfrənt (2 syllables)

opposite: similar ≠ diverse (see p.3)

Study skills

Recording word knowledge

Look at the notebook extract above. Do you record word knowledge in this way?

Use the notes in the extract to complete the sentences.

1 Chart A is different _____ Chart B.

2 Charts A and B _____ greatly.

3 There aren't many _____ between Chart A and Chart C.

Comparing sets of data

- compare sets of data
- analyse data
- use comparisons with *more/fewer/less* and *than*
- use linking words and phrases

Topic focus

1 Look at the diagram below. Do you get enough sleep for your age?

2 Work in groups and ask how much each person usually sleeps. Do you think the answers are typical for your age group?

Exam skills

Comparing data

3 Look at the table below and the diagram. What percentage of 15-year-olds do <u>not</u> get enough sleep?

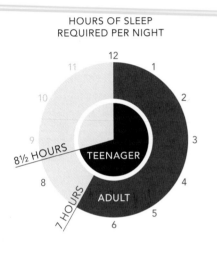

HOURS OF SLEEP
REQUIRED PER NIGHT

8½ HOURS
TEENAGER
7 HOURS
ADULT

Amount of sleep for secondary school students				
	< 3 hours	4–5 hours	6–7 hours	> 8½ hours
12-year-old boys	2%	4%	14%	80%
12-year-old girls	1%	4%	17%	78%
15-year-old boys	2%	5%	28%	65%
15-year-old girls	1%	6%	28%	65%

4 Which sentences are true or false? Write *T* (true) or *F* (false). Correct the false sentences.

1 12-year-olds sleep less than 15-year-olds.

2 Not many students sleep fewer than three hours per night.

3 Many 15-year-olds have more sleep than 12-year-olds.

4 Girls have more sleep than boys.

Grammar GRAMMAR FILE » page 114

Comparisons with *more/fewer/less* and *than*

5 Which sentences in exercise 4 give examples of:

1 *more*, *less*, or *fewer* used immediately before a noun?

2 *more than*, *less than*, or *fewer than* used immediately after a verb?

6 Add *more* and/or *than* to the sentences.

1 The table confirms that 12-year-old students sleep 15-year-old students.

2 Almost 80% of 12-years-olds have more eight hours' sleep, whereas only 65% of 15-year-olds have than eight hours' sleep.

3 There are approximately 12% 15-year-olds who sleep for just six or seven hours 12-year-olds in that category.

4 There are slightly 15-year-olds who sleep for four or five hours 12-year-olds, but overall totals in both groups are very small.

5 It should be noted that male students do not sleep female students.

6 Although younger students sleep older students, many students of both ages are not getting the recommended hours of sleep.

7 Look at the information in 1–5. Choose the correct option to complete each sentence below.

1 magazine sales: 3.7 million per day; newspaper sales: 15 million per day
People buy *less / fewer* magazines than newspapers.

2 spending on holidays: £3,000; spending on clothes: £1,500
People spend *less / fewer* money on clothes than holidays.

3 annual days of holiday in Sweden: 38; annual days of holiday in Italy: 32
Italian people get *less / fewer* holiday than Swedish people.

4 annual hours of sunshine in Spain: 2,665; in Ireland: 1,397
They have *more / a larger amount of* sunshine in Spain than in Ireland.

5 net monthly income in Portugal: €805; in France: €2,128
On average, French people earn *more / larger* than Portuguese people each month.

8 Rewrite the sentences in exercise 7. Start with the words in 1–5 below.

1 People buy more …

2 People spend more …

3 Swedish employees …

4 In Ireland …

5 Portuguese people …

Key phrases

Linking words and phrases

9 Put the words and phrases into the correct columns of the table.

> ~~Similarly,~~   ~~In contrast,~~   Also, (x2)   In conclusion,   By comparison,
> In general,   Likewise,   On the other hand,   To be specific,

Describing similar ideas	Describing different ideas	Describing additional ideas
Similarly,	In contrast,	
Describing a whole table or chart	**Giving details**	**Giving final comments**

10 Complete the paragraph with words or phrases from the table in exercise 9.

> [1] _____ the table confirms that 12-year-old students sleep more than 15-year-old students. [2] _____ almost 80% of 12-years-olds have more than eight hours' sleep, whereas only 65% of 15-year-olds have more than eight hours' sleep. [3] _____ there are 12% more 15-year-olds who sleep for just six to seven hours than 12-year-olds in that category. [4] _____ there are slightly more 15-year-olds who sleep for four to five hours than 12-year-olds, but overall totals in both groups are very small. [5] _____ it should be noted that male students do not sleep more than female students. [6] _____ although younger students sleep more than older students, many students of both ages are not getting the recommended hours of sleep.

Exam skills

Analysing data

11 Look at the bar chart on page 107. What information do you think is the most important?

12 Look at the general statement about the bar chart. How could it be improved?

> In general, we can see that people in Bangladesh have the most sleep problems.

EXAM TIP   🔊 1.22

When you write about tables (and also bar charts or pie charts), look for key similarities and differences between the categories. What should you then do with this information? » page 147

Exam practice

13 Do the task below with reference to the bar chart on page 107. Spend about 20 minutes on this task.

The chart shows differences between countries in the number of sleep problems that are reported. Summarize the information by selecting and reporting the main features and making comparisons where relevant. Write at least 150 words.

- understand difficult words
  in passages
- recognize suffixes

Topic focus

1 Discuss the questions.

1 Is it acceptable for sportspeople to use legal drugs such as food supplements?

2 Would you take a pill if doctors said it could make you more intelligent?

3 Would you ever have an operation to make yourself more beautiful?

2 Read the passage on page 25 quickly. Is it about:

1 the differences between humans and robots?

2 using new medical research to cure sick people?

3 new ways of using medical discoveries?

Exam skills

Understanding difficult words

3 How are words 1–6 used in the passage? Write the correct part of speech.

1 condition (line 12) _____noun_____   4 enhancement (line 42) _____

2 side-effects (line 17) _____   5 retinas (line 45) _____

3 temporarily (line 21) _____   6 implants (line 49) _____

EXAM TIP   🔊 1.23

You won't know the meaning of every word in the passages in the Reading test. Understanding new or difficult words can be challenging. What three things can you do to help yourself? » page 148

4 Read the sentences in the passage that contain the words in exercise 3. Then choose the correct option below without using a dictionary.

1 *Side-effects* are probably *good / bad* things.

2 *Temporarily* probably means for a *short / long* time.

3 *Implants* are probably *natural / man-made*.

4 *Retinas* are probably parts of the *eye / arms and legs*.

5 A *condition* is probably a *problem / benefit*.

6 *Enhancement* probably means something is *improved / made worse*.

5 Work in groups and scan the passage for the medical words below. Write the line number next to each word. Who can find and underline the words quickest?

_____ Modafinil   _____ Ritalin   _____ muscle atrophy   _____ ADHD

_____ TDCS   _____ strokes   _____ anabolic steroids   _____ narcolepsy

6 Which words in exercise 5 are medical treatments or problems? Write *T* (treatment) or *P* (problem). Use the context to help you.

Vocabulary   **VOCABULARY FILE » page 122**

Suffixes

7 Underline the suffix of each word in bold in the text. Then write the suffixes in the table below.

Example: *sickness*

Part of speech	Suffixes
Noun	-ness
Verb	
Adjective	
Adverb	

Medicine for the healthy

A The main purpose of medicine has always been to treat **sickness**. But recent **medical** advances are now promising to change the lives of **healthy** people, too. We are entering a new age of medicine in which pharmaceuticals and
5 bio-technology designed to treat the sick may soon make people's minds and bodies much more **powerful**.

B Students have often taken caffeine (in the form of coffee) to stay awake and think **clearly** while they study. However, one in ten students at the University of Cambridge has
10 now admitted taking **medication** to help them work for longer. The pills **commonly** used are Ritalin, a medicine used to treat the brain condition ADHD* which stops people concentrating, and Modafinil, which treats the 'sudden sleep' disorder, narcolepsy. Both these medicines
15 work by stimulating brain activity in patients, but a few healthy students take them to stay alert and focused for longer periods of time. Although short-term side-effects can appear to be minimal, regular use is likely to be dangerous. For example, one student used Modafinil for four days
20 to help her revise for an exam. She passed the exam but then collapsed, went blind temporarily and spent the night in hospital.

C Another way of enhancing brain activity in medicine is also available. TDCS* involves giving small electrical
25 currents to the brain. This therapy has been used, especially to treat people who have lost their memories after strokes. Brain scientist Roi Cohen Kadosh, at the University of Oxford, has carried out research that indicates that TDCS can also make healthy people perform better in maths tests.
30 Surprisingly, the effects seem to last for up to six months. Scientists are now discussing the possibility of a battery-powered cap (nicknamed 'The Zap Cap') that people could buy to stimulate the brain in the same way. This may prove to be relatively **inexpensive** but the success of the effects of
35 such a product cannot be guaranteed.

D Of course, it's not only the healthy brain that could benefit from medical advances. For many years, sportspeople have managed to improve their all-round physical power illegally by using anabolic steroids – drugs
40 designed originally to prevent the disappearance of muscles through muscle atrophy. However, new research is promising far more powerful forms of **enhancement**. Scientists have become increasingly more skilled at reproducing parts of the body that have stopped working.
45 For example, they can now implant new retinas into the eyes of blind people, or provide **robotic** limbs, controlled by the brain, to people who have lost arms or legs. So how could the healthy benefit from this technology? Some have **suggested** security guards could have eye implants to help
50 them see in the dark, or that soldiers might wear extra legs or 'smart trousers' to help them run across difficult terrain. In fact, the first commercially **available** 'wearable robot' has already been launched, so soon people may be able to run 20 miles to school or work without feeling tired.

55 **E** It seems likely then that medical innovations could create a society divided into three groups: the sick, the healthy, and the super-human. The question is, do people want to live in a society in which some compete and excel by using medication? It is a decision that needs to be made
60 in the coming decades.

* Attention Deficit Hyperactivity Disorder
* Transcranial Direct Current Stimulation

8 Look at the two sentences below taken from the passage. Which parts of speech are necessary to complete the sentences? Check your answers using the text.

1 _____ students also take them to stay alert and 2 _____ for longer 3 _____ of time. (lines 15–16)

Of course, it's not 4 _____ the healthy brain that could benefit from medical 5 _____ . (lines 36–7)

Exam practice

9 Complete each sentence with no more than three words and/or a number from the passage.

1 Ritalin is _____ ADHD.

2 Taking Modafinil frequently can be _____ .

3 Receiving small electric currents is a treatment for people with poor _____ .

4 Drugs have made it possible for athletes to enhance their _____ .

5 Scientists can now produce body parts like retinas and _____ arms and legs.

6 _____ machines may help us run without feeling tired.

What do you think?

10 **Choose the correct option to complete each question.**

1 What do you do to stay *health / healthy*?

2 What do you do to *enhance / enhancement* your performance in exams?

3 Is it fair for some people to take *medics / medication* when they take exams?

4 What should happen to athletes who take drugs to *improve / improvement* their performance?

5 Is it acceptable to take any drug that is *legal / legally* to improve your performance?

11 **Discuss the questions in exercise 10 with a partner.**

EXAM CHALLENGE

SPEAKING

1 **Prepare to speak about the topic on the card. Think or make notes for 1 minute.**

> Describe a place where you can go to keep fit.
> You should say:
> – where it is
> – what you can do when you are there
> – when people like to go there
> and explain how the place makes you feel.

2 **Speak for 1–2 minutes about the topic on the card. Record yourself or ask a partner to listen to you.**

3 **Check the responses you recorded and ask yourself or your partner the questions.**

1 How long did you speak for?

2 Did you use a range of positive and negative adjectives, as well as clauses of time?

3 Did you use appropriate intonation to make your voice interesting?

READING

1 **Do questions 34–36 in Practice test: Reading on page 160. Try to get at least two answers correct in 5 minutes.**

2 **Even if you did not get the correct word, did you manage to get the correct word form?**

LISTENING

1 **Do questions 11–15 in Practice test: Listening on page 150. Try to get at least three answers correct.**

2 **Before you listened, did you think about what type of word you needed to complete the table?**

WRITING

1 **Look at the table on page 107 and write a paragraph comparing the life expectancies in the countries.**

2 **Check your writing against the model answer on page 112. Did you identify the main similarities and differences? Did you use comparative structures?**

UNIT 3 Society & family

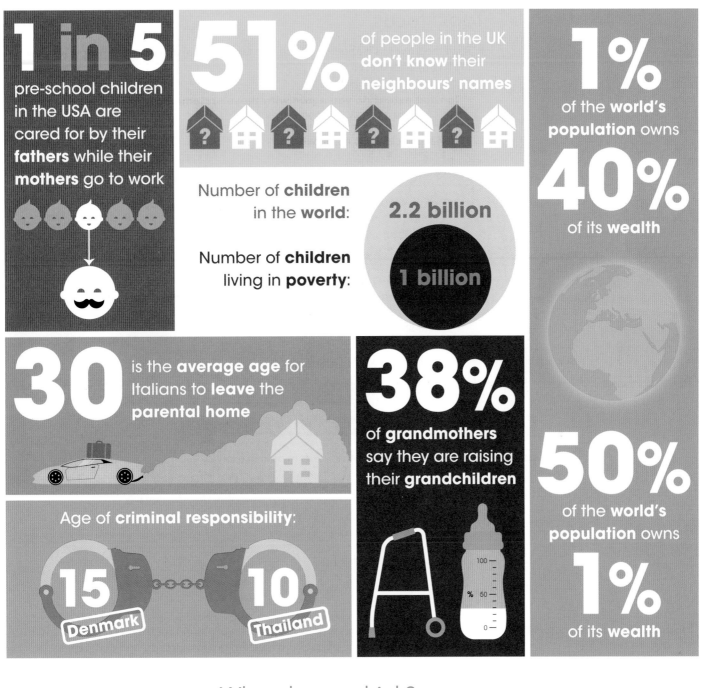

1 in 5 pre-school children in the USA are cared for by their **fathers** while their **mothers** go to work

51% of people in the UK **don't know** their **neighbours' names**

1% of the **world's population** owns **40%** of its **wealth**

Number of **children** in the **world**: **2.2 billion**

Number of **children** living in **poverty**: **1 billion**

30 is the **average age** for Italians to **leave** the **parental home**

Age of **criminal responsibility**:
15 Denmark
10 Thailand

38% of **grandmothers** say they are raising their **grandchildren**

100
% 50
0

50% of the **world's population** owns **1%** of its **wealth**

What do you think?

1 Who usually looks after children in your country?

2 How many of your neighbours do you know? How important is it to know them?

3 Do you think it's better to leave home when you are older or younger? Why?

4 At what age should people be held responsible for committing a crime?

5 Do you think wealth should be more equally distributed? Why / Why not?

▸ use *It* to give opinions
▸ speak about social issues
▸ respond to opinion questions

Topic focus

1 Read the survey. Is it about a) attitudes to family life, b) opinions about work, c) views on the law, d) all of these?

To what extent do you agree with these statements?
(1 = disagree strongly, 5 = agree strongly).

1 Men shouldn't do **housework**.
   1 2 3 4 5
2 Women should be prepared to stop paid work because of family **responsibilities**.
   1 2 3 4 5
3 People should care for the **well-being** of everyone in society.
   1 2 3 4 5
4 Everyone should have **equal opportunities** at work.
   1 2 3 4 5
5 People should always respect social **customs**.
   1 2 3 4 5
6 The government should reduce differences in **income**.
   1 2 3 4 5
7 There should be more controls on **immigration**.
   1 2 3 4 5
8 People should never break the **law**.
   1 2 3 4 5

Vocabulary VOCABULARY FILE » page 123

Social issues

2 Match 1–8 below with the words in bold in exercise 1.

1 system of rules
2 people moving to a country
3 traditions
4 commitments

5 health and happiness
6 the same chances; equality
7 salary
8 cooking and cleaning

3 Do the survey in exercise 1.

Key phrases

Responding to opinion questions

4 🔊 1.24 Listen to a person responding to questions about their views on statements in the survey. Complete the phrases the speaker uses for agreeing and disagreeing.

a No, absolutely _____.
b Well, it _____.
c Yes, _____.

d No, I _____ think so.
e Yes, to some _____.
f Yes, _____ I do.

5 Order the phrases in exercise 4 (1 = disagree strongly, 6 = agree strongly).

6 Work with a partner and take turns to ask the survey questions. Use the phrases in exercise 4. Note how strongly your partner agrees or disagrees (1–5).

Do you think that men shouldn't do housework?   *Well, it depends.*

Exam skills GRAMMAR FILE » page 113

It for giving opinions
7 The structure *it's / it is* + adjective + infinitive with *to* is often used to give opinions. Match the words and phrases in the table to make sentences.

> It's important to share housework.

It's	important	to be fair.
	difficult	to help other people.
	good	to have equality.
	necessary	to be tolerant.
	right	to obey the rules.
	useful	to have freedom of choice.
	valuable	to share housework.
	wrong	to restrict immigrant numbers.

8 Correct two mistakes in each of the responses below to statement 1 in the survey.
   1 Yes, to some extend because isn't good to change tradition.
   2 Well, it's depends because it not normal to do that in some cultures.
   3 No, I not think so because for women it's important to working, too.
   4 Yes, definitely, because is necessary for men to be relax at home.

9 Work with a partner. Ask and answer questions about the statements in the survey. Give reasons for your opinion.

> Do you think that men should do housework?

> Yes, definitely, because it's right to ...

10 ◉ 1.25 Listen to two speakers being asked for their opinion. Who sounds more interested, A or B? Why?

11 ◉ 1.26 Listen again to the survey response and repeat it. Try to copy the speaker's word stress.

Exam practice

12 Work with a partner. Student A, go to page 107. Student B, go to page 108.

EXAM TIP ◉ 1.27

Sounding enthusiastic can help you to get a better mark for pronunciation because your intonation and word stress will be more varied. What could you try to imagine in the exam to make sounding enthusiastic easier? » page 145

LISTENING
EXAM FOCUS: SECTION 3

Understanding agreement

- ▶ answer multiple-choice questions
- ▶ answer matching questions
- ▶ recognize agreement and disagreement
- ▶ consider how to manage study time

Topic focus

1 Tell a partner about the personalities of your siblings or other siblings that you know. How are they different? Use the adjectives below to help you.

| sociable | lazy | adventurous | hard-working | caring | relaxed | fun-loving |
| responsible | moody | creative | easy-going | funny | generous | clever | shy |

2 🔊 1.28 Listen to two students talking about older siblings. Do they agree?

Key phrases

Agreeing and disagreeing 3 🔊 1.29 Listen again and complete the phrases in the table.

Disagreeing	Partly agreeing	Agreeing
1 I don't __know__ about that.	3 I agree to __some__ extent.	5 That's __true__ .
2 Really? I __disagree__ .	4 That's __partly__ right.	6 __definitely__ .
		7 Yes, I think so, __too__ .

4 How do you think older and younger children differ?

> I think the oldest child in a family is often more responsible.

> I disagree.

Exam skills

Answering multiple-choice questions 5 Look at questions 1–4. Will the conversation be about a new book or a lecture?

1 New research suggests that eldest siblings
  Ⓐ are cleverer when they become adults.
  B do better in intelligence tests when they are 12.
  C are cleverer because they get more attention.

2 The students will probably be able to look at the research
  Ⓐ on the internet.
  B in both libraries.
  C in the faculty library only.

3 The research is available in the journal(s)
  A *Science*.
  B *Intelligence*.
  Ⓒ *Science* and *Intelligence*.

4 The next lecture on infant development is
  Ⓐ tomorrow morning.
  B on Wednesday.
  C tomorrow at 12.15.

EXAM TIP 🔊 1.30

In Listening Section 3, you listen to two or three speakers. Where does the conversation take place? Do the speakers often agree? » page 146

6 🔊 1.31 For question 1 in exercise 5, listen and choose the correct letter, A, B, or C.

7 Look again at question 1 in exercise 5. The male speaker says *babies who are born first are cleverer*, so why is option B <u>not</u> correct?

Exam practice

8 🔊 **1.32** For questions 2–4 in exercise 5, listen and choose the correct letter, A, B, or C.

Exam skills

Answering matching questions

9 Look at questions 5–9 from Part 3 of the Listening paper. For each answer, do you have to write a word or a letter?

> **I** Isabella agrees with the statement.
> **S** Simon agrees with the statement.
> **B** Both speakers agree with the statement.
> **N** Neither speaker agrees with the statement.
>
> 5 Isabella's brother is cleverer than Isabella. *I*
> 6 You can become more intelligent if you study hard. *B*
> 7 Isabella isn't as successful as her brother because she's female. *N*
> 8 Younger children try to avoid competing with their older brothers. *S*
> 9 Siblings affect your character more than your parents do. *N*

10 🔊 **1.33** For question 5 in exercise 9, listen and write the correct letter.

11 Explain to a partner why you chose the letter you did.

Exam practice

12 🔊 **1.34** Listen and answer questions 6–9 in exercise 9.

What do you think?

13 Discuss how the factors below can affect your personality or behaviour.

> *a large family   no siblings   strict parents   good teachers*
> *classmates who behave badly   celebrities you admire*

> *If you have a large family, you might be less shy in groups.*

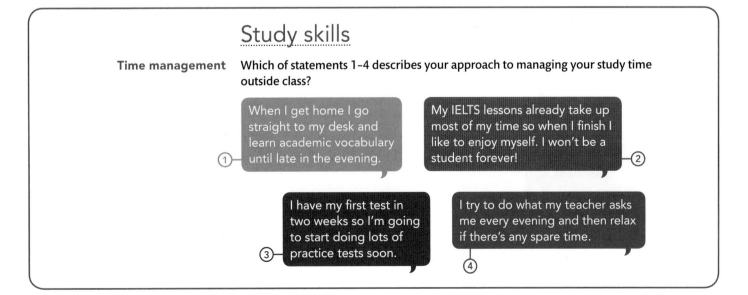

Study skills

Time management

Which of statements 1–4 describes your approach to managing your study time outside class?

① When I get home I go straight to my desk and learn academic vocabulary until late in the evening.

② My IELTS lessons already take up most of my time so when I finish I like to enjoy myself. I won't be a student forever!

③ I have my first test in two weeks so I'm going to start doing lots of practice tests soon.

④ I try to do what my teacher asks me every evening and then relax if there's any spare time.

▸ understand essay questions
▸ build an introduction
▸ understand thesis statements

Topic focus

1 **Work with a partner. Are the statements about essays true or false? Write *T* (true) or *F* (false).**

   1 The main purpose is to entertain. _____

   2 All opinion must be supported with evidence. _____

   3 The writer always gives their opinion in the introduction. _____

2 **Match the parts of an essay with definitions 1–5 below.**

> *conclusion* _____   *supporting sentence(s)* _____   *thesis statement* _____
> *background statement* _____   *topic sentence(s)* _____

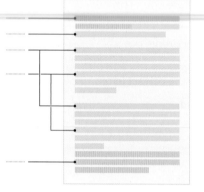

   1 provides examples, clarification, or evidence that helps the reader understand the paragraph's main idea

   2 contains the main idea of the paragraph

   3 summarizes the main ideas of the essay

   4 part of the introduction and contextualizes the essay in the real world

   5 part of the introduction and tells the reader what the writer will do; can include the main argument

3 **Label the diagram with the correct parts of an essay in exercise 2.**

Exam skills

Understanding essay questions

4 **Look at the essay question and find a) the instruction, b) the topic, c) the issue.**

> [1] In many countries women are doing jobs that men used to do. [2] This change has brought a lot of benefits to society. [3] To what extent do you agree?

5 **Match the essay questions to photos A–D.**

   1 An increase in tourism has had a significant effect on traditional society's way of life. Many people argue that this change has brought progress. Do you agree? Give reasons for your answer.

   2 Many people worry about the effects of living alone. Others think that technology is replacing the need for living together. Discuss.

   3 Population growth has been rapid in the last 50 years. This is causing high levels of unemployment. What can governments do to solve this problem?

   4 Unemployment causes many problems in society. Governments should provide jobs and income for everyone. To what extent do you agree?

6 **Identify the topic, issue, and instruction in each of the essay questions in exercise 5.**

7 **Look at the instructions in the essay questions in exercise 5. How are they different from each other?**

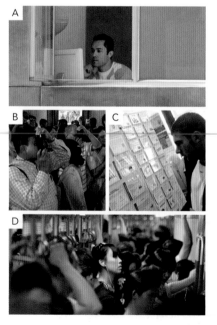

A

B   C

D

EXAM TIP 🔊 1.35

There are three main parts of an essay question. Which part is probably the most important? Why? » page 147

8 Match task descriptions 1–3 with essay types and instructions a–c.

1 You must present two opposing sides of an argument. ....

2 You must give your opinion and reasons for it. ....

3 You need to explain something with your own ideas. ....

a explanation: *What problems are associated with ...? / What can governments do to ...?* etc.

b discussion: *Discuss both views. / What are the advantages and disadvantages?* etc.

c personal opinion: *Give your opinion and support it. / Do you agree or disagree? To what extent do you agree or disagree / Present a written argument or case for ...* etc.

Building an introduction

9 Write an introduction for essay question 1 in exercise 5.

10 Compare your introduction to the model answer on page 108.

11 Synonyms and similar phrases are important in making your background statement original. Match the words in 1–4 below to similar words and phrases in the essay questions in exercise 5.

1 impact on, rise

2 are concerned, numerous, individuals, consequences

3 number of people, five decades, shot up, past

4 a number of, issues, leads to

12 Complete the background statements for the essay questions in exercise 5. Use the words and phrases from exercise 11.

1 The .... in tourism has had a great .... many parts of the world.

2 .... about the .... of living alone.

3 The .... has .... in the ....

4 Unemployment .... in society.

Understanding thesis statements

13 Match thesis statements a–d to essay questions 1–4 in exercise 5.

a This essay will discuss both sides of the issue.

b This essay will argue that the change is actually progress.

c This essay will suggest that it is the responsibility of individuals, not governments.

d This essay will outline the main ways that the issue can be dealt with.

14 Which two thesis statements in exercise 13 include the writer's opinion? What words show this?

Exam practice

15 Write essay introductions for the questions below. Each introduction should contain a background statement and a thesis statement.

1 The rise in people living alone is causing negative changes to society. To what extent do you agree?

2 Research suggests that older brothers and sisters are more successful than younger ones. Why might this be true?

Short answer questions

► scan a passage to find information quickly
► understand expressions with prepositions

Topic focus

1 Which of the following factors do you most associate with being an adult?

> *getting married   living alone*
> *paying your own bills   starting work*
> *reaching the age of 18   becoming a parent*

Exam skills

Scanning

2 Underline the key words in the four short answer questions below.

1 What percentage of people live alone in Sweden?

2 What percentage of young people lived alone in the USA in 2012?

3 Who is living with their children less than they did 100 years ago?

4 How much rubbish does a person living alone create each year?

3 Scan the passage on page 35 and answer the questions in exercise 2. Try to use no more than three words or a number for each answer.

4 Are the words you underlined in exercise 2 the same words you found in the passage?

EXAM TIP   ◆)) 1.36

Scanning is a reading strategy which is common in real life. Which type of question in the Reading test can scanning particularly help you with? » page 148

Exam practice

5 Answer the questions below. Choose no more than three words or a number from the passage for each answer.

1 What percentage of people live on their own in Norway?

2 What can't many young people get?

3 What things are young Americans happy to give up?

4 Who consumes the most goods and services?

5 What do individual households consume nearly two-thirds more of?

6 Who produces 1,000kg of rubbish each year?

6 Work with a partner and answer the questions below about exercise 5.

1 Did you read every word and sentence of the text?

2 Can you underline the sentences that contain the answers to the questions?

3 Approximately how much of the text did you have to read to answer the questions?

Vocabulary   **VOCABULARY FILE » page 123**

Expressions with prepositions

7 Replace the phrases in bold with phrases in *italics* from the passage.

1 People are less **dependent on** each other today.

2 Physical distance is less of an issue **because of** technology.

3 Some people worry that the changes have a negative **effect on** society.

4 Independence in old age is **leading to** more people choosing to live alone.

5 Many people are not **happy about** living in larger groups.

6 Organizations are right to be **concerned about** the impact of these changes.

INDEPENDENT LIVING

A The global number of people living alone is rapidly increasing. Numbers increased from about 153 million in 1996 to 277 million in 2011 – around 80% in 15 years. In the UK, 34% of households consist of one individual, while
5 in the USA the figure stands at 27%. Sweden has more people living on their own than anywhere in the world, with 47% of households having one person; followed by Norway at 40%. China, India, and Brazil have the fastest growing number of individual households. So why has this
10 happened and what impact on society has this change had?

B As far as the younger generation is concerned, many are unable to find good jobs so are forced to remain with or move back in with their parents. However, the surprising thing is that even though the economy was weak, between
15 2007 and 2012 the percentage of young people living alone in the USA hardly changed – dropping from 12% to 11%. The reality is that it has become an enormous priority for young adults to live alone. The explanation is perhaps that they are prepared to do without 'luxuries' like gym
20 membership, as well as to spend less on clothes, travel, and all kinds of other things because they want the experience of living alone. Starting work or getting married were once the indicators of adulthood, now it seems that living alone is the way to achieve it.

25 **C** It is not only the younger generation and their families that have been affected – independence is increasingly important to much older adults as well. A century ago, 70% of elderly American widows lived with a grown child; today, only 20% do, *thanks to* increased wealth and government
30 support. According to Eric Klinenberg, Professor of Sociology at New York University, they do value their relationships with their children but they would much prefer 'intimacy at a distance'. In other words, they do not want just to go back into their children's homes and live
35 in a bedroom. So again, we have a situation where society values independence as much as being part of a group. This is a massive cultural change in how society is organized and how it operates.

D The changing roles of family and society and these issues
40 are a concern for many, but are we actually *worried about* the wrong thing? Arguably, many people are *satisfied with* their new living arrangement. The extended family and its role has changed, people move away for work more and they are less *reliant on* their family and more so on their
45 friends. Perhaps what we should really be questioning is the environmental *impact* these decisions are actually having *on* our planet.

E According to research, one-person households are the biggest consumers of energy, land and household goods (e.g.
50 washing machines, TVs, etc.). Per person, they consume 38% more products, 42% more packaging, 55% more electricity, and 61% more gas than individuals in a four-person household. In addition, in four-person households each person produces 1,000 kilograms of waste annually,
55 while those living alone create 1,600 kilograms of waste each year. In an era of environmental challenges, this is clearly a great concern. Some also argue that single living is a factor in the breakdown of community, *resulting in* greater isolation and less respect for others. People are
60 perhaps less willing to help or support others as they no longer see a mutual benefit to these relationships.

8 Complete the questions with a preposition.

1 Are you satisfied _____ where and how you live?

2 Are you reliant _____ others or quite independent?

3 What problems in society do you / people you know worry _____ most?

4 Do you think unemployment leads _____ an increase in crime?

5 Thanks _____ social networking sites, fewer people are lonely. Do you agree?

6 What effect has technology had _____ how people behave in your society?

What do you think?

9 Discuss the questions in exercise 8 with a partner.

EXAM CHALLENGE

SPEAKING

1 **You have just talked about a family relationship in Speaking Part 2. Now respond to questions 1–3 below. Try to speak for 25 seconds each time. Record your responses or ask a partner to listen to you.**

   1 Do you think new parents should attend a parenting course?

   2 Should we always tell the truth to young children?

   3 If you have an argument with a friend, should you always apologize – even if it's not your fault?

2 **Check the responses you recorded and ask yourself or your partner the following questions.**

   1 Did you use phrases to show how strongly you agreed or disagreed?

   2 Did you state your opinions and give a reason for them?

   3 Did you use intonation and stress to make your voice interesting?

READING

1 **Do questions 23–26 in Practice test: Reading on page 157. Try to get at least three answers correct in 6 minutes.**

2 **Did you use your scanning skills to answer all the questions in the time given?**

LISTENING

1 **Do questions 21–24 in Practice test: Listening on page 151. Try to get at least three answers correct.**

2 **Did you understand agreement and disagreement between the speakers?**

WRITING

1 **Read the Task 2 question below. Then write an introduction for the essay. Try to finish it in 5 minutes.**

   Many people think that individuals should be free to wear what they want when they go to school or work.

   To what extent do you agree?

2 **Check your introduction against the model introduction on page 108. Discuss any differences using the following questions.**

   1 Did you manage to write a background statement *and* a thesis statement?

   2 Did your background statement focus on the same topic as the one in the model?

   3 How does your thesis statement compare to the one in the model?

BEFORE

AFTER

TEMPERATURE
↓ 4.6°C
Decrease in local temperature

AIR POLLUTION
↓ 35%
Decrease in air pollution

PUBLIC TRANSPORT
↑ 15.1%
Increase in use of buses

BIODIVERSITY
↑ 639%
Increase in different plants and animals

What do you think?

1 The infographic shows the same part of Seoul in South Korea before and after an environmental restoration project. What similarities and differences can you see?

2 Which statistic is the most surprising? Why?

3 Why do you think the changes shown by the statistics happened?

4 What are the main environmental problems where you live now?

5 How *green* (concerned about the environment) are you and your family / friends?

SPEAKING
EXAM FOCUS: PART 2

Describing cause and effect

- ▶ connect causes and effects
- ▶ use *too much / many* and *there is / are*
- ▶ speak about population problems and solutions

Topic focus

1 **Complete the text with the correct letters of pictures A–D.**

> Overcrowding is common in many urban environments and often leads to further problems. Exhaust emissions from the high number of vehicles can cause diseases, such as asthma (*picture* ＿＿) and even cancer. Also, there aren't enough green spaces where people can exercise, so obesity (*picture* ＿＿) may also become a problem. In developing countries, uncontrolled migration can result in extra challenges. For example, unplanned development of housing can lead to lack of sanitation (*picture* ＿＿) and to the creation of illegal rubbish dumps (*picture* ＿＿).

2 **Match definitions 1–6 with words and phrases in the text in exercise 1.**

1 being very fat
2 gases from vehicles
3 places where waste is taken and left without permission
4 no checks on large numbers of people moving from one place to another
5 no system for keeping things clean
6 too many people living in one place

3 **Are there problems related to population in any cities you know? What other problems can overcrowding lead to?**

Vocabulary   VOCABULARY FILE » page 124

Population problems and solutions

4 **Discuss the meaning of the words in bold in sentences 1–5. Use a dictionary to help you.**

1 **Conservation projects**, recycling centres, and **safe disposal sites** can help reduce ＿＿＿＿＿＿＿ .

2 **Rural development** may prevent ＿＿＿＿＿＿＿ .

3 **Public transport** systems and **cycle lanes** may lead to a reduction in ＿＿＿＿＿＿＿ .

4 **Sewage systems** will help where there is a ＿＿＿＿＿＿＿ .

5 **Planning regulations** will protect parks and public spaces and help to reduce ＿＿＿＿＿＿＿ .

5 **Complete the sentences in exercise 4 with words and phrases from exercise 1.**

Grammar GRAMMAR FILE » page 113 and 114

Too much/many, there is/are 6 Connect phrases in the table to make sentences.

Example: *Too much packaging is used so there is a lot of household waste.*

Causes			Effects		
Too much Too many	packaging is used			household waste.
	tourists visit the city			obesity and poor public health.
	green spaces are destroyed	so	there is a lot of there are a lot of	illegal settlements.
	waste enters rivers			water pollution.
	workers migrate to cities			litter in the streets.
	people use cars			traffic jams.

7 Write sentences for the problems you discussed in exercise 3. Use the structure in the table in exercise 6 to help you.

8 🔊 1.37 Listen to the sentences below. What sound can you hear between *There* and the words that follow it?

There is a lot of household waste.
There are a lot of traffic jams.

9 Read the complete sentences from exercise 6. Practise linking *There is / are.*

> Too many workers migrate to cities so **there are** a lot of illegal settlements.

Exam skills

Connecting causes and effects 10 Put the words in the correct order to make sentences.

1 a lot of / so / shops / too much / use / plastic packaging / there / household waste / is

2 there / household waste / is / use / shops / plastic packaging / because / a lot of / too much

11 Complete the stem in four different ways. Use *so* or *because* in each sentence.

Where I come from, there is / are a lot of …

EXAM TIP 🔊 1.38

In Speaking Part 2, you may have to talk about a problem and its causes and effects. What else might you be asked to do? » page 145

12 Read your sentences from exercise 11 to a partner. Stop after the word *so* or *because.* Can your partner complete the sentences?

> *Where I come from, there is a lot of household waste **because** …*

> *… too many products are bought online.*

Exam practice

13 Speak for 1–2 minutes about the topic on the card.

> Talk about an environmental problem where you live.
> You should say:
> – what the problem is
> – when it happens
> – what caused or causes it
> and explain how people help to solve the problem.

LISTENING

Completing sentences

- ▶ find key words in sentence completion and multiple-choice questions
- ▶ recognize phrases for environmental problems
- ▶ consider studying in groups

Topic focus

1 What environmental problem is shown in the picture on page 41? Can you think of any other problems it creates or effects it has?

Vocabulary VOCABULARY FILE » page 124

Environmental problems 2 Match pictures A–E with problems 1–5 caused by deforestation.

1 the impact of climate change
2 the loss of natural habitats
3 the risk of areas becoming deserts
4 the loss of potential cures for diseases
5 the loss of traditional ways of life

3 Put the problems in exercise 2 in order from the most serious to the least serious. Then explain your order to a partner.

> I think the loss of natural habitats is the most serious problem because ...

Exam skills

Finding key words 4 Underline the key words in the sentences.

1 Forests are mainly chopped down for financial reasons or to ....

2 Many farmers clear a little space to produce crops or to ....

3 Companies also create roads to reach ....

4 Some deforestation happens by accident when fires burn ....

5 Match the synonyms below to some of the key words you underlined in exercise 4.

> destroy   cut down   money   small   area
> access   chance   purposes   plants   construct

6 🔊 1.40 Listen to part 1 of a lecture about deforestation. Complete the sentences in exercise 4 with no more than three words.

EXAM TIP 🔊 1.39

When you're preparing to listen, you should read all the questions carefully and underline key words. What else can you do? » page 146

Exam practice

7 🔊 1.41 **Listen to part 2 of the lecture. Complete the sentences with no more than three words and/or a number.**

1 Scientists say that there are over .... species yet to be discovered.

2 Agricultural businesses depend on small organisms to break down ....

3 Plants need around .... different insects to help them survive.

4 Researchers have estimated that the value of services provided by .... is 2.9 trillion dollars.

5 As a result of climate change, species are looking for areas with ....

6 Plants and animals that don't come from a particular area can cause local species to ....

8 🔊 1.42 **Listen to part 3 of the lecture. Answer the multiple-choice questions.**

1 Rainforests cover
  A 7% of the Earth.
  B 2% of the Earth.
  C 36% of the Earth.

2 The lecturer thinks that
  A logging and mining companies are to blame.
  B local people are to blame.
  C the economic situation is to blame.

9 **Work with a partner. Compare any key words you underlined in exercises 7 and 8. Did you also think of similar synonyms as preparation?**

What do you think?

10 **Discuss the questions in groups.**

1 Is deforestation a problem in your country?

2 What other environmental problems are there in your country?

3 What do you think is the single most important environmental problem in the world today?

11 **Make a list of possible solutions for any of the problems you discussed in exercise 10.**

12 **Work with a partner from a different group. Present some of your solutions.**

> *Deforestation is a big problem in my country. The best solution is to ...*

Study skills

Studying in groups

Which factors are advantages or disadvantages of studying in groups?
Write *A* (advantages) or *D* (disadvantages).

.... share ideas

.... one or two people dominate

.... easily distracted

.... learn from other people's methods of working

.... progress not obvious

.... learn from other people's experiences

.... no clear focus

.... clarify your own thoughts

Can you add any other factors to the list?

WRITING

EXAM FOCUS: TASK 2

Brainstorming ideas

- ▶ analyse solution questions
- ▶ brainstorm essay ideas
- ▶ use *could* and *would*
- ▶ use verbs describing change

Topic focus

1 Read the problem. Work in groups and choose a solution a–e.

You have a problem! There is illegal dumping of waste near where you live, which is unattractive and unsafe. Choose from the solutions below to deal with the problem.

a Confront the people dumping the waste directly.

b Report the vehicle number plates of people dumping the waste to the police.

c Raise the issue with the local environmental authorities.

d Move somewhere else.

e Other (your suggestion).

2 How did you choose which solution was the best?

Exam skills

Analysing solution questions

3 Which essay question a–c below:

1 asks you to decide if a solution is good? ....

2 asks you to give your own solutions? ....

3 does *not* ask you to discuss a solution? ....

a How can governments help to reduce traffic congestion?

b To what extent would a tax on household waste help improve the environment?

c Destruction of forests is the most serious environmental problem we face today. Discuss.

Grammar **GRAMMAR FILE » page 118**

Could and *would*

4 Read the essay paragraphs below. Which essay question from exercise 3 is each one answering? Which paragraph is more effective? Why?

Paragraph A

> There are many reasons why a tax on household waste helps the environment. First, it encourages people to recycle more because they save money. It also provides income for the government which they can spend on conservation. Finally, people see packaging as a cost and they change their buying habits.

Paragraph B

> There are many steps that authorities could take to reduce traffic. Most importantly, they could ban cars from the city centre. This would improve air quality and attract more tourists. It would also help create more room for green spaces in the city because parking spaces would not be necessary.

5 Complete the rule.

To propose a solution, add .... before the verb. To explain an effect you're certain of, add .... before the verb. To explain a possible effect, use .... Remember to use the base form of the verb.

6 Rewrite paragraph A in exercise 4 using *could* and *would*.

Example: *There are many reasons why a tax on household waste **could help** the environment ...*

Vocabulary VOCABULARY FILE » page 124

Verbs describing change

7 Put the verbs into the correct columns of the table below.

> ~~decrease~~   develop   construct   reduce   alter
> improve   modify   limit   introduce   adapt

Make less	Make different	Make better	Create
decrease			

EXAM TIP   🔊 1.43

Always brainstorm ideas or reasons
<u>before</u> you start writing an essay.
How many ideas should there be in
your brainstorm for a discussion essay?
» page 147

8 Complete the sentences with words from exercise 7. Change the parts of speech where necessary. More than one answer may be possible.

1 _____ public transport would help to _____ air pollution.
2 People won't change completely but _____ our behaviour could help.
3 It's important to _____ new laws to _____ CO_2 emissions.
4 Constructing new roads may help to _____ the economy.
5 People need to _____ their use of plastic.

Exam skills

Brainstorming essay ideas

9 Work in groups. How many ideas can you brainstorm for the following essay question?

> How would a ban on private cars affect people?

10 When brainstorming ideas, it can help to consider the opinions of other groups of people. Match the descriptions below to pictures A–E. More than one answer may be possible.

_____ **I**ndustry leaders care about economic growth, developing skills, and trade.
_____ **D**octors care about our health and emotional well-being.
_____ **E**nvironmentalists care about protecting nature and natural resources.
_____ **A**rtists care about beauty and the freedom to make choices and express ideas.
_____ **S**ocial workers care for people who are disadvantaged, such as children, the elderly, the poor, and the disabled.

11 Match opinions 1–5 to the groups of people in exercise 10.

1 People would spend less time driving and this would help businesses.
2 I need my car to visit galleries and sell my work.
3 A ban on cars would reduce air pollution.
4 Parents would stop taking their children into the countryside.
5 A ban on cars could reduce breathing-related illnesses.

Exam practice

12 Brainstorm ideas for the following essay question.

> We must limit tourism if we want to save the environment. Discuss.

13 Write a paragraph starting with the sentence below. Use three of your best ideas from exercise 12.

> Limiting tourism would have many positive effects on the environment.
> For example, …

▸ predict text organization
▸ match phrases in questions and the passage
▸ use key phrases for evaluating solutions to problems

Topic focus

1 Look at the diagram below. What does it tell you about global car ownership from 1990 to 2010?

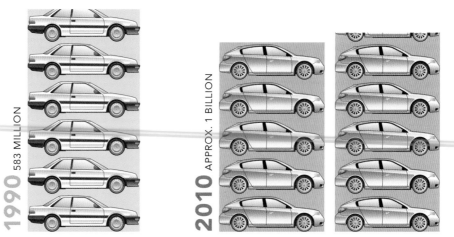

583 MILLION
1990

APPROX. 1 BILLION
2010

2 How important is having a car for you – now or in the future? Discuss with a partner.

Exam skills

Predicting text organization

3 For each text type a–c, number the sections in the order you would expect to read them.

a problem–solution: _____ poor solutions _____ good solution _____ description of problem

b information: _____ current situation _____ original or past situation _____ future situation

c discussion: _____ disadvantages _____ advantages _____ your personal opinion

EXAM TIP 🔊 1.44

In the test, there are many different types of passage. Three common types are problem-solution, information, and discussion. How does knowing the type help you to find information quickly?
» page 148

4 Read the passage on page 45 quickly. Decide if it is about:

1 solving the problem of traffic congestion

2 information about how traffic congestion has been controlled

3 the author's opinion about how to reduce the level of car ownership.

5 Read the passage again. Decide which paragraphs are about:

1 poor solutions   paragraphs _____ and _____

2 a good / new solution   paragraphs _____ and _____

3 problems   paragraphs _____ and _____

6 Check if the information in the passage is in the same order you predicted in a) in exercise 3.

Matching phrases

7 Look at the exam question. Underline four key words in 1.

Which paragraph contains information about:

1 a solution that has not worked in cities?

8 Look at the paragraphs of the passage about solutions that have <u>not</u> worked. Then find a phrase with a similar meaning to 1 in exercise 7. Does it contain ideas that match all the words you underlined?

STARTING TO DRIVE AT 25?

A High traffic levels remain a problem for many governments. Car ownership in the world's fast-developing countries continues to double each year, and migration to cities is also rising quickly, resulting in high levels of
5 congestion and pollution.

B Until recently, governments successfully controlled traffic levels by imposing financial obligations on drivers. Initially, they made it more expensive to drive by raising taxes on petrol or increasing parking costs. At the same time, they
10 made it cheaper to use public transport by investing in rail and bus travel. However, these 'tax and spend' approaches are no longer possible to introduce easily. This is because living costs are growing in many countries and the global economy is not strong, so governments can't spend as much
15 money and people are angry when they have to pay more. New controls are therefore needed.

C Legal solutions to congestion issues are now attracting greater interest. However, traffic laws and regulations have often proved ineffective. For example, banning cars in city
20 centres has simply transferred problems to the edge of cities. Similarly, controlling speed limits has been effective on fast roads but has done little to solve congestion in urban areas.

D A more effective legal intervention might be to stop some people from driving altogether – but who exactly?
25 If workers were stopped from driving, they might not be able to get to work. Many older citizens and families also rely on cars to move around easily. Furthermore, both these groups vote frequently so it would be a political disaster to prevent them from driving.

30 **E** This leaves young people. Many people, including road safety campaigners, would agree with raising the minimum driving age. Young people make up over 25% of road deaths in many countries and, according to recent research, parts of the brain that help to calculate risk and
35 consequences are not fully developed until the age of 25. Consequently, there have already been discussions in the media about stopping young people driving or carrying passengers. Above all, raising the minimum driving age to 25 would reduce the number of drivers on the road by over
40 10% and therefore cut pollution.

F Of course, young people would have to be given financial help to make sure public transport remained affordable for them. But as pressure grows on the governments to reduce congestion, it surely makes sense to postpone the time that
45 young drivers get their licenses until a little later in life.

Exam practice

9 Which paragraphs (A–F) of the passage contain the information in 1–6 below?

1 an opinion on whether young people should drive _____
2 a social group that depends on cars _____
3 the relationship between driving age and serious accidents _____
4 an environmental benefit of raising the age you can drive _____
5 a continuing increase in the car's popularity _____
6 a general rise in prices across much of the world _____

Key phrases

Evaluating solutions 10 Look at the words and phrases below from the passage. Which suggest a positive evaluation or a negative evaluation? Write + (positive) or – (negative).

> *successfully   no longer possible   ineffective   simply transferred the problem*
> *has done little to solve   might not be able   makes sense*

11 Complete the sentences with words and phrases from exercise 10.

1 Congestion has been _____ reduced with the introduction of a congestion charge.

2 The government _____ to continue with the project due to the high costs.

3 It is _____ to invest a lot of money in public transport.

4 While there is now less congestion in cities, the solution _____ traffic problems on the motorways.

5 The solution was _____ as it _____ from inner-city areas to the suburbs.

6 It _____ to lower speed limits as there are more accidents at higher speeds.

What do you think?

12 Discuss in groups how raising the minimum driving age to 25 would affect you. Use the phrases below to help you.

It would affect me a lot because I would have to ...

A possible impact could be that I wouldn't be able to ...

EXAM CHALLENGE

SPEAKING

1 Prepare to speak about the topic on the card. Think or make notes for 1 minute.

> Talk about cities in your country and the problems they have. You should say:
> – what the main problems are
> – which is the biggest problem
> – what is being done to deal with the problems
> and explain what effects the problems have on society.

2 Speak for 1–2 minutes about the topic on the card. Ask a partner to listen to you or record your responses.

3 Ask your partner or yourself the questions.
1 Did you use *There is / are* accurately?
2 Did you use countable / uncountable nouns accurately?
3 Did you talk about causes and effects?

READING

1 Do questions 27–30 in Practice test: Reading on page 159. Try to get at least three answers correct in 6 minutes.

2 Did you use your predicting skills to help you answer the questions?

LISTENING

1 Do questions 28–30 in Practice test: Listening on page 151. Try to get at least two answers correct.

2 Did you use your knowledge of word formation to help you?

WRITING

1 Work alone and brainstorm ideas for the following question. Spend 2 minutes thinking about your ideas.

What problems are linked to traffic congestion?

2 Exchange your ideas with a partner. Then discuss the questions.
1 How many different ideas did you think of?
2 Did you use IDEAS (see page 43, exercise 10) to include the opinions of other groups of people?

3 Write a paragraph starting with the sentence below. Use three of your best ideas from exercise 1.

Traffic congestion can have many negative effects. For example, ...

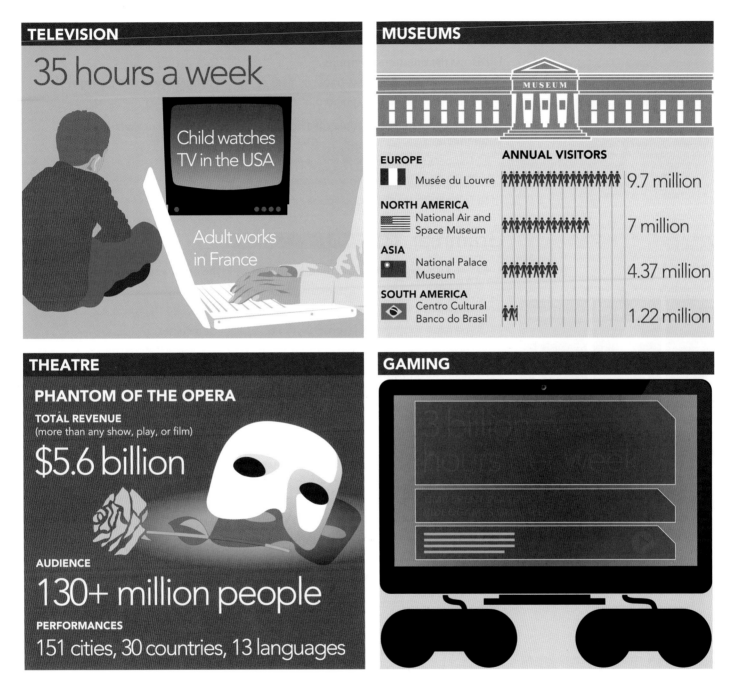

TELEVISION

35 hours a week

Child watches TV in the USA

Adult works in France

MUSEUMS

MUSEUM

		ANNUAL VISITORS
EUROPE	Musée du Louvre	9.7 million
NORTH AMERICA	National Air and Space Museum	7 million
ASIA	National Palace Museum	4.37 million
SOUTH AMERICA	Centro Cultural Banco do Brasil	1.22 million

THEATRE

PHANTOM OF THE OPERA

TOTAL REVENUE
(more than any show, play, or film)

$5.6 billion

AUDIENCE

130+ million people

PERFORMANCES
151 cities, 30 countries, 13 languages

GAMING

What do you think?

1 How much TV do you watch a week? Is this more or less than the average amount in your country?

2 Have you visited any of the museums listed in the infographic? Which museums are the most popular in your country?

3 Have you ever seen a play or show at the theatre?

4 Why do you think gaming is so popular? Which games do <u>you</u> most like to play?

5 What are any negative aspects of the forms of entertainment shown?

47

Structuring responses

▸ extend responses
▸ predict Part 1 and Part 3 questions
▸ use adverbs of frequency
▸ speak about types of book

Topic focus

1 Discuss the questions in groups.

1 Have you read any of the books in pictures A–F in English or your first language?

2 Have you seen film adaptations of any of them?

2 ◀)1.45 Listen to three people speaking about e-books. Match speakers 1–3 with summaries a–c.

a This person reads e-books and paper books.

b This person reads celebrity biographies.

c This person spends a lot of money on e-books.

Grammar   GRAMMAR FILE » page 115

A   B   C

D   E   F

Adverbs

3 ◀)1.46 Listen again. Number the adverbs below in the order you hear them.

.... actually   .... basically   .... generally

.... maybe   .... regularly   .... often

.... perhaps   .... possibly   .... sometimes

.... occasionally

4 Write the adverbs from exercise 3 that are used to suggest:

a the speaker is going to say something surprising

....

b the speaker is giving the most important information

....

c the speaker is saying how often something is true

....

d the speaker is going to make a guess about something

....

e the speaker is saying how often something happens.

....

5 Which of the adverbs from exercise 4 can go in positions 1–3 in the sentence below?

(1), when my friends choose books, they (2) choose fantasy stories. (3) it's because they like the characters.

6 Add at least one adverb from exercise 4 to each of the sentences below. Make sure the adverbs are in the correct position.

1 The young people I know only read for their studies.

2 When I read in cars or on buses, I feel sick.

3 I'll read a novel on my next holiday.

4 I like to read. I can read in three different languages.

5 I don't like fantasies. It's because the plots are silly.

7 Change words in the sentences in exercise 6 so that they are true for you. Then compare your ideas with a partner.

EXAM TIP   ◀)1.47

Using adverbs correctly can really improve your English. In which parts of the Speaking test are adverbs particularly helpful? Which two adverbs are useful in all parts of the test? » page 145

Vocabulary VOCABULARY FILE » page 125

Types of book 8 Match books A–F shown on page 48 with types 1–6 below. Can you think of any other types of book?

1 biography _____ | 4 historical novel _____
2 crime novel _____ | 5 drama _____
3 romance _____ | 6 thriller _____

9 Tell a partner what types of book or e-book you like reading. Give reasons.

Pronunciation 10 🔊 1.48 Look at the questions and responses. Underline the word that would be stressed in each response. Then listen and check.

1 What do you drink when you read? | I often drink coffee when I read.
2 When do you drink coffee? | I often drink coffee when I read.

11 Look at the stressed words in responses 1–3. Write the question that would be asked for each one.

1 I sometimes read *magazines* on planes.

2 I *sometimes* read magazines on planes.

3 I sometimes read magazines on *planes*.

12 Ask and answer the questions from exercise 11 with a partner. Give true information and use appropriate stress.

Exam skills

Extending responses 2 13 Extend responses 1–4 by matching them with a–d.

1 Generally, I prefer films to books. | a Maybe one day I'll read more in English.
2 Basically, paper books won't be common in the future. | b I usually go to the cinema twice a month.
3 I often read in my first language. | c Possibly, people have more time on holiday.
4 Generally, people don't have time to read. | d Perhaps we'll buy them on special occasions.

14 Add adverbs to the responses below. Then extend the responses and tell a partner.

1 I prefer books with pictures …

2 People read to make themselves look clever …

3 I read non-fiction …

4 I think we won't need 'real' libraries in the future …

> *Generally*, I prefer books with pictures. I often read comics and manga.

Predicting Part 1 and Part 3 questions 15 Which questions are asked in Part 1 or in Part 3? Write *P1* (Part 1) or *P3* (Part 3).

1 How often do you read books?

2 Would you like to write a book one day?

3 Why do some people read on trains?

4 What are the advantages of e-books compared to paper books?

5 What stories did your parents or teachers read to you when you were young?

6 How could teachers get students more interested in books?

Exam practice

16 Ask and answer the questions from exercise 15 with a partner. Ask the Part 1 questions first.

LISTENING

Labelling plans and maps

- ▶ complete plans and maps
- ▶ recognize words and phrases for entertainment facilities
- ▶ prioritize vocabulary learning

Topic focus

1 What type of entertainment venue is shown in the picture below?

2 Make a list of as many different types of entertainment venue as you can. Then compare with a partner.

Vocabulary   VOCABULARY FILE » page 125

Entertainment facilities

3 In which types of venue would you find the facilities in the list below? More than one answer is possible.

_____ balcony	_____ ticket office	_____ screen
_____ VIP boxes	_____ dance floor	_____ cloakroom
_____ aisles	_____ fire exits	_____ snack bar

4 Describe your favourite entertainment venue. Use words from exercise 3.

> I love going to the IMAX cinema in London. It has an enormous **screen** and the **snack bar** is amazing.

Exam skills

Completing plans and maps

EXAM TIP   🔊 1.49

On plans and maps, it's sometimes difficult to find all the question numbers. Make sure you find the gaps for all the questions <u>before</u> you begin listening. What else can you do to prepare?
» page 146

5 Look at the plan of the Pitt Lane Theatre. With a partner, try to predict where the facilities in the list are. Label them using the letters in brackets.

> main entrance (M)   snack bar (SB)   stage (S)   ticket office (TO)   toilets (T)
> seating area (SA)   cloakroom (C)   main auditorium (MA)   fire exit (FE)

6 🔊 1.50 Listen and complete the information for people at the Pitt Lane Theatre.

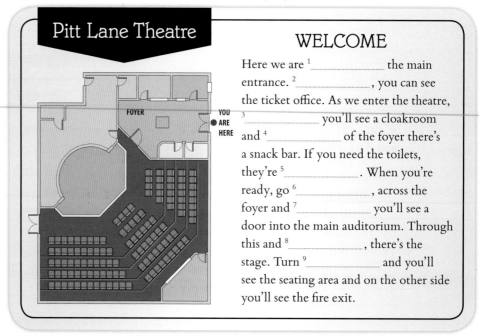

Pitt Lane Theatre

FOYER

YOU ARE HERE

WELCOME

Here we are ¹_____ the main entrance. ²_____, you can see the ticket office. As we enter the theatre, ³_____ you'll see a cloakroom and ⁴_____ of the foyer there's a snack bar. If you need the toilets, they're ⁵_____. When you're ready, go ⁶_____, across the foyer and ⁷_____ you'll see a door into the main auditorium. Through this and ⁸_____, there's the stage. Turn ⁹_____ and you'll see the seating area and on the other side you'll see the fire exit.

7 Use the instructions in exercise 6 to check your predictions in exercise 5.

Exam practice

8 🔊 **1.51** Listen and label the map below. Write no more than two words for each answer.

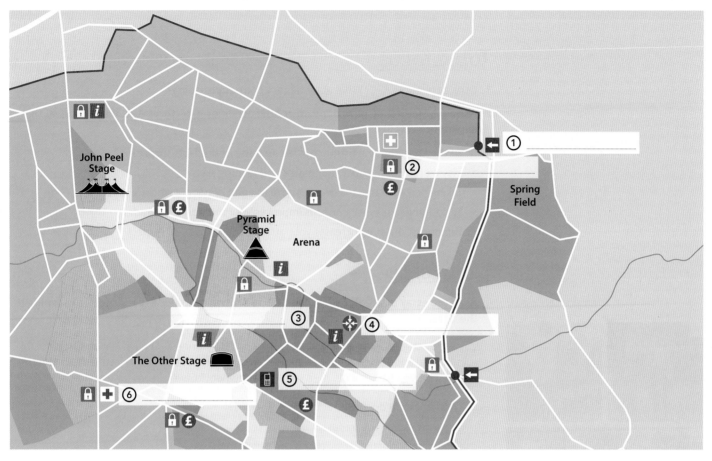

What do you think?

9 Look at the information. Discuss what you think the ages are in your country.

The average age of people going to …

| THE THEATRE *in the USA is* **44** | THE OPERA *in Germany is* **55–60** | THE CINEMA *in the USA is* **25–34** | MUSIC FESTIVALS *in the UK is* **35–37** |

Study skills

Prioritizing vocabulary learning

Look at the two groups of words. How is group 1 different from group 2?

① purpose opinion explanation benefit trend cause

② fantasy fire exit cloakroom e-reader novel stage

Which group of words would you choose to learn first? Why?

From brainstorm to plan

▸ plan a personal opinion essay
▸ use verbs for positive effects

Topic focus

1 Look at pictures A–C. What activities are the people doing?

2 Ask a partner if they have done any of the activities in pictures A–C. If so, ask what the experience was like.

3 Read the facts about artistic activities. Are any of the facts surprising?
- Playing music improves your maths and reading skills.
- Taking part in drama makes you more tolerant of people who are different.
- Performing in plays or concerts improves your memory and grades.
- Painting or drawing increases your attention level and self-respect.

Exam skills

Planning an essay

4 Read the essay question below. Then decide which sentence a–c is closest in meaning to the question.

> Artistic activities, such as music, drama, or painting, bring a range of benefits to the individual and society and so should receive greater government investment. To what extent do you agree or disagree with this statement? Give reasons for your answer.

a To what extent do artistic activities change us?

b Are artistic activities useful for us?

c Should artistic activities receive more public money?

5 Read the brainstorm below. Does it have points which agree and disagree with the statement in exercise 4? Why / Why not?

B improve school grades

A improve young people's self-respect and confidence

C develop understanding and tolerance of others

ARTISTIC ACTIVITIES

D provide social life for old and young people

F bring together people of different backgrounds and languages

E can be watched / seen by everyone in society

EXAM TIP ◀)) 1.52

Before you start writing your essay, it's important to write a plan with paragraph topics. How do you choose good paragraph topics? » page 147

6 Which of a–c below would make a good paragraph topic for the essay which answers the question in exercise 4. Why?

a all the effects of artistic activities

b the academic benefits of artistic activities

c the positive effect of finger-painting on five-year-olds' maths results

7 Look at the essay plan. Underline the best paragraph topic in each pair.

My opinion: The government should support artistic activities.

Paragraph topic 1: Social benefits of art / Advantages for old people

Brainstorm points: _____ _____

Paragraph topic 2: Increase in self-respect / Benefits to individuals

Brainstorm points: _____ _____

Paragraph topic 3: Effects on community relations / Increase in tolerance

Brainstorm points: _____ _____

8 Add points from the brainstorm in exercise 5 to the paragraphs in exercise 7.

Exam practice

9 **Discuss the essay question.**

> Technology has had a positive influence on performing arts such as music and theatre. Do you agree or disagree?

10 **Read the brainstorm below. Which points A–H could you put under the possible paragraph topics in the list? Some points can be used more than once.**

> performers   variety in art   business   audiences   the internet   participation in art

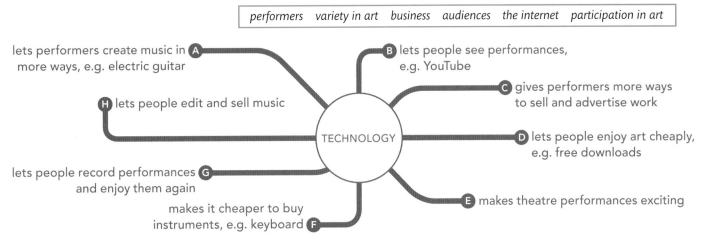

11 **With a partner, decide which three paragraph topics from exercise 10 you would use in an essay plan. Include as many brainstorm points as possible without repetition.**

Vocabulary   **VOCABULARY FILE » page 125**

Verbs for positive effects   12 **Put the verbs in bold in 1–8 into categories a–c below. The first one is done for you.**

> a to reach a target
> b to make something better
> c to give, get, or make something new

1 Street art (like graffiti) can **improve** the local environment. _b_

2 Real-life performances **provide** a more valuable experience than recordings. _____

3 Looking at paintings helps people **develop** knowledge of other cultures. _____

4 Everyone can take part in artistic activities but most people can't **create** a work of art. _____

5 People **gain** an important skill when they learn to play an instrument. _____

6 You **accomplish** more by learning traditional instruments or styles of painting than by learning modern ones. _____

7 Paintings, sculptures, and music **enhance** all our lives greatly. _____

8 It's difficult to **achieve** success in more than one artistic activity. _____

13 **Discuss the statements in exercise 12 with a partner.**

- locate information in a passage
- locate and match opinions in a passage
- understand and use phrases for examples, reasons, and effects

Topic focus

1 How much do other people influence the films you choose to watch? Circle an option 1–5 for each group.

	No influence ——————→ Significant influence				
Friends	1	2	3	4	5
Family	1	2	3	4	5
Film critics	1	2	3	4	5
Bloggers	1	2	3	4	5

2 Compare your answers with a partner. Explain your reasons.

> *My friends have the most influence, but I like to see what film critics write because …*

Exam skills

Locating information

3 Read the question below. Underline one key word that will help you to locate the information in the passage.

Which paragraph tells you about …

1 a reason for a recent improvement in reviews? _____

4 Now scan the passage on page 55 to answer the question in exercise 3. Did the key word you chose help you to find the information quickly?

EXAM TIP 🔊 1.53

Some matching questions ask you to look for specific information. What *two* things should you do before you start looking?
» page 148

Exam practice

5 The passage has five paragraphs, A–E. Which paragraph contains the following information? You may use any letter more than once.

1 _____ the effects of a change in how we communicate
2 _____ an example of where you can read many opinions about films
3 _____ an innovation from the 1920s that was not liked by everyone
4 _____ a change in the popularity of films
5 _____ an event that was copied by others
6 _____ the result of a new way of watching films

Exam skills

Locating and matching opinions

6 Look at the question asking about an opinion. What would you scan the passage for first to find the answer?

Which is W.G. Faulkner's opinion?

1 Cinema has become popular in a certain country.
2 Films are generally of a low standard.
3 The cinema should have a higher status in society.

7 Views are often given with reporting or opinion verbs such as *believe*, *consider*, or *think*. Underline the sentence in the passage that expresses Faulkner's view.

THE RISE AND FALL OF THE FILM CRITIC

A Long before Hollywood began to dominate the industry, watching films was already a popular leisure activity in the UK. At first, these films had relatively low status since people preferred other forms of entertainment and they were only shown after other performances in theatres or in empty shops. But at the start of the twentieth century the first purpose-built 'electric palaces' – in other words 'cinemas' – arrived and, as a result, films started to gain higher status. Soon afterwards, film critics started to appear.

B Professional film criticism has a history of about 100 years. In 1912, a journalist by the name of W.G. Faulkner observed that the cinema had now 'become an everyday part of the national life.' A year later, he became the author of the first regular criticisms of films in any British newspaper. Subsequently, many methods of criticizing and rating films evolved, such as Hollywood's famous 'star system'. This was born in 1928 in the New York Daily News, and some historians see it as a key moment in the development of film criticism. However, many professional film critics did not (and still do not) like the star system due to its simplicity.

C In America, some critics believed that standards in the 'movie' industry in general needed raising. Consequently, in 1929 the Academy of Motion Pictures, Arts and Sciences, set up by MGM film studios, organized the word's first media awards ceremony, now called 'The Oscars'. In an effort to preserve the neutrality and professionalism of film criticism, several independent organizations, for instance the New York Film Critics Circle (founded in 1935), soon followed with their own awards ceremonies.

D A century after the birth of film criticism, some critics feel that their professionalism is under attack. Arguably, they are no longer respected as individual thinkers but are seen as part of the advertising machine of the film industry. This is partly because the internet now allows anyone who is interested in films to write reviews, resulting in a mass of comments by amateurs and fans. Some film critics, such as Armond White, argue that the outcome of this has been to lower the standards of the profession – potentially because film criticism is no longer written by people who have studied cinema at university but by film-loving bloggers instead.

E So has film criticism ceased to exist in a form that is worth reading? Not necessarily. According to the media guru Roger Ebert, reviews are much clearer now since they are no longer written by academics who, arguably, don't always write clearly. Not only this, but websites, for instance Rotten Tomatoes or IMDb, can bring together many reviews in one place. While these may not always offer academic insights, they offer a broader view of a film than 'expert' reviewers can. In short, film criticism, like the films we watch, has evolved. Whether this change is for the better continues to be a matter of debate.

8 Which of the sentences in exercise 6 means the same as the sentence you underlined in the passage?

Exam practice

9 Look at the names of people / organizations A–E and statements 1–5 below. Match each statement with the correct name.

A Academy of Motion Pictures, Arts and Sciences

B Professional film critics

C New York Film Critics Circle

D Armond White

E Roger Ebert

1 Film criticism should be professional.

2 Improvements are necessary in all parts of the film business.

3 The internet has improved film reviews.

4 The internet has made film criticism worse.

5 The star system is not sophisticated.

Vocabulary VOCABULARY FILE » page 125

Examples, reasons, effects **10** Decide if the words in bold in sentences 1–3 refer to an example, a reason, or an effect.

1 Watching films at home is now common, **so** fewer people go to the cinema.

2 The *New York Daily News* said *Lawless* was excellent, but the *New York Post* said it was weak, which **illustrates** how reviews can differ.

3 English spread around the world partly **because** American films were so popular.

11 Put the words in bold in exercise 10 into the correct columns of the table. Then add those from the list below.

> as   for instance   since   such as   as a result   consequently
> for example   outcome   due to   resulting in

Introducing examples	Introducing reasons	Introducing effects

12 Write a short paragraph about an entertainment trend in your country and its effect.

Example: *People in my country watch action films a lot as they are exciting. As a result, society is becoming more violent.*

What do you think?

13 Tell your partner your opinion of a film you watched recently.

EXAM CHALLENGE

SPEAKING

1 Respond to the Part 1 and Part 3 questions below. Ask a partner to listen to you or record your responses.

1 What kind of stories or books do you mostly enjoy reading?

2 Why do some people like to read in a foreign language?

3 Do you think stories will be written by computers one day?

2 Ask your partner or yourself the questions.

1 Did you use adverbs in your responses?

2 Did you use appropriate sentence stress?

LISTENING

1 Do questions 16–20 in Practice test: Listening on page 150. Try to get at least four answers correct.

2 Did you predict any information on the plan? Could you follow the directions clearly?

READING

1 Do questions 31–33 in Practice test: Reading on page 159. Get at least two answers correct in 5 minutes.

2 Did you use your scanning skills and knowledge of synonyms to locate parts of the text quickly?

WRITING

1 Work alone. Write a brainstorm and plan for the following essay question. Finish them in 5 minutes.

> Home entertainment is becoming so good that we no longer need traditional entertainment venues like cinemas, theatres, or concert halls. To what extent do you agree?

2 Compare your brainstorm and plan with the model answer on page 108. Then answer the questions.

1 Did you select an appropriate number of ideas from your brainstorm?

2 Did your plan have a similar structure to the model answer?

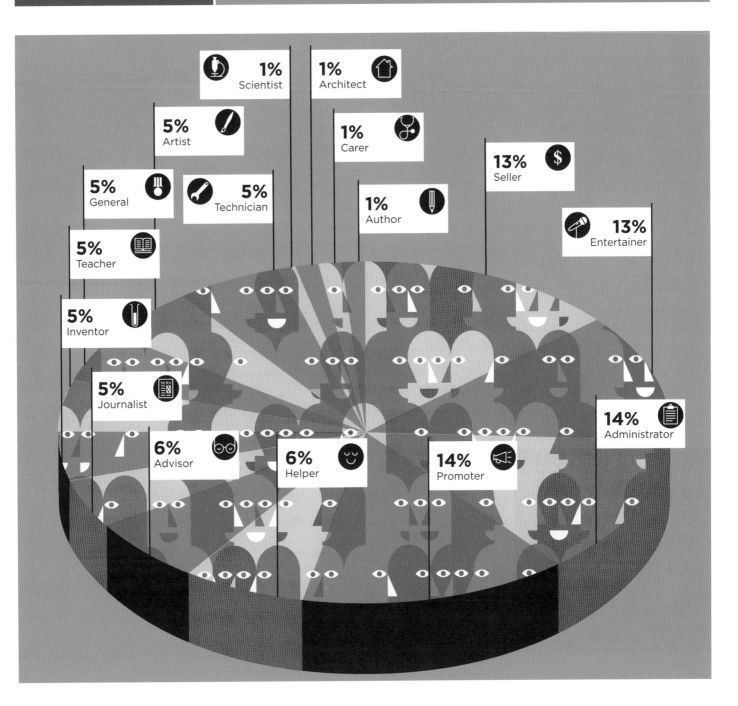

1% Scientist

1% Architect

5% Artist

1% Carer

13% Seller

5% General

5% Technician

1% Author

5% Teacher

13% Entertainer

5% Inventor

5% Journalist

14% Administrator

6% Advisor

6% Helper

14% Promoter

What do you think?

1 Experts believe people naturally belong to the career groups in the infographic. Which group do you think *you* belong to?

2 Which groups do you think are most important for a) society, b) the economy?

3 Are you naturally suited to your academic subject or career? How do you know?

4 Why do some people do the 'wrong' jobs?

5 Success is being able to earn money by doing what you enjoy. Do you agree?

SPEAKING

EXAM FOCUS: PART 2

Varying language

- vary language
- use the second conditional
- use character adjectives and nouns

Topic focus

1 **Read statements a–j about what makes a good leader. Decide which two are the least important. Why?**

A good leader:

a has enough skill to do the job well
b gives help and encouragement
c treats everyone equally
d is brave
e doesn't give in easily
f is enthusiastic
g plans for the future
h makes you feel excited
i has new and exciting ideas
j wants to be successful

Vocabulary

VOCABULARY FILE » page 126

Character adjectives and nouns

2 **Match the adjectives below with the statements in exercise 1. Which two adjectives are not defined in exercise 1?**

inspiring intelligent fair determined imaginative passionate ambitious courageous forward-looking competent honest supportive

3 **With a partner, choose five adjectives from exercise 2 that you think are the most important in a leader.**

4 **Read the information on page 108. Compare your answer to the order. Is the Top 5 surprising?**

5 **Complete the table below with the noun forms of the adjectives in exercise 2. Use a dictionary to help you. Which adjective does not have a noun form?**

Adjective	Noun
inspiring	inspiration
ambitious	ambition

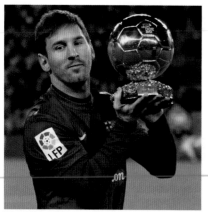

Lionel Messi
Captain, Argentina / Striker, Barcelona

6 **Discuss the questions with a partner.**

1 Which three characteristics are your strongest? Give examples of how you show them.
2 What characteristics do you most admire in other people? Why?

Exam skills

Varying language 2

7 **Read the sentences. Which one is better and why?**

1 Lionel Messi is really amazing. He's really skilful, he's really courageous and he's really friendly, too. He's really amazing.
2 My hero's Lionel Messi. He's so skilful. He's also got lots of courage and his friendliness is obvious to everyone.

EXAM TIP 🔊 1.54

Varying your language helps you to get a
higher mark for vocabulary and grammar.
In which part of the Speaking test is it
most difficult to vary language? Why?

» page 145

8 **Complete the second sentence so it has the same meaning as the first. Vary the language where possible. The first one is done for you.**

1 My mother is very supportive. She gives ____me a lot of support____ .

2 My cousin is passionate about his job. He has _____ .

3 My teacher behaves very fairly. She _____ .

4 My friend is determined and I respect this. I admire _____ .

5 My brother is ambitious and is going to succeed. My brother's

_____ .

9 **Think about a famous person or someone who you admire. Tell a partner about the person. Use adjectives and nouns from exercise 5 to describe their character.**

> *I admire my sister, Sara. She's **intelligent** and **ambitious**. Her **determination** is amazing.*

Grammar GRAMMAR FILE » page 118

Second conditional 10 **Complete the sentences with the correct form of the verbs in brackets. The first one is done for you.**

1 If I _had to choose_ (have to choose) one word to describe my favourite author, it _would be_ (be) *imaginative*.

2 If I _____ (have to describe) my hero in one word, it _____ (be) *courageous*.

3 If I _____ (can meet) any famous person, it _____ (be) a world leader.

4 I think many actors _____ (be) successful if they _____ (be) models, too.

5 If a young woman _____ (want to look up to) a strong female role model, I _____ (suggest) Marissa Mayer for her ambition.

11 **Change the sentences in exercise 10 so they are true for you.**

12 **How are the sentences below different from 1 and 5 in exercise 10?**

1 If I had to choose one word to describe my favourite author, it'd be *imaginative*.

2 If a young woman wanted to look up to a strong female role model, I'd suggest Marissa Mayer for her ambition.

13 **When are contractions normally used in English?**

14 **Practise saying the sentences in exercise 12.**

Exam practice

15 **Speak for 1–2 minutes about the topic on the card.**

> Describe a famous person that you admire. You should say:
> – what they do
> – what their characteristics are
> – what you would like to say to them
> and explain why you admire them.

Marissa Mayer
President and CEO, Yahoo!

LISTENING
EXAM FOCUS: SECTION 3

Completing notes

- complete notes from a recording
- recognize and use words and phrases for working conditions
- look at how to learn new vocabulary

Topic focus

1 Tell a partner which of the options below you would choose. Give reasons.

1 a job with a salary of $50,000 a year (everyone else earns $25,000 a year)

2 a job with a salary of $100,000 a year (everyone else earns $200,000 a year)

2 Read the information on page 108. Does it surprise you?

Vocabulary VOCABULARY FILE » page 126

Working conditions **3 Put the items into the correct columns of the table.**

| ~~salary~~ ~~full time~~ ~~company car~~ company pension overtime promotion |
| flexitime bonus training opportunities attractive location pay rise holiday |

Financial	Working hours	Other benefits
salary	full time	company car

4 Look at the numbers. Which items in exercise 3 could they refer to?

1 40 hours   5 10%
2 2 hours   6 20 days
3 £25,000   7 9 a.m.–3 p.m.
4 £1,000   8 £5,000

5 🔊 1.55 Listen to a conversation about a job offer. Check your answers to exercise 4.

6 Tell a partner which items from exercise 3 would be the most important to you in a job. Give reasons.

Exam skills

Completing notes from a recording

7 🔊 1.56 Listen and complete the sentences. Change the words you hear to fit the gaps.

1 Students who are interested are asked to fill in a _____.

2 When their courses _____, students have to _____ _____.

3 Employees have access to both a _____ _____.

8 Read the notes about *Sterne Consulting Group* on page 61. Match the types of information (a–h) below with gaps 1–9 in the notes.

a a benefit (x2) _____   e something you learn _____

b a grade or mark _____   f a plural noun _____

c a type of payment _____   g an action (verb) _____

d a course or programme _____   h a describing word (adjective) _____

9 🔊 1.58 Listen and complete the notes on page 61. Write no more than two words or a number.

EXAM TIP 🔊 1.57

When you complete notes from a recording, make sure you read the notes before you listen. What should you do while you read them? » page 146

Exam practice

10 🔊 1.59 **Listen and complete the notes below. Write no more than three words and/or a number for each answer.**

Notes on teacher training:
– Trainee teachers work in four different ¹_____ during the year.
– Each placement lasts from ²_____ weeks and then trainees return to college in order to
  ³_____ the experience.
– The course is assessed through both observations of teaching and the marks given for ⁴_____.
– The biggest challenge for many trainees is to ⁵_____.
– The salary isn't high but there are twelve ⁶_____ every year and a generous ⁷_____.

What do you think?

11 **What things do you think are important for getting a job? Number a–e in order of importance (1 = most important, 5 = least important).**

a making personal contacts ......   d being good at interviews ......
b getting qualifications ......   e being prepared to work for free at first ......
c getting experience ......

12 **Compare your answers to exercise 11 with a partner. Explain your reasons.**

Study skills

Learning vocabulary   **What things do you need to know when you learn new words?**

Example: *definition, pronunciation, spelling*

Look at the ideas for learning vocabulary. Tell a partner which ideas work best for you.

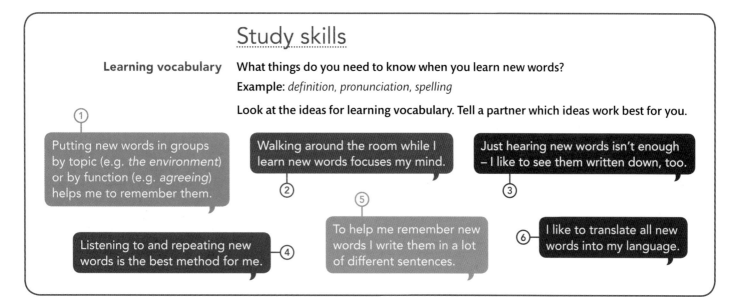

① Putting new words in groups by topic (e.g. *the environment*) or by function (e.g. *agreeing*) helps me to remember them.

② Walking around the room while I learn new words focuses my mind.

③ Just hearing new words isn't enough – I like to see them written down, too.

④ Listening to and repeating new words is the best method for me.

⑤ To help me remember new words I write them in a lot of different sentences.

⑥ I like to translate all new words into my language.

From plan to topic sentences

- write topic sentences from plans
- use linkers *is / is that* in topic sentences
- use words for academic ideas in topic sentences

Topic focus

1 How much would the rewards below motivate you? Number them 1–5 (1 = a little, 5 = a lot).

> *friendship* *fame* *job satisfaction* *a medal or trophy* *a large financial bonus*
> *a good pension* *a comfortable lifestyle* *respect from colleagues* *making parents proud*

2 Compare your answers to exercise 1 with a partner. Give reasons and examples.

Exam skills

Writing topic sentences from plans

3 Read the essay question. Discuss your opinions with a partner.

Some professionals, like bankers, receive large financial rewards while the pay of teachers and nurses remains relatively low. Some people think it is right to pay workers in some professions more than we pay others. To what extent do you agree or disagree?

4 Look at the plan below. Then match reasons 1–3 with topic sentences a–c.

> <u>Thesis:</u>
> I will argue that big differences in pay between professions are fair.
> <u>Reasons:</u>
> 1 Highly paid work often requires extra experience and training.
> 2 People can choose if they enter a high-paid profession or a low-paid profession.
> 3 Money is not the only important thing in life.
> <u>Topic sentences:</u>
> a) The first reason for my position is that school-leavers or graduates can easily predict the impact their career decisions will have on their income.
> b) Secondly, I would argue that most highly paid jobs involve a higher level of knowledge and skill than lower-paid jobs.
> c) The final reason for my view is that although teachers and nurses receive low pay, they are rewarded for their work in other ways.

EXAM TIP 🔊 1.60

The first sentence in each paragraph of an essay is often a topic sentence. What's one example of how each topic sentence might connect to the thesis statement?
» page 147

5 The topic sentence below is divided into three parts (1–3). Match a description (a–c) to a part of the sentence.

[1]The final reason for my view is that / [2]teachers and nurses / [3]are rewarded for their work in other ways.

a main subject of paragraph
b claim about subject of paragraph
c phrase to connect paragraph to other paragraphs

6 Look at topic sentences 1–3 from three different essays. Divide each sentence into three parts following the model in exercise 5.

1 The second reason for my position in this debate is that public sector employees have more job security.

2 The final explanation for salary differences is that companies are free to decide how much they pay.

3 One negative effect of giving a lot of bonuses is that the people who want them may take risks in their work.

Vocabulary VOCABULARY FILE » page 126

Academic ideas

7 Match each definition below with a word in column A of the table in exercise 8.

> *result   positive effect   negative effect   method   cause   reason / excuse*

8 Connect phrases in columns A–C of the table to make six sentences.

A	B	C
1 An explanation	of	working from home is that you can't attend meetings.
2 A drawback	of	raising university fees is that it will improve standards of education.
3 An advantage	of	low motivation is a lack of support from managers.
4 A consequence	to	employing younger people is that they are easier to train.
5 A justification	for	motivate staff is to increase pay.
6 A way	for	modern communications is that more people work from home.

9 Describe 1–6 with your own ideas. The first one is done for you.

1 reduced travel time   = an advantage   *of working from home*

2 working at night   = a drawback

3 stress at work   = a consequence

4 closure of factories   = an explanation

5 limits on pay   = a way

6 increased profits   = a justification

Grammar GRAMMAR FILE » page 116

Linkers: *is / is that*

10 Underline examples of the linkers *is* and *is that* in column C of exercise 8. Which linker is followed by:

a an infinitive or noun?

b a subject + verb?

11 Put *is* or *is that* in the correct place in the sentences.

1 A consequence of low pay workers are less motivated.

2 A way to get job satisfaction to do something you are good at.

3 An advantage of paying people the same they will work better with others.

4 A drawback of fame lack of privacy.

12 Complete the topic sentences for the essay question below with your own ideas.

What are the advantages of going to university?

1 The first advantage   .

2 Another consequence   .

3 A final justification   .

Exam practice

13 Write a plan and topic sentences for one of the essay questions below.

1 Nowadays, too many young people want to become famous. Do you agree or disagree?

2 What can bosses do to motivate their staff?

3 Success at work brings happiness. Do you agree?

14 Work with a partner and take turns. Read your topic sentences from exercise 13. Can you guess which essay question they refer to?

- match headings with paragraphs using topic sentences
- understand and speak about factors for success

Topic focus

1 Read passages A–C. Which advice do you think is the most useful?

Tips from the top:
Successful people share their secrets

A 'More than any other element, fun is the secret of Virgin's success,' says businessman Richard Branson. When he started his company Virgin from a basement flat in West London, he simply set out to create something that would be enjoyable and pay the bills. The business empire was a bonus.

B You have to admire the ability of top sports people. But ex-paralympic athlete Linda Mastandrea believes that the key to success is really determination. She claims it's the drive to work hard every single day that separates a winner from the rest of the pack. 'Go after your dream no matter how unattainable others think it is,' she says.

C Lisa Tse, businesswoman, is modest about her success. She believes it's the people around her that have made the difference to her life. Her parents told her to surround herself with people of good reputation, so that she would be viewed positively, too. And, she adds, if you associate with top professionals, you'll soon learn what makes them successful.

2 How successful are you at working or studying? Give a partner some advice of your own.

Exam skills

Matching headings with paragraphs

3 Read the passages in exercise 1 again. Underline the sentence in each text that gives the main idea most simply.

4 The sentences you underlined in exercise 3 are *topic sentences*. Use them to help you to match the passages in exercise 1 with one of the headings below.

1 Being determined will make you successful.
2 Always enjoy your success.
3 Not everyone can be successful.
4 Success is about being with the right people.
5 To be successful, you must have a good time.
6 Parents are responsible for our success.

5 Underline the topic sentence in each paragraph A–G of the passage on page 65. According to the author, which two of the factors below result in career success?

1 hard work   3 appearance   5 other people
2 intelligence   4 luck

6 Look at the task in exercise 7. Can all the headings i–viii be matched with the paragraphs?

EXAM TIP 🔊 1.61

Finding topic sentences is an important skill. Where do you usually find them?
» page 148

SOURCES OF SUCCESS

A Why do some achieve more than others? Ask a successful person and they may point to their talents and all their hard work. Investor Warren Buffet, for instance, suggests that integrity, **intelligence**, and energy are essential,
5 whereas for millionaire Marc Andreessen it's about **motivation, drive**, ethics, and **curiosity**. In short, what's on the inside is key. Or is it? Research suggests that what's on the outside counts for more than we may think.

B Few could deny that intelligence is essential to success
10 in early life. Brighter students, particularly those whose parents are well educated, tend to do well at school and they then usually go on to the better universities and enter the higher-paid professions. But it seems to account for at most a third of personal wealth in later life, and the
15 impact of intelligence and **family background** *after* leaving university is less clear.

C In fact, it seems that during working life, **educational background** has much less impact than it once did. Recent research into legal careers shows that while students from
20 well-educated families tend to enter the profession more easily, the less advantaged students that enter usually earn more and work for better firms. Some causes of success clearly lie beyond academic achievement.

D Admittedly, the capacity for hard work is probably
25 important, too. A recent study found that people who earn less than $20,000 a year, for instance, spent more than a third of their time in passive leisure. By contrast, those earning more than $100,000 a year spent less than a fifth of their time relaxing. But hard work can often be the result of
30 success, as well as the cause, and there is certainly room for exploring other causes.

E Indeed, new research suggests that a wide variety of external factors also assist high achievers. Rice University, in Texas, found that a person's **looks** and smile particularly
35 help them to gain trust and so bring employment or promotion opportunities. A person's **height** and the depth of their voice are also significant, it would seem. Male Chief Executive Officers (CEOs) are over 7 centimetres taller than the average man, according to Harvard University,
40 and those with lower-pitched voices apparently have better social connections than other CEOs.

F Self-presentation and the way we **dress** may also play a role. For example, a typical pink shirt wearer earns £1,000 more per year than males who wear more sober colours
45 for work. While clothing could simply be a product of personality, another study showed that women who wear make-up are far more likely to be taken seriously than those who don't, demonstrating that appearance itself can bring rewards.

50 G So, is style becoming more important than substance? Given the importance of the visual image in the modern media, it would not be surprising. Perhaps teaching the art of making an impression on others may be as valuable to today's generation as a traditional schooling.

Exam practice

7 Match headings i–viii with the paragraphs in 1–5.

i	It's all about the voice	1	Paragraph B
ii	Our bodies talk	2	Paragraph C
iii	The effects of a good education	3	Paragraph D
iv	The lifestyles of successful people	4	Paragraph E
v	We can all be successful now	5	Paragraph F
vi	Dressing for success		
vii	The importance of academic success in adult life		
viii	The views of successful people		

Vocabulary   VOCABULARY FILE » page 126

Factors for success **8 Put the bold words in the text into the correct columns of the table.**

External factors (things people can see)	Internal factors (things people can't see)	Situational factors (the world around us)

MOST IMPORTANT
FACTORS FOR SUCCESS

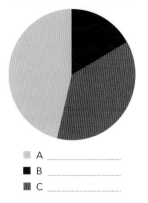

- ■ A _____
- ■ B _____
- ■ C _____

9 Read the passage on page 65. Then label the parts of the pie chart *external*, *internal*, and *situational* according to the opinion of the author.

10 Do you agree with the author's opinion in the passage? Would you label the pie chart in a different way? Tell a partner and give examples.

> *I think situational factors are the most important. For example, family background is essential because children often follow the career choices of parents.*

What do you think?

11 Which factors are most important for the careers below? Write *E* (external), *I* (internal), or *S* (situational).

> musician _____ teacher _____ banker _____ air traffic controller _____
> web designer _____ scientist _____ soldier _____ fashion model _____

12 Compare your answers to exercise 11 with a partner. Give reasons and examples.

> *I think situational factors are important for a soldier because you need a good team to support you.*

EXAM CHALLENGE

SPEAKING

1 Speak for 1-2 minutes about the topic on the card. Ask a partner to listen to you or record your responses.

> Describe someone you know who has an interesting job.
> You should say:
> – who they are
> – what they do in their job
> – why they are good at their job
> and explain how well you think you would do their job.

2 Ask your partner or yourself the questions.

   1 Did you make an effort to vary your language?

   2 Did you use a second conditional in response to the last prompt?

LISTENING

1 Do questions 8–10 in Practice test: Listening on page 149.

2 Did you manage to predict any of the information in the notes?

WRITING

1 Read the essay question below. Work alone and write a plan and topic sentences for the essay. Finish them in 5 minutes.

   > Some people think that job satisfaction is more important than high pay. What do you think?

2 Compare your plan and topic sentences with the model answer on page 108. Then answer the questions.

   1 Are your topic sentences in a logical order?

   2 Does each topic sentence provide a clear reason for your opinion?

READING

1 Do questions 14–19 in Practice test: Reading on page 156. Try to get at least four answers correct in 8 minutes.

2 Did you find the topic sentence each time?

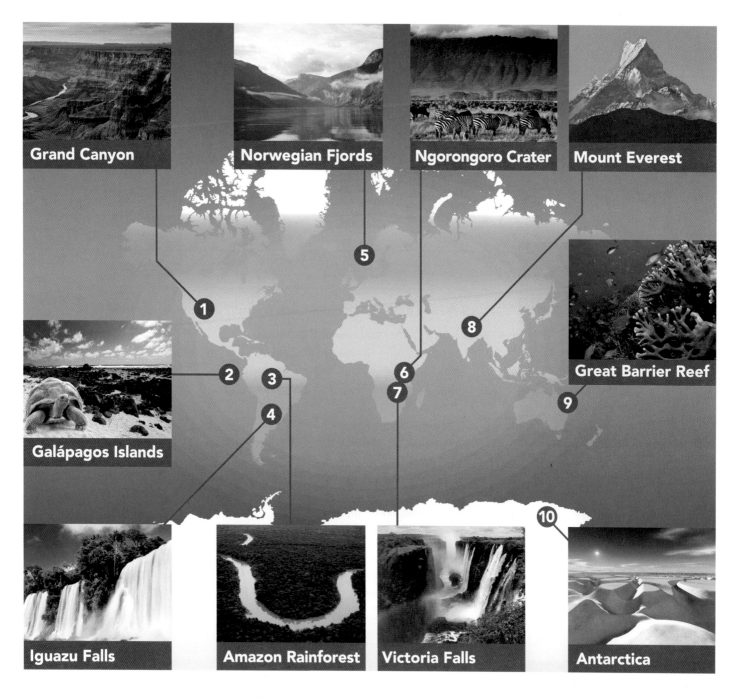

Grand Canyon

Norwegian Fjords

Ngorongoro Crater

Mount Everest

Great Barrier Reef

Galápagos Islands

Iguazu Falls

Amazon Rainforest

Victoria Falls

Antarctica

What do you think?

1 The map shows ten of the world's natural wonders. How many have you heard of?

2 Which country / countries are the natural wonders located in?

3 Which natural wonder would you most like to visit? Why?

4 What other locations or events would you add to the list of natural wonders?

5 Why is it important to protect and conserve the natural environment?

Adding detail to descriptions

- ▶ remember details about places
- ▶ use sentences with 'empty' subjects
- ▶ use adverbs of degree in descriptions
- ▶ speak about the weather

Topic focus

1 What are the best natural places to visit in your country (not in a town or city)?

2 What is the best time of year to go there? Why?

Vocabulary   VOCABULARY FILE » page 127

Weather   3 🔊 1.62 Listen to three people speaking about different regions of the world. Match each speaker with a region.

    a Northern Europe   b Caribbean   c Eastern Asia

4 🔊 1.63 Listen again. Which adjectives does each speaker use? Write 1, 2, or 3 next to each word.

changeable _____	pleasant _____	chilly _____	overcast _____	wet _____
stormy _____	mild _____	humid _____	sunny _____	cool _____	dry _____	windy _____

5 Circle the adjectives from exercise 4 which usually describe temperature.

6 Work with a partner and answer the questions.

  1 What is the difference between the following pairs of words?
    a mild, cool   b overcast, stormy

  2 Which adjectives from exercise 4 do you associate with the following nouns?
    a showers   b thunder   c mist

  3 What kind of weather and temperature do you associate with the following?
    a a mountainous area   b the rainy season   c a region by the sea

Grammar   GRAMMAR FILE » page 113

'Empty' subjects   7 Add *it* to the text in four places.

> In Ecuador the temperature varies by region. By the coast, to the west of Ecuador, is usually warm – about 25°C on average. However, the capital, Quito, is in the mountains and so its climate is fairly cool. During the day is just 18.9°C and 10°C at night. There are seasonal changes, too. Between January and April is particularly hot and it rains a lot because is the middle of the wet season.

8 Complete sentences 1–4 with *it* or *there.*

  1 _____ snows a lot.   3 _____ is some mist.
  2 _____ is a lot of wind.   4 _____ is sunny.

Exam practice

9 Work with a partner and take turns. Student A, go to page 109. Student B, go to page 112.

EXAM TIP   🔊 1.64

In Speaking Part 2, you may be asked to talk about a place. What's one way of remembering details about different places? » page 145

Exam skills

Remembering details 10 Add the adjectives to the diagram on the left.

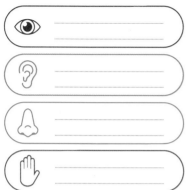

> thrilled   pretty   noisy   sweet   colourful   impressed   disgusting   peaceful

11 🔊 1.65 Listen to someone talking about a place of great natural beauty. Write one example they give for each of the categories below.

sights: _scenic beaches_

sounds: ....

smells: ....

sensations: ....

Grammar   **GRAMMAR FILE » page 116**

Adverbs of degree 12 🔊 1.66 Listen again. Tick the adverbs you hear below.

> absolutely   a little   fairly   pretty   extremely   a bit   completely   quite   really

13 Put the adverbs from exercise 12 on the line below.

smallest degree ◄————— *quite* —————► largest degree

14 Which adverbs from exercise 12 are usually used before:
  1 strong adjectives, e.g. *amazing*? ....
  2 non-gradable adjectives, e.g. *silent*? ....
  3 adjectives with negative meanings, e.g. *crowded*? ....

15 Choose the best adverbs to complete the text.

The ¹*fairly / absolutely* spectacular fjords of Musandam are one of the best places to visit. Although part of Oman, it's ²*really / completely* separated from the rest of the country by the surrounding United Arab Emirates. You can explore the ³*really / absolutely* attractive fishing villages and you have a ⁴*pretty / completely* good chance of seeing dolphins. ⁵*An absolutely / A fairly* small number of tourists visit Musandam but it's ⁶*a little / really* beautiful. It's ⁷*pretty / extremely* hot all year round but the best time to visit is between November and March when it's ⁸*a little / quite* comfortable. The trip can be ⁹*a bit / completely* long and tiring, but it's well worth it.

Exam practice

16 Speak for 1–2 minutes about the topic on the card.

> Describe a place of great natural beauty in your country.
> You should say:
> – where it is
> – what the place is like
> – when the best time of year to visit is
> and explain why people should visit it.

LISTENING
EXAM FOCUS: SECTION 4

Labelling diagrams

- ▶ predict content of a lecture
- ▶ recognize and transcribe compound nouns
- ▶ recognize key phrases for direction and location in diagrams
- ▶ consider how to practise test preparation independently

Topic focus

1 What do pictures A–C show? What things in nature do they look like?

A   B   C

Exam skills

Predicting content

2 You are going to listen to parts of a biology lecture. Look again at the pictures on this page and the diagram on page 71. What do you think the topic will be? Choose from 1–4 below. Then explain your choice to a partner.

1 plant and animal products in the things we make
2 amazing designs in nature
3 uses of living plants and animals
4 using nature to solve problems

3 🔊 2.1 Listen to part 1 of the lecture. Check your answer to exercise 2.

Key phrases

Location and direction

4 Look at the diagram of a natural pool on page 71. What can you see in the places below?

> *in the top right corner   on the left   in the centre   on the right*

5 Look at the arrows showing water flow in the diagram. Starting at point X, number the phrases below in the order you would expect to hear them.

> *to the left   below   downwards   to the right*

6 🔊 2.2 Listen to part 2 of the lecture and check.

Vocabulary   VOCABULARY FILE » page 127

Compound nouns

7 Use the words to make compound nouns for definitions 1–8 below.

> *fall (x2)   level   cap   line   pressure   pool   bed*

1 sea _____: the floor of the sea
2 rain _____: the total amount of rain in one area in a period of time
3 coast _____: the land along the edge of a country next to the sea
4 rock _____: a small amount of water that collects between the rocks by the sea

5 ice _____ : a layer of frozen water permanently covering part of the Earth, especially in the North and South Poles

6 water _____ : a place where a stream or river drops from a high place, e.g. a cliff or rock

7 sea _____ : the average height of the sea, used to measure the height of other things such as mountains

8 air _____ : the force from the Earth's atmosphere

Exam skills

Transcribing compound nouns

8 🔊 2.3 Listen and write the compound nouns you hear. Why is it sometimes difficult to hear them correctly?

9 🔊 2.4 Listen to part 2 of the lecture again. Label 1–5 in the diagram.

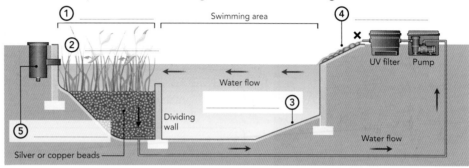

EXAM TIP 🔊 2.5

In Listening Section 4, you may have to label diagrams with technical words that are unfamiliar. How can you write words accurately if you don't know them?
» page 146

Exam practice

10 🔊 2.6 Listen to part 3 of the lecture. Label the diagram on page 109.

11 🔊 2.7 Listen to part 4 of the lecture. Match plants and animals 1–4 with ideas A–F that they have inspired.

1 Namibian beetle
2 Locust
3 Whales
4 Lotus leaves

A preventing diseases
B creating safer roads
C cleaning surfaces
D getting water from a natural source
E saving energy
F making travel quicker

What do you think?

12 Choose a statement to discuss in groups.

1 The natural world can teach us many useful things.
2 We shouldn't waste the world's natural resources.
3 The natural world is often dangerous and needs to be controlled.

Study skills

Practising independently

Circle which IELTS test you can prepare for most easily by yourself. Why?

Listening   Reading   Speaking   Writing

What activities could you do to prepare for the Speaking and Writing tests?

> I could record my voice then write down what I said.

> I could practise describing the main trends of diagrams on the internet.

WRITING

From topic sentence to paragraph

- ▸ write structured paragraphs
- ▸ use the zero conditional for causes and effects
- ▸ write about natural threats and their effects

Topic focus

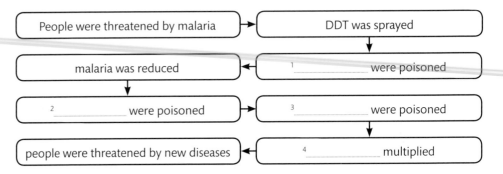

A   B   C   D

1 Match the words with pictures A–D.

> *gecko   mosquito   cat   rat*

2 What is happening to the cats in the picture on the left? Read the text on page 109 to find out why.

3 Read the text on page 109 again. Then complete the flow chart with animals from exercise 1.

| People were threatened by malaria | → | DDT was sprayed |

| malaria was reduced | ← | 1 _____ were poisoned |

| 2 _____ were poisoned | → | 3 _____ were poisoned |

| people were threatened by new diseases | ← | 4 _____ multiplied |

Vocabulary   **VOCABULARY FILE » page 127**

Natural threats

4 What do each of the natural threats below have an effect on?

Example: *flood – buildings, food supplies, wildlife, farmland*

> *flood   food shortage   volcano   asteroid   drought   earthquake*
> *disease   predator   erosion   climate change*

5 What can people do about the effects of the natural threats in exercise 4?

Example: *When there is a flood, people can move to higher areas.*

Exam skills

Writing structured paragraphs

6 Look at the pictures below. How do the activities control nature?

A Harvesting of water hyacinth

B Building a dam

EXAM TIP 🔊 2.8

Make sure your paragraphs are well structured. What exactly does this mean?
» page 147

7 Use a–d to label sentences 1–4 in the paragraph below.

a result
b example
c explanation
d topic sentence

¹Plant species can be a challenge to control. ²For instance, water hyacinth, once only found in South America, is now found on lakes in all continents and causes huge problems. ³In Africa's Lake Victoria the plant currently covers 70,000 hectares, blocking sunlight, killing fish, and stopping boats from crossing the lake. ⁴As a consequence, lakeside communities, which depend on fishing, are losing income and are suffering from severe food shortages.

8 Put sentences a–d into the correct order to make a paragraph.

a For example, if a country builds a dam, it often has several negative effects.

b A dam causes a change in the water level for many miles down a river – affecting farming, fishing, and water transport industries.

c It can be dangerous to try to control nature.

d If this happens, people's jobs and important animal species are then lost.

Grammar   GRAMMAR FILE » page 117

Zero conditional for causes and effects

9 Match causes 1–4 with effects a–d.

1 flood
2 earthquake
3 disease
4 hurricane

a trees fall over
b buildings are damaged
c buildings collapse
d people need medication

10 Write sentences to connect the causes and effects in exercise 9. Use *if* in the sentences.

Example: *If there is a flood, buildings are often damaged.*

Exam practice

11 Read the question and the topic sentences. Does the writer agree or disagree with the statement in the question?

Question: Modern science has learnt to control natural threats and we have much less to fear than we did in the past. To what extent do you agree?

Topic sentences:

– Human interventions often cause more problems than they solve.
– Not all natural threats can be controlled.
– New natural threats continue to emerge.
– Some natural disasters are difficult to predict.
– It takes money and resources to control nature, which few governments have.

12 Choose one of the topic sentences in exercise 11. Write the rest of the paragraph (but do not include the topic sentence).

13 Work with a partner. Exchange your paragraphs from exercise 12. Can you guess which topic sentence your partner chose?

- answer *True / False / Not Given* questions
- understand pronoun referents in a passage

Topic focus

1 What are the animals in pictures A–E? What do you think they have in common? Discuss with a partner.

Exam skills

Answering True / False / Not Given questions

2 Read the passage on page 75. Circle which statements are true and which are false.

1 The elephants have migrated through a hotel.	True / False
2 The monarch butterfly migrates north because of the temperatures.	True / False
3 The red crab travels to lay eggs.	True / False
4 The Arctic tern travels in a straight line.	True / False

EXAM TIP 🔊 2.9

In *True / False / Not Given* questions, you have to compare several statements with information in the passage. Which of the three options can be confusing? Why?

» page 148

3 Read the passage again quickly. Which of statements 1–5 does the author disagree with? Which facts in statements 1–5 does the author not give? Circle which statements are *False* and which are *Not Given*.

1 The elephant migration is dangerous for hotel guests.	False / Not Given
2 Most monarch butterflies die before completing their journey.	False / Not Given
3 Red crabs move a lot during the year.	False / Not Given
4 Animals use the moon to tell them when to migrate.	False / Not Given
5 The number of monarch butterflies is rising.	False / Not Given

4 Discuss the questions about exercise 3 with a partner.

1 How confident did you feel about putting *Not Given* for an answer?

2 How many times did you read each section to decide if the information is *Not Given*?

Exam practice

5 Do statements 1–5 agree with the information in the passage? Write:
True if the statement agrees with the information
False if the statement contradicts the information
Not Given if there is no information on this.

1 Monarch butterflies use the sun to navigate. _____

2 Red crabs spend most of their lives in the ocean. _____

3 Red crab migration is being threatened by tourists. _____

4 Arctic terns face many challenges on their journey. _____

5 Arctic terns don't stop to find food. _____

6 Match animals A–E with facts 1–7.

A

B  C

D

E

A Arctic tern	1 were altered by scientists
B Monarch butterfly	2 have large brains
C Elephant	3 like to eat fruit
D Red crab	4 change biologically before migrating
E Trout	5 use the wind
	6 use their noses to navigate
	7 carry scientific equipment

Secrets of migration

A Every year in November a herd of elephants in Zambia returns to eat fruit from the same group of mango trees. But one year they returned to find that a luxury hotel, Mfuwe Lodge, had been built around their trees. So, what did
5 the elephants do? We might expect them to have turned away, confused. However, it seems their memory was so strong that they simply walked through the reception, into the hotel garden, and found the fruit. Such remarkable stories of animal migration have long fascinated humans
10 and attracted biologists, whose research is revealing some amazing insights.

B Whereas elephants can rely on large brains and incredible memories to find their migration paths, smaller species carry other special equipment. Take for example,
15 the monarch butterfly in the USA. It migrates further than any insect species, flying 2,000 km south to Mexico to escape winter temperatures, and then north again to feed. By painting one of their antennae black and observing the resulting confusion, scientists have concluded that
20 the butterfly uses them to sense the position of the sun and navigate effectively. In another recent study, on trout, scientists discovered cells in the fish's nose that respond to the Earth's magnetic field, just like an internal compass, helping them to swim either up or down a river.

25 **C** Other animals have been shown to make amazing biological changes just before they travel. Christmas Island, an isolated Australian territory located in the Indian Ocean, accommodates up to 120 million red crabs, which migrate each year from the island's high central rainforest to the
30 sea to lay their eggs. The 'red tide' of young crabs that journey 5 km through towns and along roads has to be seen to be believed, but their journey is more incredible when you consider that under normal circumstances they can only walk for 10 minutes before needing to rest. Tests have
35 shown that high levels of sugar are released into the blood before each migration, enabling them to keep going for several days.

D Some species cleverly use their environments to gain fuel and support for their journeys. The Arctic tern is a
40 prime example. It holds the record for the longest migration route of any known creature, travelling for most of the year from breeding grounds in northern Canada down to the Southern Ocean of Antarctica and back, an annual journey of over 70,000 km. But its journey is not direct. By
45 attaching electronic tracking devices to birds, researchers have discovered that they fly in a giant 'S' shape, using air currents to help them save energy and adapting their route to stop at particular islands that are known to offer feeding opportunities.

50 **E** Such research may be interesting but it has great value, too. Tracking animals as they migrate and monitoring their numbers can help scientists protect them better in the face of a number of threats. For instance, research has shown that numbers of monarch butterflies have been declining for
55 the last seven years, falling 59% in 2013 alone, and this has highlighted the need for controls on logging, land clearing, and use of pesticides in Mexico and the USA. Tracking elephants has proved how illegal killing is stopping them from passing on the knowledge of migration routes to
60 younger elephants. Despite this knowledge, if we are not careful, some of the greatest spectacles of nature could change radically or even be lost forever.

Grammar GRAMMAR FILE » page 113

Pronoun referents **7** Find pronouns 1–8 in the passage. What does each one refer to in the passage? The first one is done for you.

1 their (line 4) ___elephants___

2 them (line 20) _____

3 them (line 24) _____

4 they (line 26) _____

5 them (line 36) _____

6 its (line 44) _____

7 this (line 55) _____

8 them (line 58) _____

8 Use the words to complete the text below.

| they | them | it | these | their |

Emperor penguins aren't the only species of this bird that migrate, but [1]_____ are perhaps the most famous. [2]_____ magnificent creatures have adapted well to the difficult conditions that surround [3]_____. Though the migration of emperor penguins to and from [4]_____ nesting areas is short compared to that of many animals, [5]_____ is full of challenges and the risks are great.

What do you think?

9 Discuss the questions with a partner.

1 How popular are TV programmes or channels about nature and wildlife in your country?

2 Why could learning about how animals navigate be useful to humans?

3 Animals migrate to find food, raise their young, or find better weather. Do people 'migrate' or move for similar reasons?

EXAM CHALLENGE

SPEAKING

1 Prepare to speak about the topic on the card. Think or make notes for 1 minute.

Talk about a visit you made to the countryside.
You should say:
– where you went
– why you went there
– what the weather was like
and explain what you enjoyed about the place.

2 Speak for 1–2 minutes about the topic on the card. Ask a partner to listen to you or record your responses.

3 Ask your partner or yourself the questions.

1 Did you use *used to* and/or other past forms?

2 Did you describe details about the sights, smells, sounds, and sensations?

LISTENING

1 Do questions 35–37 in Practice test: Listening on page 152. Try to get at least two answers correct.

2 Did you use your knowledge of individual words to spell the compounds correctly?

WRITING

1 Write a paragraph to follow the topic sentence below.

Governments can now control the effects of extreme weather effectively.

2 Check your paragraph with the model answer on page 109. Did you include:

a supporting examples?

b a conditional sentence to show cause and effect?

READING

1 Do questions 8–13 in Practice test: Reading on page 155. Try to get at least four answers correct in 9 minutes.

2 Did you understand the difference between *Not Given* and *False* information?

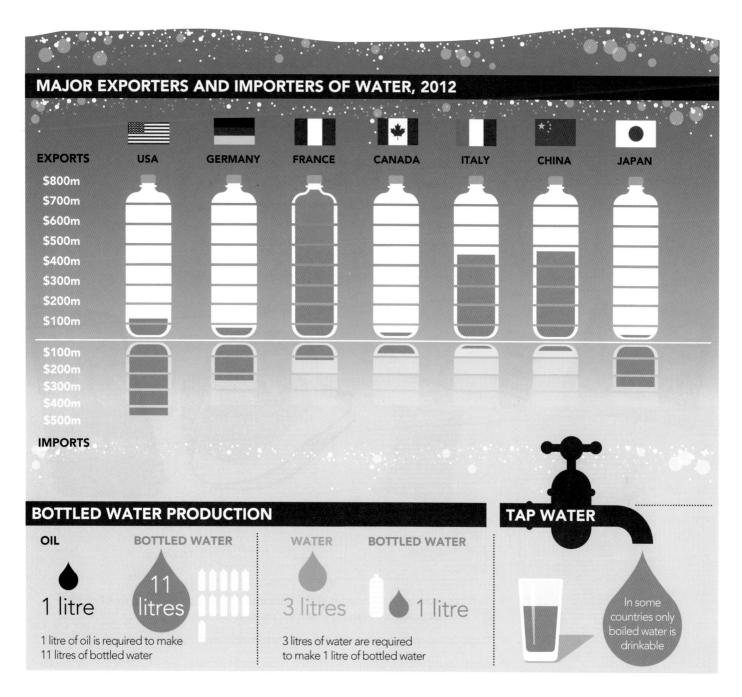

MAJOR EXPORTERS AND IMPORTERS OF WATER, 2012

EXPORTS	USA	GERMANY	FRANCE	CANADA	ITALY	CHINA	JAPAN

$800m
$700m
$600m
$500m
$400m
$300m
$200m
$100m

$100m
$200m
$300m
$400m
$500m

IMPORTS

BOTTLED WATER PRODUCTION

OIL

1 litre

BOTTLED WATER

11 litres

1 litre of oil is required to make 11 litres of bottled water

WATER

3 litres

BOTTLED WATER

1 litre

3 litres of water are required to make 1 litre of bottled water

TAP WATER

In some countries only boiled water is drinkable

What do you think?

1 Why is French water so popular?

2 Why does the USA import so much water?

3 Do you drink tap water or do you buy bottled water? Why?

4 What other products does your country import and export?

5 What are the advantages and disadvantages of international trade?

- recognize question types for Part 3
- speak about consumer products
- use key phrases to respond to different question types

Topic focus

1 How do you like to shop? Underline one option in each of 1–6.

   1 I buy what I need **OR** I buy what I want

   2 I ask for advice **OR** I choose by myself

   3 I buy immediately **OR** I wait until it's cheaper

   4 I buy online **OR** I buy in shops

   5 I only buy my favourite brands **OR** I try new brands

   6 I plan my shopping **OR** I shop when I like

2 Compare your answers to exercise 1 with a partner. Give reasons and examples.

Vocabulary   VOCABULARY FILE » page 128

Consumer products

3 Look at pictures A–F. What are the products? Put them into the categories below.

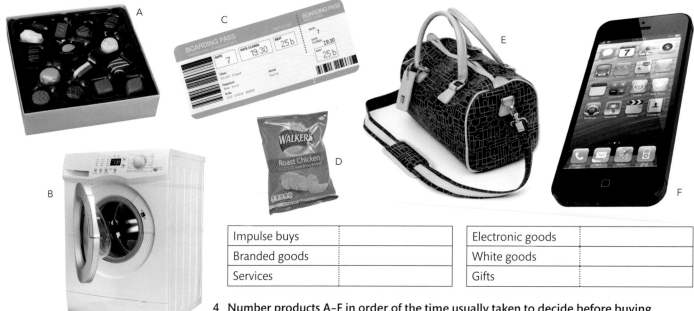

Impulse buys			Electronic goods	
Branded goods			White goods	
Services			Gifts	

4 Number products A–F in order of the time usually taken to decide before buying. (1 = shortest amount of time, 6 = longest amount of time).

5 Think of two more items to add to each category in exercise 3.

6 What would you do before buying the products in pictures A–F? Choose 1–6 below for each product. Then compare with a partner.

   1 Check a comparison website.

   2 Read online reviews by other consumers.

   3 Look for special offers.

   4 Get a personal recommendation.

   5 Browse through a catalogue.

   6 Look at / Try a sample in a shop.

7 Tell a partner how you would buy each of the things below.

> *coat   bicycle   sunglasses   printer ink cartridges   tablet computer*

Exam skills

Recognizing question types

8 Match questions 1–4 with functions a–d below.

1 Which is better? Going to an out-of-town shopping centre or to local shops?

2 What are the most important exports in your country?

3 Why do you think some people prefer to write shopping lists?

4 Will we buy everything online in the future?

a prediction

b speculation

c comparison

d evaluation

9 🔊 2.11 Listen to eight different questions. Match each question with a function (a–d) in exercise 8.

1 ....   5 ....

2 ....   6 ....

3 ....   7 ....

4 ....   8 ....

Key phrases

Responses to different question types

10 🔊 2.12 Listen again. Choose the correct response (a–h) for each question you hear.

a **It's probably because** they enjoy shopping.

b It depends on the person. **The main thing is** to buy what you need.

c **Maybe it's because** they think that children are already spoilt.

d Gifts, **more than anything**. I think some husbands hate choosing things for their wives.

e **My guess is that** there'll be more factories and more pollution.

f **They're totally different**. Women make more impulse buys, I think.

g I think **both are important** but the second is more fun!

h I'd say **they're likely to become** smaller.

11 Put the phrases in bold from exercise 10 into the table below.

Prediction	Speculation	Comparison	Evaluation

Exam practice

12 Work in groups of three and take turns. Student A, go to page 109. Student B, answer Student A's questions. Student C, make a note of the key phrases that Student B uses.

LISTENING

EXAM FOCUS: SECTION 3

Choosing options from lists

- ▶ choose multiple items in a list
- ▶ recognize and use words to describe money and value
- ▶ deal with test-related stress

Money and value

Topic focus

1 Work alone and answer the questions. Circle option a, b, or c.

1 If you received a large amount of money, would you:
   a have a holiday with friends? b save it? c buy a new car?

2 If your home was on fire, which item would you save first?
   a pictures or photos b wallet or purse c electronic goods

3 If you bought a present for a colleague, what would it be like?
   a expensive b expensive (and buy yourself one) c as cheap as possible

4 If a colleague won a car, would you think:
   a I'm happy for them b I wish I were them c That's so unfair!

5 A friend asks if they can borrow your new bicycle. Do you:
   a agree happily? b agree but say 'Be careful'? c refuse?

2 Which option in exercise 1 did you circle most? What do you think your answers say about you?

Vocabulary VOCABULARY FILE » page 128

3 Would you normally use the words and phrases below to describe products, people, or experiences? Put them into the correct column.

> priceless   worthless   wealthy   good value   rich
> valuable   a waste of money   wasteful   pricey   poor

Products only	Products or experiences	People

4 Complete the sentences with words or phrases from exercise 3.

1 This antique collection is worth a fortune. It's ....

2 We can't afford that house. It's too ....

3 Who would buy that jacket? It's totally ....

4 You shouldn't spend so much on clothes. You're so ....

5 How much did you buy? Are you feeling ....?

6 His parents send him a lot of money because they're very ....

7 Oh, look! If you buy one bottle, you get one free. That's ....

8 How .... is that painting?

9 I never buy new textbooks. They're ....

10 I give a percentage of my income to .... people.

5 With a partner, discuss the value of each item in the list below. Decide which item you would buy.

> I think the home cinema system would be **pricey** ...

home cinema system   meal in a top restaurant   designer watch
two tickets for a music festival   new suit / dress   piece of original artwork

80   **UNIT 8   PRODUCERS & CONSUMERS**

Exam skills

Choosing multiple items in a list

6 Answer questions 1-3 about the task below.

1 Do you have to write letters or words?

2 How many items do you have to choose?

3 Does it matter in what order you write the answers?

Which three things are discussed in the tutorial? Choose three letters (A–G).

A why being happy is important

B examples of important possessions

C the meaning of 'materialism'

D human motivation and the brain

E the objects that make us unhappy

F how long researchers have studied materialism

G the theory of evolution

7 Underline the key words in options A–G in exercise 6.

EXAM TIP	◢ 2.13

In addition to basic multiple-choice questions, you may have to choose more than one option from a list. Why can this be difficult? » page 146

8 ◢ 2.14 Two students have done the survey in exercise 1 as preparation for a sociology tutorial. Listen to part 1 of the tutorial. Circle the three correct options A–G in exercise 6.

Exam practice

9 ◢ 2.15 Listen to part 2 of the tutorial. Which three things are mentioned by the speakers? Choose three letters (A–G).

A social events

B marriage

C sports activities

D family vacations

E branded goods

F traditional toys

G giving gifts

10 ◢ 2.16 Listen to part 3 of the tutorial. Complete the summary. Write one word for each answer.

People with materialistic values are often [1]_____ and care about their possessions. Research shows that they become less [2]_____ than others. This may be because they feel [3]_____ about their possessions or stop [4]_____ other people. To be happy, it may be better to spend money on having [5]_____ with others.

What do you think?

11 Discuss the questions with a partner.

1 Is it important for you to feel in control of a situation?

2 Do things or experiences make you happier? Why?

3 Do you think it's useful to compare yourself to other people?

Study skills

Dealing with test-related stress

Which of the things below make you feel stressed about tests?

- having unrealistic goals
- what other students say or do
- parents' expectations
- having too much work to do
- feeling unprepared
- needing to remember a lot

What other things make you feel stressed about tests? How do you deal with stress?

- structure discussion essays
- write topic sentences for discussion essays
- use linking words and phrases

Topic focus

1 **Read the text. Answer questions a and b.**

> Two supermarkets are offering the chance to taste some jam. Supermarket 1 has six flavours; Supermarket 2 has 24 flavours. In which supermarket are you more likely to a) stop and try some jam, b) buy some jam?

2 **Read the text on page 109. Do the results surprise you? Why / Why not?**

Exam skills

Structuring discussion essays

EXAM TIP 🔊 2.17

If a Task 2 essay question asks about opinions, check whether you have to write a discussion essay or a personal opinion essay. Why is this important?
» page 147

3 **Read the essay question below. Does it require you to give your opinion? How many points of view should you present?**

> Many people believe that having more choice is always a good thing. Others believe we have to make too many choices in modern life. Discuss both points of view.

4 **Which statements (a–f) give a reason for choice being a positive thing?**

a it can also stop us feeling happy

b we look forward to things that we have chosen

c it gives us the power to improve our lives

d sometimes we are not able to make the right choices

e it can motivate us to work harder

f too many options can stop us making good decisions

5 **Complete the two paragraphs from a discussion essay below with statements a–f from exercise 4.**

> On the one hand, there are several reasons why choice can be beneficial. **Firstly,** ¹_____. **For example**, if we do not like the service a doctor provides we can choose a different surgery. **Secondly,** ²_____. **For instance**, if our parents chose a holiday destination for us we would not anticipate or enjoy the trip as much as if we had chosen it. **Finally,** ³_____. **For example**, a child who is given a choice of school subjects may work harder to prove their choice was good or for the pleasure of doing something they have chosen themselves.
>
>   **On the other hand**, being able to choose can also have many negative consequences. **Firstly,** ⁴_____. **For instance**, research has shown that when presented with a wide range of different savings accounts, people often don't choose the best option or make no decisions. **Secondly,** ⁵_____. **For example**, we let schoolchildren choose what subjects they want to do even though teachers might be better able to decide what is best for them. **Finally,** ⁶_____. **For instance**, research shows that we are more likely to be happy with something we are given and cannot return than something we could easily exchange.

Key phrases   VOCABULARY FILE » page 128

Linking words and phrases

6 Match 1–5 below with similar linking words and phrases in bold from the paragraphs in exercise 5.

1 Lastly ....

2 Furthermore ....

3 To begin with ....

4 However ....

5 As a case in point ....

7 Complete the text with linking words or phrases from exercises 5 and 6.

> Many people believe that large shopping centres have a range of negative effects on an area. This may be true. [1] ...., they also have a generally positive economic impact. [2] ...., they encourage people to shop because parking is more convenient. [3] ...., people tend to spend more in shopping centres as they have less distance to walk and can load up their cars more easily. [4] ...., they attract tourists to areas that don't have popular city centres. [5] ...., the city of Bloomington in the American state of Minnesota has attracted $1 billion of income from tourism because of its 'Mall of America'.

Exam skills

Writing topic sentences for discussion essays

8 Read the topic sentences in the paragraphs in exercise 5. Which words or phrases tell you there will be more than one idea in the paragraphs?

9 Complete the two topic sentences for each essay question below. Vary your language. The first one is done for you.

1 We consume too much in modern society. Discuss.

On the one hand, high levels of consumption bring many benefits.
On the other hand, consuming too much can have negative effects.

2 In the future, we will do all our shopping online. Discuss.

Some people think ...
However, others believe ...

3 Electricity is the world's greatest discovery. Discuss.

To some extent, ...
However, ...

Exam practice

10 Write two paragraphs for one of the essay questions in exercise 9. Follow the structure below. Use the plans on pages 109–10 to help you if necessary.

Paragraph 1	Paragraph 2
Topic sentence	Topic sentence
Point 1, example 1	Point 1, example 1
Point 2, example 2	Point 2, example 2
Point 3, example 3	Point 3, example 3

- ▶ read for the main idea in a passage
- ▶ complete summaries of a passage
- ▶ use modal verbs to talk about ability

Topic focus

1 Look at the photo. Choose one of functions 1–3 for what you think the machine does.

  1 It makes objects bigger or smaller.

  2 It prints objects in three dimensions (3D).

  3 It allows objects to 'travel' through space.

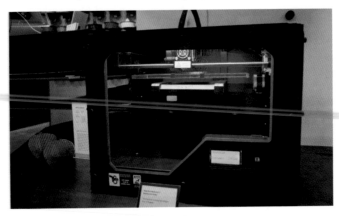

2 How do you think the machine in the picture works? Discuss with a partner.

Exam skills

Reading for the main idea

3 Read only the first sentence of the paragraph below. Choose the best heading a–c.

  a How 3D printing is changing

  (b) A description of 3D printing

  c How 3D printing was developed

> 3D printing works by reproducing whole objects in layers. The machine first scans an object with great precision and then rebuilds it from bottom to top using a special material. The process can be used to produce tools, shoes, clothes, guitars ... in fact, almost anything, including objects with moving parts. Furthermore, the objects are produced as single pieces, removing the need to put parts together.

EXAM TIP 🔊 2.18

To understand the main idea of a passage, you often need to read only the topic sentence. Which type of question is this particularly useful for? » page 148

4 Now read the complete paragraph. Is your answer to exercise 3 the same?

5 Read the passage on page 85 quickly, focusing on the topic sentences of paragraphs A–F. Is the passage about:

  ① the advantages and disadvantages of producing things at home?   *some passage*

  2 the advantages of 3D printing?

  3 why we should change the current system of production?   *no*

Completing summaries

6 Read the sentence below. Which paragraph of the passage discusses this problem?

  However, people without money, large houses, or _____ may not be able to participate in this new economy.

HW 2/18 6~10

7 Which part of speech is the missing word in the sentence in exercise 6: verb, noun, or adjective? Try to guess the word.

8 Scan the paragraph you chose in exercise 6. Find a suitable word or phrase to complete the sentence in exercise 6.

THE THIRD INDUSTRIAL REVOLUTION

A 'Today is the beginning of the third industrial revolution.' These words were spoken by the Vice President of the EU, Antonio Tajani, in 2012. But what did he mean? In the first industrial revolution of the 19th century, machines started
5 doing the tasks once done by hand. The second industrial revolution, 100 years later, saw electricity being used to mass-produce objects like cars in large factories. Now, many believe that these factories will disappear because technology permits us to produce much of what we need
10 in our houses or locally. We can already produce renewable energy at home using solar panels or turbines, and 3D printing technology now allows us to print a range of objects. But should we, like Mr Tajani, be excited about this 'third industrial revolution'?

15 **B** The idea that we may all become producers is certainly attractive to many. Homeowners will be able to make money producing renewable energy and selling it over the internet, or print wonderful products – designing and producing them without having to build a large factory.
20 Working under production managers will become a thing of the past and we will be able to print off whatever we need whenever we want.

C There will also be benefits for society in general. In the current world economy, various parts of a product like
25 a mobile phone are made in different countries, sent to another country to be put together and packaged, and then shipped to shops all around the world. So, by downloading the product directly in our homes we will dramatically reduce production and distribution costs. We will also
30 waste less energy and reduce levels of industrial pollution.

D However, perhaps not everyone will benefit from the third industrial revolution. In a world of small-scale domestic industry, people who don't have the space at home, the money for equipment, or the skills to design
35 objects won't be able to profit. Worse still, 3D printers and energy generators may replace many of the jobs in factories and shops that less skilled workers could previously do. Poorer countries with lower levels of capital, education, and technology may be particularly affected.

40 **E** There is also doubt over whether governments will be able to regulate production. For example, currently, governments are able to restrict the sale of dangerous goods such as guns and knives by making sure buyers and sellers have a licence. But who will control what millions of 3D
45 printers produce? Also, if production of copied 'designer' goods is already a problem for brands, how much greater will the problem be when we can scan and print off any object we find? Finally, how will governments tax goods or energy produced domestically?

50 **F** These are just a few of the questions that need to be answered during the third industrial revolution. In the meantime, technicians from all countries are busy exploring the applications of 3D printing and other exciting inventions. The main problem is whether the governments
55 of the world will be able to keep up with them and deal with the consequences.

Exam practice

9 **Complete the summary with words from the passage. Write no more than two words each time.**

The third industrial revolution will have many advantages. For instance, we will produce more things at home, rather than in a [1]_____. This will reduce the [2]_____ of making products, as well as levels of [3]_____ and energy use. However, unskilled workers and poorer people may not be able to participate in this new economy. People will need financial capital for [4]_____ and they will need a range of new skills. There may also be a negative impact on [5]_____ in production and distribution. Furthermore, governments will need to [6]_____ the new economy to stop people making things that are [7]_____.

Grammar **GRAMMAR FILE » page 118**

Modal verbs of ability 10 **Complete the sentences from the passage. Use *could, can,* or *will / won't be able to.***

1 We _____ already produce renewable energy at home using solar panels or turbines.

2 People who don't have the space at home, the money for equipment, or the skills to design objects _____ profit.

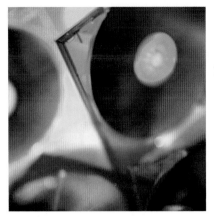

3 3D printers and energy generators may replace many of the jobs in factories and shops that less skilled workers _____ previously do.

4 There is also doubt over whether governments _____ regulate production.

11 Discuss the activities below using *could*, *can*, or *will / won't be able to*. Use the stems to help you.

Example: *In the past, we could get a free university education.*

> In the past ...   At the moment ...   In the future ...

- get a free university education
- buy CD players
- touch and smell objects on webpages

- have a meal for under 5 euros
- watch 3D televisions
- go on holiday in space

What do you think?

12 Read the complete passage on page 85. Will the production of home energy and 3D printing really change the world? Think about the points below. Then discuss with a partner.

- quality of home-produced goods / energy
- technical limits

- enjoyment of shopping
- needs of travellers

EXAM CHALLENGE

SPEAKING

1 With a partner, choose three questions to ask each other.
  1 Do you think shops will exist in the future?
  2 What are the most popular products for teenagers to buy?
  3 Is it better to buy local products or imported products?
  4 Why do some people avoid asking sales assistants for help?
  5 Will we buy the same things in the future as we buy now?
  6 How are older people and younger people different in their shopping habits?

2 Take turns to ask and answer the three questions you chose in exercise 1. Ask your partner to listen to you or record your responses.

3 Did you or your partner use key phrases appropriate to the question type?

LISTENING

1 Do questions 25–27 in Practice test: Listening on page 151.

WRITING

1 Write two main paragraphs for the essay question below.

   Children in modern society receive too many gifts. Discuss.

2 Check your paragraphs with the model answer on page 110. Did you write one paragraph for and one paragraph against the idea?

READING

1 Do questions 1–4 in Practice test: Reading on page 154. Try to get at least three answers correct in 6 minutes.

2 Did you read the topic sentences first to help you to locate the information?

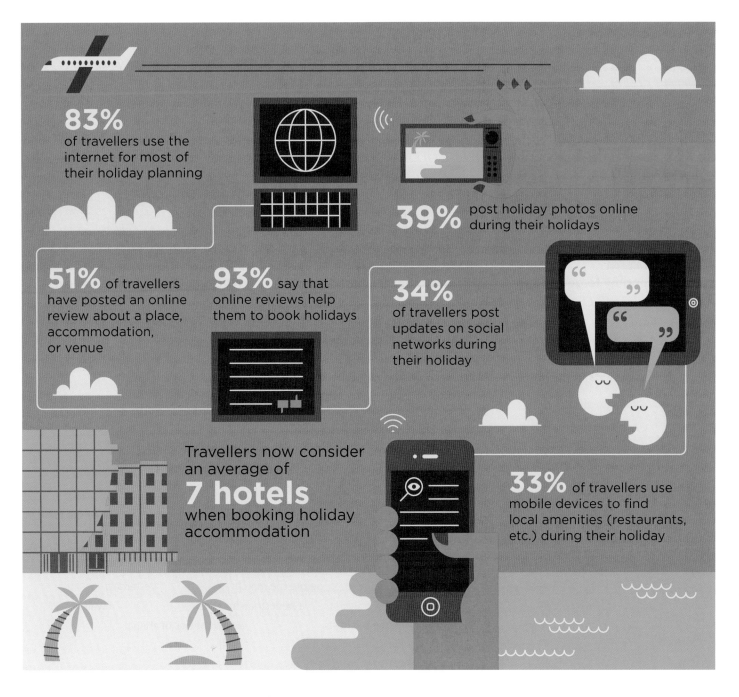

83% of travellers use the internet for most of their holiday planning

39% post holiday photos online during their holidays

51% of travellers have posted an online review about a place, accommodation, or venue

93% say that online reviews help them to book holidays

34% of travellers post updates on social networks during their holiday

Travellers now consider an average of **7 hotels** when booking holiday accommodation

33% of travellers use mobile devices to find local amenities (restaurants, etc.) during their holiday

What do you think?

1 How do you find out information before you travel?

2 Do you ever post online reviews of a place you have visited?

3 Previously, do you think people considered more or fewer than seven hotels when booking holiday accommodation? Why?

4 What information do you share with others about your holiday? How?

5 Do you think social media will continue to change travel in the future? How?

SPEAKING

Narrating

▸ use sequencing markers
▸ use the past simple and past continuous
▸ speak about events in the news
▸ say the endings of regular past tense verbs

Topic focus

1 Look at pictures and headlines A–C. Which of the news stories would you most like to read? Why?

2 Number the stories according to how popular you think they were (1 = most popular, 3 = least popular).

3 How are news websites different from newspapers?

A

Global economy to get weaker

B

Man who fights shark loses job

C

NASA: Life on Mars could exist

Vocabulary   VOCABULARY FILE » page 129

Events in the news

4 Match the phrasal verbs with nouns 1–6.

> break out   break into sth   take place   run over sb
> go off   run off   come across sth   crash into sth

1 an event   4 a driver (x2)
2 an alarm or a bomb   5 thieves (x2)
3 scientists   6 violence or a fire

5 Complete the sentences with verbs from exercise 4. You may need to change the form of the verbs.

1 When the thieves _____ the factory, the alarm _____ and so they quickly

   _____ .

2 Some violence _____ before the match _____ yesterday.

3 Last night, a driver _____ a pedestrian and then _____ a wall.

4 During their trip, the scientists _____ a new species of animal.

Exam skills

Using sequencing markers

6 Match the events to the pictures (A–E), then put them in order to make a narrative.

   _____ The family was rescued.   _____ The firefighters arrived.   _____ The fire was put out.

   _____ A fire broke out.   _____ The family screamed for help.

A   B   C   D   E

In Speaking Part 2, you may be asked to describe or 'narrate' past events. Remember to use mostly past simple verb forms. What tense can give background to your narrative? » page 145

Past simple and past continuous

Contact lens solution

7 Tell a partner your narrative from exercise 6, using the sequence markers below. Did you tell the same version?

| Next   Then   In the end   Soon   First |

First, a fire broke out. Then, ...

Grammar   **GRAMMAR FILE » page 119**

8 Look at tasks a–c. Read the narrative below. Which task does it refer to?

a Describe a difficult journey.

b Describe the plot of a book you enjoyed.

c Describe an interesting news story.

I recently ¹_____ (read) about a backpacker. He ²_____ (get lost) in the Australian Outback while he ³_____ (walk). If I remember correctly, he ⁴_____ (work) at a farm, many miles from the nearest town. To survive, he first ⁵_____ (drink) some contact lens solution that he ⁶_____ (carry) with him. But then this ⁷_____ (run out) and he ⁸_____ (become) weak. After three days in the sun he nearly ⁹_____ (die) but in the end, a helicopter ¹⁰_____ (discover) him while he ¹¹_____ (cross) an area of open land. They ¹²_____ (rescue) him and ¹³_____ (take) him to hospital. I ¹⁴_____ (think) the story was really interesting because ...

9 Complete the narrative in exercise 8. Put the verbs in brackets into the past simple or past continuous.

10 Work with a partner. Use only the list of verbs to retell the narrative from exercise 8.

| read   get lost   walk   work   drink   carry   run out
| become   die   discover   cross   rescue   take   think |

11 ◄)) 2.20 Listen to the final sound of the regular past tense verbs. Put each one into the correct column of the table.

| discovered   reported   crashed   arrived   screamed   visited
| attacked   survived   worked   rescued   posted   photographed |

/d/	/t/	/ɪd/

12 Continue one of the stories below. Use as many verbs from exercise 11 as you can.

1 The pilot was feeling tired as his plane approached Madrid airport ...

2 The tourist was enjoying the boat trip along the Amazon River ...

Exam practice

13 Speak for 1–2 minutes about the topic on the card.

Describe an interesting news story. You should say:

– how you found out about the story

– what it was about

– why you chose to read it / watch it / listen to it

and explain why you thought the story was interesting.

Understanding connected speech

▶ separate connected speech
▶ recognize and use vocabulary for tourist city sights
▶ consider resources you can use to prepare for the test

Topic focus

1 Cities 1–6 are among some of the most visited cities in the world. Match them with countries a–f.

1	Kuala Lumpur	a	Thailand
2	Istanbul	b	Spain
3	Barcelona	c	Malaysia
4	Dubai	d	USA
5	Bangkok	e	Turkey
6	New York	f	UAE

2 Tell a partner what you know about the cities in exercise 1. Why do you think they are popular?

3 Can you think of any other cities that are popular with tourists?

Vocabulary   VOCABULARY FILE » page 129

City sights   4 Look at pictures A–F. Which sights from the list below are shown?

> street market   harbour   monument   mall   art gallery   fountain
> cathedral   mosque   main square   city wall   public gardens   statue

A  B  C  D E  F

5 Complete the questions with the correct form of the verb *visit*.

1 Do you enjoy _____ monuments?

2 Would you prefer _____ public gardens or a street market?

3 Have you _____ an art gallery recently?

4 Can you _____ any famous buildings where you live?

5 What can you see if you _____ the main square in your town or city?

6 Work with a partner. Take it in turns to ask and answer the questions in exercise 5.

Exam skills

Separating connected speech   7 ◀)) 2.21 Listen to four sentences. How many words do you hear in each sentence? (Count contractions, e.g. *it's*, as one word.)

8 ◀)) 2.23 Listen to the recording and rewrite sentences 1–3 correctly.

1 It's a really grey town.

2 You'll soon see his stories everywhere.

3 Is that the woman you meant?

EXAM TIP   ◀)) 2.22

In the Listening test, you often have to write down individual words that you hear. What makes this difficult? » page 146

9 🔊 **2.24 Listen to Aimee's audio diary about Mexico City. Complete the notes. Write no more than three words for each gap.**

MEXICO CITY

Good points:
– The ¹_____ of the buildings
– The ²_____ in the churches

Interesting facts:
– The towers in Mexico City aren't ³_____ .
– This is because it was built on a ⁴_____ lake.

Getting around:
– Easy to travel around the city on ⁵_____ .
– It stops at all the key ⁶_____ .

What next?
– Cancún! The flight there takes ⁷_____ .
– There, you can go dancing in some ⁸_____ and spend time on ⁹_____ .

Exam practice

10 🔊 **2.25 Listen and answer the questions.**

1 Which is the correct position of Dubrovnik Airport in the diagram: A, B or C?

2 Which three things does the guide say you can see as you walk through Dubrovnik?

A cars	D an old fountain
B small mansions	E some birds
C lively cafés	F bookshops

11 🔊 **2.26 Listen and complete the notes. Write no more than two words for each gap.**

Tourist sights and activities in Dubrovnik:
– The ¹_____ Limited gallery
– A coffee bar that ²_____ during the recent war
– Views of the tall ³_____
– A ⁴_____ to the island of Lokrum
– A view of the harbour from the ⁵_____
– A dance on ⁶_____

What do you think?

12 Think of a city you know well. Which sights would you take a foreign visitor to on a one-day tour?

13 Compare your ideas with a partner. Give reasons. How could they improve their tour?

Study skills

Using resources **How would you use the resources below to help you to prepare for the test?**

- your coursebook
- your study notes
- practice tests
- the internet
- your teacher
- your friends and family
- your classmates
- free time

Are some resources more important as you get closer to the test date? Why / Why not?

WRITING

Conclusions

▶ write conclusions for essays
▶ use compound nouns to write about the media

Topic focus

1 Look at the headline and the pictures. What do you think happened?

Change of luck for homeless man

2 Read the news story on page 110. Compare your prediction from exercise 1.

3 Discuss the questions with a partner.

1 Why was there such a positive reaction to the news story?

2 Would you give money to a 'viral' campaign like the one started by Sarah Darling's husband?

Vocabulary · VOCABULARY FILE » page 129

Compounds: media

4 Create compound nouns by matching nouns in group A with nouns in group B.

A | *news   Web   social   TV*

B | *story   content   programme   users*
  | *page   media   network   broadcast*

5 Discuss the questions with a partner.

1 Which news network do you trust the most?

2 Which social media sites do you use?

3 Have you ever created a web page about yourself?

4 How do you decide which TV programmes to watch?

Exam skills

Writing conclusions

6 Look at the essay questions. Which one asks you to show if your opinion is the same as the one given?

1 The internet has allowed the public to be better informed about world events. To what extent do you agree or disagree with this view? Give reasons for your answer.

2 How does the internet affect people's views of the world?

7 Look at the parts from an essay below. Are they from an answer to question 1 or 2 in exercise 6?

> Thesis statement:
> Arguably, the internet has not increased the public's knowledge of world issues.
>
> Topic sentences:
> It is true that the internet has allowed people to find a wide variety of news stories and articles online …
> However, internet users tend to select more entertaining stories to read and listen to …
> Furthermore, web publishers show us only the information they know we like …

8 Read the conclusion. Which sentences repeat the information in a) the thesis statement and b) the topic sentences from exercise 7?

> ¹In conclusion, the internet has not made us better informed about global news. ²It may have helped the public access information, but the quality of information we are given is often poor and web users generally choose to watch less serious content. ³Consequently, if we want to educate people, it is essential that we preserve traditional forms of media as far as possible.

9 Rewrite thesis statements 1–4 to make different sentences for conclusions. Use vocabulary from exercise 4 where possible. The first one is done for you.

1 This essay will argue that broadcasters have less control over news than they used to.
   This essay has argued that <u>news networks have less control than they used to</u>.

2 This essay will argue that online communities are replacing traditional friendships.
   This essay has argued that _____.

3 This essay will argue that the public controls the material it sees on the internet.
   This essay has argued that _____.

4 This essay will argue that live visual media will be replaced by recorded video content.
   This essay has argued that _____.

10 Put sentences a–c in the correct order to make a conclusion for essay question 2 in exercise 6.

a The question is whether we can trust the public to access important information.

b The internet has changed our view of the world in two very different ways.

c It has made information about other countries readily available and has given us freedom to choose the content we see.

EXAM TIP   🔊 2.27

In a conclusion, you should include a summary of your main points and a sentence that directly answers the question. What else could you include?
» page 147

Exam practice

11 Read the thesis statement and topic sentences. Then write a conclusion for the essay.

> Thesis statement: This essay will outline how digital communications can help us to create change in our world.
> Topic sentence 1: Firstly, the internet helps people raise awareness of key issues around the world.
> Topic sentence 2: Secondly, mobile media, like smartphones, makes it easy to meet or act together.
> Topic sentence 3: Thirdly, online payment systems enable money to be raised and sent quickly.

▶ understand *Yes / No / Not Given* questions
▶ understand vocabulary of advertising

Topic focus

1 Look at the advert for New Zealand. Would you like to go there? Why / Why not?

2 What picture and phrase would you use to advertise your country?

Vocabulary **VOCABULARY FILE » page 129**

Advertising

3 Match 1–10 with definitions a–j.

100% PURE NEW ZEALAND

Flowering in late Spring the Mount Cook Lily is one of 415 mountain plants that are unique to the South Island's magnificent Mount Cook region. Whether you're there to take in the snow clad peaks or heli-ski down them, the alpine air and piercing light will refresh you like nothing else on earth. www.newzealand.com

1	advert	6	blog
2	(hash)tag	7	trending list
3	campaign	8	review
4	brand	9	slogan
5	logo	10	search engine ranking

a .... a website where a person writes regularly about recent topics or events

b .... a design or symbol that a company or an organization uses as its special sign

c .... the position something has on the internet depending on its popularity

d .... a phrase used to attract people's attention or to suggest an idea quickly

e .... topics being discussed frequently on a social media site such as Twitter would appear here

f .... a type of article in which somebody gives an opinion on something

g .... a notice, picture, or film telling people about a product, job, or service

h .... a symbol which highlights a topic being discussed on Twitter

i .... the associations connected to a product name

j .... a series of planned activities that are intended to promote a product or service

4 Are items 1–10 in exercise 3 usually created by companies or the public?

Exam skills

Understanding *Yes / No / Not Given* questions

5 Read paragraph G of the passage on page 95. According to the author, which group of people helps to create national brands?

6 Is the author likely to agree or disagree with the statements below?

1 Governments need to spend more money on printed adverts.

2 Tourists can't get useful information about countries online.

Exam practice

EXAM TIP ◀) 2.28

Yes / No / Not Given questions are different to *True / False / Not Given* questions. How? Where can you often find the author's main opinion? » page 148

7 Do the statements agree with the ideas expressed by the author of the passage? Write *Yes, No,* or *Not Given.*

1 Countries spend more than you would expect on national branding.

2 Traditional rebranding campaigns have worked well in many cases.

3 Britain and Las Vegas have recently had successful rebranding campaigns.

4 It is harder for authorities to control branding than it was in the past.

5 Films and music now have more effect on branding than all other sources of information.

6 The experience of South Korea shows that slogans can still be effective.

BRANDING PLACES

A The travel and tourism industry contributes $6 trillion to global GDP*, almost as much as banking. With the industry still growing, it is not surprising that many countries are spending tens of millions of dollars trying to increase their
5 share of the prize. What then should countries be doing to promote themselves?

B One traditional approach has been to use rebranding campaigns, with logos and slogans, to create a fresh, new image for the country. This approach has seen notable
10 successes. Perhaps most famously, in the 1980s, Spain managed to transform itself into the world's eighth largest tourist economy with its 'Everything under the sun' campaign, which emphasized its variety of attractions. Similarly, in the 1990s, the 'Scotland the brand' campaign
15 resulted in a 200% rise in cultural exports like food and drink, and a decade later the '100% Pure New Zealand' campaign helped to make this small nation the adventure sports capital of the world.

C However, tourist authorities have not always found
20 it easy to impose a brand on a country. For example, the 'Cool Britannia' brand message of the mid-1990s was soon ridiculed in the British media as it didn't reflect important, traditional values. Similarly, Las Vegas failed to rebrand in the 1990s when it created the 'It's anything and everything'
25 message to try and attract a range of tourists, including families, to the world's party capital. Tourist authorities in both places were quickly forced to change their advertising to reflect more popular views of the destinations.

D In fact, in the modern world it is becoming increasingly
30 difficult for authorities to control the brand of destinations. The growing number of travel bloggers, reviewers, and social media users all contribute their own views (and photos) of destinations. Similarly, cultural products like films and music, which create vivid images of places, are
35 exchanged on a growing scale. Comparatively bland advertising slogans fail to compete with this rising tide of information. For example, the 'South Korea – Sparkling' and the 'Soul of Asia' advertising messages have certainly made less impact on the national brand than the country's
40 'K-pop' music genre.

E This does not mean that public spending on tourist promotion is wasted, but it has to work together with existing media. Consequently, many countries now promote themselves through popular blogs or travel websites and
45 create adverts that connect with 'trending' topics. For example, when, on one day in 2012, an ancient Mayan prediction led nervous internet users to worry that the world was about to end, the Australian government placed a clever advert on the web. It said: 'Tomorrow has already
50 arrived in Australia', reminding people where to go for sanity and calm.

F But the days of the big, planned campaign are not over. Clever tourist authorities have been able to organize social media campaigns, and they've often used their own
55 citizens to do this. For example, the Colombian government launched a page on Facebook entitled: 'It's not Columbia; it's Colombia', to highlight the common spelling error. In the first two weeks the page had been 'liked' by 70,000 proud Colombians, and it went high up in search engine
60 rankings. The Philippine government had even greater impact with its tag '#itsmorefuninthephilippines'. It invited Philippinos to upload and tag photos of themselves having fun and many did, making their campaign the number one trending topic on Twitter. Both countries are reporting
65 growth in tourism.

G Perhaps then, the key to successful place branding is to turn millions of patriotic social media users into a giant sales force. The messages they spread are certainly likely to be more powerful and authentic than advertising slogans.

Glossary
GDP abbreviation for Gross Domestic Product (total value of all goods and services produced by a country in one year)

---

8 Complete the text below with words from the list.

> adverts   proud   believable   web pages   traveller   attractive
> social media   support   create   pictures   countries   messages

Tourist authorities use online media in a variety of ways. They can make [1]_____ that are linked to popular internet discussion topics, but they can also start campaigns in [2]_____ communities. The campaigns have often been most successful when authorities involve the people of their own countries. For example, citizens may be encouraged to [3]_____ a particular web page or even put [4]_____ online with an official tag. These work well because people are very proud of their [5]_____ and their contributions on social media sites are usually [6]_____ and influential.

What do you think?

9 **Discuss the questions with a partner.**

1 Do you think it's important for a country to develop a brand? Why / Why not?

2 Does your country have a slogan? If so, do you think it is an effective slogan for your country?

3 Think of countries you know well. How would you brand them?

10 **In 2013, experts predicted the countries below would have strong brands in the future. What do you know about the countries? Do you think the predictions will be correct?**

 Chile    Estonia   Qatar

China   Malaysia   United Arab Emirates

EXAM CHALLENGE

SPEAKING

1 **Prepare to speak about the topic on the card. Think or make notes for 1 minute.**

> Talk about a difficult journey you have made.
> You should say:
> – where you were travelling to
> – how you were travelling
> – who you were travelling with
> and explain why the journey was so difficult.

2 **Speak for 1–2 minutes about the topic on the card. Ask a partner to listen to you or record your responses.**

3 **Ask your partner or yourself the questions.**

1 Did you use a variety of regular and irregular past tense verbs?

2 Did you make sure the -ed endings were pronounced clearly?

3 Did you include sequence markers (*First, next, then,* etc.) in your narrative?

LISTENING

1 **Do questions 38–40 in Practice test: Listening on page 152. Try to get at least two answers correct.**

2 **Did you manage to identify individual words that you knew?**

WRITING

1 **Write a conclusion to follow the thesis statement and the three topic sentences below.**

> Thesis statement
> This essay will argue that guidebooks are still a useful resource for travellers.
>
> Topic sentences
> First, the high quality of writing can inspire travellers.
>
> Secondly, the information in guidebooks is selected and edited to make it clear and concise.
>
> Finally, guidebooks can be used in remote places where digital media cannot.

2 **Compare your conclusion with the model answer on page 110. Then answer the questions.**

1 Did you include all the necessary parts of the conclusion?

2 Did you try to paraphrase some of the vocabulary from the topic sentences in exercise 1?

3 Now do Task 2 in Practice test: Writing on page 161.

READING

1 **Do questions 37–40 in Practice test: Reading on page 160. Try to get at least three answers correct in 6 minutes.**

2 **Did you use your knowledge of the author's opinion to help you to choose the answers correctly?**

UNIT 10 | Science & progress

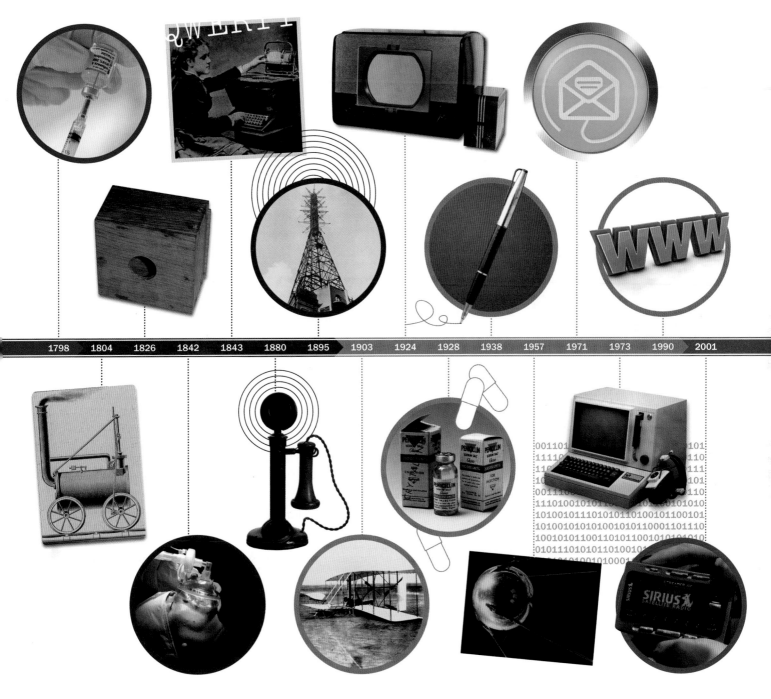

1798 1804 1826 1842 1843 1880 1895 1903 1924 1928 1938 1957 1971 1973 1990 2001

What do you think?

1 What are the inventions in the infographic?

2 Do you know any of the people who invented them?

3 How do you think each invention changed people's lives?

4 Which invention has most affected your life today?

5 Can you extend the timeline with any more recent inventions?

Comparing past and present

▸ avoid common errors in Speaking Part 3
▸ use *used to*
▸ speak about areas of progress in a country
▸ ask for clarification

Topic focus

1 **Label photos A–C with the words below.**

> *education   income   health*

2 **Which area in exercise 1 do you think gives the best indication of progress in a country?**

Vocabulary   VOCABULARY FILE » page 130

Areas of progress

3 **Look at areas 1–11 used to assess progress. Match them with descriptions a–k.**

1 housing
2 income
3 jobs
4 community
5 education
6 environment
7 civic engagement
8 health
9 life satisfaction
10 safety
11 work-life balance

a .... qualifications, number of years studying, skills development
b .... interest in issues of public concern
c .... number of rooms per person, basic facilities, and cost
d .... number of serious crimes
e .... total wealth and money available after paying taxes, etc.
f .... feeling good about life
g .... life expectancy and feeling fit
h .... social support network
i .... air pollution and water purity
j .... working less and having more leisure time
k .... level of unemployment, salary, job security

4 **Underline the words or phrases in a–k in exercise 3 that helped you to match the descriptions with areas 1–11.**

5 **Work with a partner and look at the map. Write areas 1–11 from exercise 3 next to the countries which you think have the highest level/quality of each.**

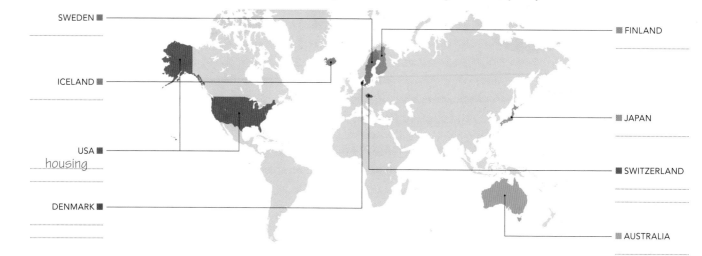

SWEDEN ■
ICELAND ■
USA ■
housing
DENMARK ■
FINLAND
JAPAN
SWITZERLAND
AUSTRALIA

6 Choose a country (A–D) according to what is important to you. Then turn to page 110 to find out the name of the country.

Country A	Country C
higher levels of health and community	higher levels of education and income
lower levels of education and jobs	lower levels of environment and work-life balance
Country B	**Country D**
higher levels of education and jobs	higher levels of life satisfaction and health
lower levels of health and wealth	lower levels of safety and income

7 Compare your choice in exercise 6 with a partner. Give your reaction.

Grammar GRAMMAR FILE » page 119

Used to

8 ◀)) 2.29 Listen to a student in Speaking Part 3. Complete the sentences.

1 People _____ have larger homes.

2 The standard of accommodation _____ be so high.

3 Our country _____ export much.

4 Workers earn more money than they _____ .

9 Decide which examples of *used to* in exercise 8 describe:

a a regular action in the past
b an action that didn't happen in the past

c a situation in the past
d a situation that didn't exist in the past.

10 ◀)) 2.30 Listen to the sentence and answer the questions.

In the past, people didn't use to use cars and they used to walk more.

1 Do you hear the /d/ sound in *used*?

2 Do you hear the /uː/ sound in *to*?

3 How is the letter *s* pronounced differently in the first *use* and the second *use*?

11 Think about your lifetime. What changes have happened in the areas below in your country? Discuss with a partner.

> education   jobs   health   safety

> *Many people used to leave school at sixteen but nowadays they usually study longer.*

Exam skills

Avoiding common errors

12 ◀)) 2.31 Listen to a different student in Speaking Part 3. Match his three responses with the common errors (a–c).

a too short

b too personal

c doesn't respond to the question

13 ◀)) 2.33 Complete the phrases to ask for clarification. Then listen and check.

1 Sorry, but what do you _____ by *community*?

2 Please could you _____ the question?

3 Sorry, I'm not sure _____ you mean.

EXAM TIP ◀) 2.32

In Speaking Part 3, if you don't understand, you can ask the examiner for clarification. How can you begin your question to sound more natural?
» page 145

Exam practice

14 Work with a partner and take turns. Student A, go to page 110. Student B, go to page 112.

LISTENING
EXAM FOCUS: SECTION 4

Following exam instructions

- ▸ avoid common errors in the listening test
- ▸ use *can* and *may* to describe possibility
- ▸ use key phrases for discussing cause and effect
- ▸ discuss online study resources

Topic focus

1 **Look at the ideas below. Which ones have you heard about before? Discuss with a partner.**

1 A coin dropped from a tall building can kill someone.

2 Eating chocolate can make a country win more Nobel prizes.

3 A full moon can make people go mad.

2 🔊 **2.34 Which idea in exercise 1 is most likely to be true? Listen and check.**

Key phrases

Discussing effects

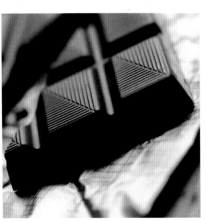

3 **Match 1-5 with a-e to make complete sentences.**

1 In poor countries, junk food can be expensive and **consequently**

2 A diet that is high in salt, sugar, and saturated fats can **lead to**

3 Changes in technology may **account for**

4 We rely on the internet more and more and **as a result**

5 We have greater access to private transport, **which means that**

a higher rates of obesity.

b changes in the way future generations will learn.

c people are less active than they used to be.

d it is consumed by rich sections of society.

e our memories may be becoming less effective.

4 **Complete 1-5 in exercise 3 with your own ideas about effects.**

Example: *In poor countries, junk food can be expensive and consequently not many people eat it.*

Grammar **GRAMMAR FILE » page 118**

Can and may for possibility

5 **Underline examples of *can* and *may* in the sentences in exercise 3. Which one means *possible now* / *generally possible* and which one means *possible in the future*?**

6 **Choose the correct option to complete the sentences.**

1 Smoking *can* / *may* cause cancer.

2 Human activity *can* / *may* account for future climate change.

3 Modern technology *can* / *may* lead to more people working from home in the future.

4 Media reports on science *can* / *may* be inaccurate.

7 **Talk to a partner about the possible effects of 1-4 below.**

> *People eat a lot of chocolate and this can lead to obesity.*

1 People eat a lot of chocolate …

2 Scientists have discovered planets similar to Earth …

3 You need advanced laboratories and equipment to study science …

4 People spend more time on computers than they used to …

UNIT 10 SCIENCE & PROGRESS

Exam skills

8 Read questions 31–40 below. What types of common error might students make?

Example: *Students might write too many words.*

Questions 31–34

Complete the text below. Write no more than **TWO WORDS OR A NUMBER** *for each answer.*

In the media, there is often confusion with the terms 'correlate' and 'cause'. This error is particularly common in the reporting of **31** .... When two things happen at the same time, it does not mean there is a cause and effect relationship, even though this kind of relationship may **32** .... For instance, people have often connected being a better learner with having **33** ...., but in fact people who don't eat properly before school often **34** ...., too, and this plays a more important role.

Question 35

Which two problems with scientific experiments are mentioned? Choose **TWO** *letters A–E.*

A The method is often bad.
B Too many people are tested.
C Some experiments are not legal.
D Some scientists just want to make a profit.
E Experiments can be expensive.

Question 36

Which of the following do modern data journalists have?

A Increasing pressure at work
B Improved statistical training
C Good critical thinking skills

Questions 37–40

Decide how each factor changed. Write:

I if the factor increased
D if the factor decreased
N if there was no change

37 Number of depressed people ....
38 The amount of drugs in doctors' prescriptions ....
39 Sales of fish oil tablets ....
40 Academic results of students ....

EXAM TIP 🔊 2.35

A few simple steps can help you to avoid common errors in the Listening test. What three things should you do when transferring your answers to the answer sheet? » page 146

9 Look at the answers on page 111 for questions 31–40 in exercise 8. What types of error did the student make?

Exam practice

10 🔊 2.36 Listen and answer questions 31–40 in exercise 8.

11 Copy your answers to the questions in exercise 8 onto the answer sheet on page 111.

What do you think?

12 How reliable do you think the media is? Who or what do you trust as a reliable source of information? Why?

Study skills

Using online study resources There are many online resources to help you to practise for the exam. Tell your partner about:

1 any websites you know and have already used
2 what is good about the website(s)
3 how often you use the website(s) and what activities you usually do.

WRITING
EXAM FOCUS: TASK 1

Describing processes

- summarize a process
- check for common errors in writing
- use the passive to describe a process
- use sequencing words

Topic focus

1 Read the descriptions of three new items of technology. Then tick if you think they are useful (*progress*) or not useful (*pointless*).

Invisibility cover
A cover that makes objects seem to 'disappear' ☐ ☐

Location tracking
An application that enables you to locate friends and family ☐ ☐

Virtual fitting room
A device that shows you wearing any item of clothing ☐ ☐

Grammar   **GRAMMAR FILE » page 120**

Passive for a process

2 Look at the sentences about the invisibility cover. Complete them with the passive of the verb in brackets. The first one is done for you.

a The image is _reflected off_ the cover. (reflect off)

b The image _____ by a computer. (process)

c The background image _____ 'through' the cover. (see)

d The image _____ to a projector. (send)

e The image _____ onto the cover. (project)

f A video image of the background _____. (record)

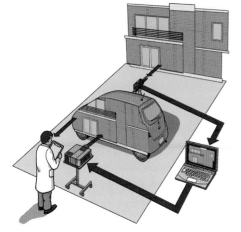

3 Look at the diagram of how the invisibility cover works. Number a–f in exercise 2 in the order that the steps happen.

Example: *1 f*

4 Why is the passive often used to describe a process? Choose from options a–c.

a We don't know who or what does the action.

b The important part of a process is what happens, not who does it.

c Verbs used in a process don't have active forms.

Key phrases

Sequencing words

5 Which five words or phrases can be used to complete the sentence below?

> next   then   firstly   now   lastly   after that
> meanwhile   subsequently   secondly   and

A video image is recorded. _____, the image is sent to a computer.

6 Tell a partner why the other five words or phrases in exercise 5 <u>cannot</u> be used to complete the sentence.

7 Choose the correct option in 1–6 below to complete the description.

> [1]*At first / Firstly*, an image of the background is recorded [2]*next / and* is sent to a computer. [3]*Then / And* the image is processed. [4]*After that / Meanwhile*, it is sent to a projector, [5]*now / where* it is projected onto the cover. [6]*Lastly / In the end*, it is reflected off the cover to the viewer.

Exam skills

8 Use the words to complete the summary.

> *general   achieve   diagram   suggests   complex*

The ¹_____ shows one way that an object can appear invisible. In ²_____, we can see that achieving even a simple illusion is a very ³_____ process and this ⁴_____ that true 'invisibility' may take many years to ⁵_____.

9 Look at the diagram of the robotic vacuum cleaner below. Write a summary about how it works. Use the summary in exercise 8 as a model. (Y = Yes; N = No)

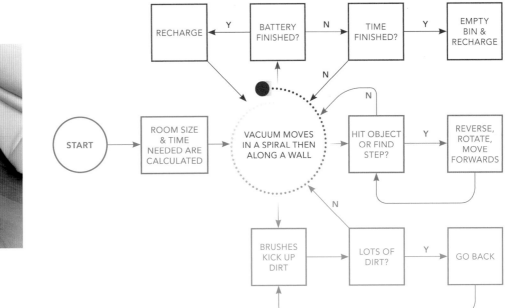

10 Put errors 1–10 into three groups. Write *G* (grammar), *V* (vocabulary), or *P* (punctuation).

1 not using a comma after a linking word which needs one, e.g. *Next_the image is ...*

2 not using a full stop at the end of a sentence, e.g. *This is how the machine works_*

3 missing the verb *be* from a passive, e.g. *the image _ sent*

4 missing *s* or *es* endings from a plural, e.g. *a lot of student_*

5 missing *s* or *es* endings from third-person verbs, e.g. *it travel_ quickly*

6 not putting a subject before a verb, e.g. *After that _ is sent electronically ...*

7 spelling words incorrectly, e.g. ~~miror~~ *mirror*

8 using the wrong part of speech, e.g. *The ~~develop~~ development of the process ...*

9 using a linking word incorrectly, e.g. *Secondly, the process starts ...*

10 not putting in an article, e.g. *_ Process is quite complicated.*

11 Read the text about the robotic vacuum cleaner on page 111. Find an example of each of the errors 1–10 in exercise 10.

Exam practice

12 Look at the diagram on page 111. Describe the process, selecting and reporting the main features.

13 Exchange your description from exercise 12 with a partner. Check for any errors. Label them *G* (grammar), *V* (vocabulary), and *P* (punctuation).

- ▶ label graphics
- ▶ understand scientific words
- ▶ speak about scientific issues

Topic focus

1 Some people believe the moon landings didn't happen because the pictures don't look real. Match reasons 1–3 with explanations a–c.

1 There are no stars in the background.
2 There is a letter 'C' on one of the rocks.
3 The flag seems to move but there's no wind on the moon.

a A hair got onto the film.
b It was constructed to stand upright and look like it was moving.
c Sunlight reflected off the moon's surface was too bright for a camera to pick up things in the distance.

2 Do you believe the moon landings happened? Why / Why not?

Vocabulary   VOCABULARY FILE » page 130

Scientific words

3 Complete the table with the correct word forms.

Verb	Noun
	design
discover	
	experiment
invent	
	prediction
prove	
	research
test	

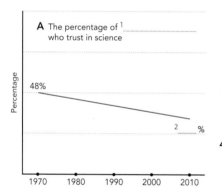

A The percentage of ¹........................ who trust in science

48%

² .... %

1970 1980 1990 2000 2010

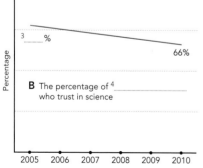

³ .... %

66%

B The percentage of ⁴........................ who trust in science

2005 2006 2007 2008 2009 2010

4 Complete the sentences with the correct word from the table in exercise 3.

1 I don't believe new ideas until scientists .... them.
2 Japanese scientists .... that flights without fossil fuel will be possible by 2038.
3 Products only become popular if they have an attractive ....
4 Many people say we should .... drugs on animals before humans use them.
5 Scientists often do .... to make a profit.
6 The .... to discover the Higgs boson particle cost too much money.
7 Scientists will .... fewer products in the future because we have everything we need.
8 The .... of antibiotics changed our lives more than anything else.

5 Discuss the sentences in exercise 4 with a partner. Say which ones you agree / disagree with and why.

Exam skills

Labelling graphics

6 Do graphs A and B above show that more or fewer people now trust scientists?

7 Read the first paragraph of the passage on page 105. Complete labels 1–4 on graphs A and B.

TRUST ME, I'M A SCIENTIST!

A Trust in scientists seems to be decreasing. Since 2005 the percentage of Europeans who trust in science has declined from 78% to 66%, while among conservative Americans trust in science has declined by 13% since the 1970s to
5 35%. So, first, are we right not to trust in science? Secondly, how can we explain this trend?

B The answer to the first question is quite simple. No. Over the last century the world has made huge advances in life expectancy and wealth and this is largely due to
10 scientists. For example, they have discovered cures to some of the world's most dangerous diseases, like smallpox, and discovered how to modify crops to prevent crop failures. Such discoveries have far-reaching consequences. They save lives, especially among children, and so families then choose
15 to have fewer children and invest more money in educating them. Populations then become more skilled and economies grow. In short, we have progress.

C It is surprising then that scientists today face such hostility and criticism. When scientists modify a crop
20 to increase growth or to add vitamins, they are accused of 'playing with nature'. When they discover that we are changing our climate, they are criticized for trying to scare us. When scientists invent a vaccine, they are wrongly accused of trying to make a profit from fear of illness.
25 When the swine-flu epidemic occurred in 2009–10, some conspiracy theorists even suggested that scientists created it.

D So, what is behind this distrust of science? Many have argued that it is simply a lack of education. But this can't be true. We are all becoming more intelligent, at a rate of
30 three IQ points per decade, and better educated. In fact, research has shown that it is the more educated people who often distrust science the most. Dan Kahan of Yale University did an experiment which showed that members of the public who had a high level of scientific knowledge
35 were slightly less likely to believe what scientists say about climate change than those with little knowledge. So why do we doubt science?

E The first reason is that science is becoming political. In his research, Kahan also discovered that people's
40 willingness to accept climate change depended on their view of the world. People who believed strongly in individual freedom tended to disagree with the science, whereas people who believed strongly in communities were more happy to accept scientists' warnings. This is probably because
45 climate scientists often recommend government control or collective action, which challenge individual freedom.

F The second reason is that conspiracy theorists who believe that scientists are trying to make money are partly right. An increasing amount of research is indeed supported
50 by companies who will often sign contracts with scientists that allow the companies to view results before they are published. Surveys have proved that the public is not only aware of such practices but that these contracts have weakened their trust in science. However, while money may
55 lead to bias in some research, it would be unlikely to affect all of it. Why then, when a majority of scientists agree we should do something, do we still doubt them?

G There is perhaps a psychological explanation which a recent example will illustrate. In 1998, there was a report
60 that suggested a link between a vaccine (for the disease measles) and autism in children. Subsequent research found no proof for the link but, despite this fact, rates of immunization began to fall – resulting in the first rise in measles cases for decades. It seems that sometimes humans
65 are happy to reject the beliefs of the majority and accept the claims of a few, especially when the minority view causes people to worry.

H In short, suspicion is weakening our faith in science: suspicion of political agendas, suspicion of big money,
70 and suspicion of consensus. This is a great shame because science is based on evidence and the scientific community should largely be beyond suspicion.

Exam practice

EXAM TIP   ◆◎ 2.38

You may be given a series of graphics and be asked to complete labels or to choose the correct graphic. What reading skill can you use to complete labels?
» page 148

8 Complete the labels for the graphics below with words from the passage. Write no more than three words and/or a number.

BELIEF IN CLIMATE CHANGE

A People who have a lot of [1] _____

B People who believe in personal [2] _____

C People who believe in strong [3] _____

9 Do statements 1–6 agree with the information in the text? Write:
Yes if the statement agrees with the claims of the author
No if the statement contradicts the claims of the author
Not Given if it is impossible to say what the author thinks about this

1 Medical scientists are motivated by a desire to make money.

2 Most scientists do not believe in individual freedom.

3 Scientists have contributed more to progress than rich individuals.

4 A lot of modern research is controlled by companies.

5 The world will probably be a worse place in the future.

6 Modern scientific communities are normally right.

10 Choose the option which best describes the author's main point.

A Progress will probably stop.

B Scientists do a valuable job.

C We should trust scientists more.

D Scientists help the world make progress.

What do you think?

11 Do you agree with the author's claim in the final sentence of the text? Why / Why not? Discuss with a partner. Support your argument with ideas from the text.

EXAM CHALLENGE

SPEAKING

1 **Respond to the questions. Ask a partner to listen to you or record your responses.**

1 How have scientists made our lives better?

2 Do you think the world is becoming a safer or more dangerous place?

3 Are standards of education higher in your country today than in the past?

4 How were working conditions in your country different in the past?

5 In what ways has your country made progress in recent years?

6 What progress would you like to see in your country in the future?

2 **Ask your partner or yourself the questions.**

1 Was your answer long enough?

2 Did you avoid talking about your personal experiences?

3 Did you clarify any ideas you weren't sure about?

3 **Now do Practice test: Speaking Parts 1–3 on page 162 with your partner. Take turns to be the examiner.**

LISTENING

1 **Do questions 31–34 in Practice test: Listening on page 152. Try to get at least three answers correct.**

2 **Did you use your knowledge of common errors to avoid simple mistakes?**

WRITING

1 **Look at the diagram on page 111. It shows how carton manufacturers can use location tracking for a product such as a carton of milk. Describe the process, selecting and reporting the main features.**

2 **Compare your paragraph to the model answer on page 112. Did you use the passive and remember to include an overview statement?**

3 **Now try Task 1 in Practice test: Writing on page 161.**

READING

1 **Do questions 20–22 in Practice test: Reading on page 157. Try to get at least two answers correct in 5 minutes.**

2 **Did you use the relevant parts of the text to label the graphs correctly?**

INFORMATION FILE

UNIT 1 SPEAKING page 9 exercise 15

STUDENT A

1 Ask Student B questions 1–3. Time the responses to make sure they speak for 15 seconds each time.

1 What subject would you like to study in the future?

2 What was your favourite subject at primary school?

3 What do you like about the place where you study?

2 Answer Student B's questions. Try to speak for 15 seconds each time.

UNIT 1 WRITING page 13 exercise 13

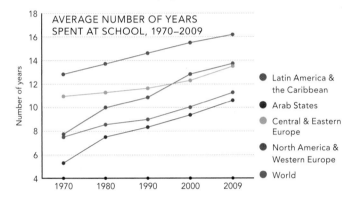

AVERAGE NUMBER OF YEARS SPENT AT SCHOOL, 1970–2009

● Latin America & the Caribbean
● Arab States
● Central & Eastern Europe
● North America & Western Europe
● World

UNIT 1 EXAM CHALLENGE: WRITING
page 16 exercise 1

The pie charts below show the changes in the percentage of people taking different subjects at university in the UK. Summarize the key information. Write at least 150 words.

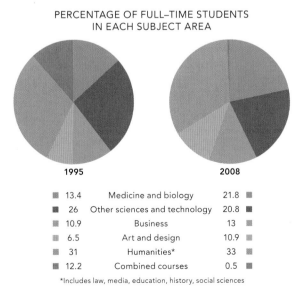

PERCENTAGE OF FULL–TIME STUDENTS IN EACH SUBJECT AREA

1995   2008

13.4	Medicine and biology	21.8
26	Other sciences and technology	20.8
10.9	Business	13
6.5	Art and design	10.9
31	Humanities*	33
12.2	Combined courses	0.5

*Includes law, media, education, history, social sciences

UNIT 2 WRITING page 23 exercises 11–13

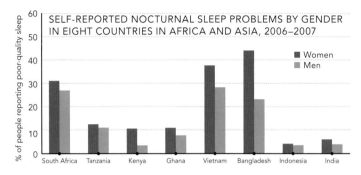

SELF-REPORTED NOCTURNAL SLEEP PROBLEMS BY GENDER IN EIGHT COUNTRIES IN AFRICA AND ASIA, 2006–2007

■ Women
■ Men

(% of people reporting poor-quality sleep — South Africa, Tanzania, Kenya, Ghana, Vietnam, Bangladesh, Indonesia, India)

UNIT 2 EXAM CHALLENGE: WRITING
page 26 exercise 1

Country	Life expectancy at birth (years)
Bangladesh	70
Japan	83
Nepal	68
Nigeria	53
Paraguay	75
Poland	77
Singapore	83
Sweden	82
United Arab Emirates	76
Zimbabwe	54

UNIT 3 SPEAKING page 28 exercise 12

STUDENT A

Ask Student B questions 1–4 in the survey on page 29. Give points each time they:

a show how strongly they agree or disagree with the statement (1 point)

b give their opinion in their own words (1 point)

c give a reason for their opinion (1 point).

UNIT 3 SPEAKING page 28 exercise 12

page 28 exercise 12

> **STUDENT B**
>
> **Ask Student A questions 5–8 in the survey on page 28.
> Give points each time they:**
>
> a show how strongly they agree or disagree with the
>   statement (1 point)
>
> b give their opinion in their own words (1 point)
>
> c give a reason for their opinion (1 point).

UNIT 3 WRITING page 33 exercise 10

The rise in tourism has had a great impact on many parts of the
world. But has it had a positive impact on development? This essay
will argue that the change is actually progress.

UNIT 3 EXAM CHALLENGE: WRITING
page 36 exercise 2

In many countries, students wear a uniform when they attend
school and workers also follow dress codes. But are such rules
about clothing really good for society? This essay will argue that
we would all work and study more effectively if we could choose
the clothing we wear.

UNIT 5 EXAM CHALLENGE: WRITING
page 56 exercise 2

Possible answer

Brainstorm:

Home entertainment can replace traditional entertainment
venues:

- You can eat while you enjoy home entertainment.
- You can pause the 'performance'.
- It costs very little.
- You can enjoy a greater variety of things.
- You can watch on computers or on mobile devices – anywhere.
- We already have 3D technology – similar to live performance.
- Entertainment at cinemas, etc., is overpriced.

Home entertainment cannot replace traditional entertainment
venues:

- Young people need to see live performances to inspire them.
- You can meet friends there.
- A live audience makes the performers perform better.
- Being part of a large audience is fun.
- You usually remember live performances for a long time.
- Travelling to venues is part of the fun.
- You get more risky (less commercial) art in local venues.
- We don't want to make the home entertainment corporations
  too powerful.

Plan:

I agree that we no longer need traditional entertainment venues:

- Home entertainment is more convenient.
- It is also cheaper.
- It is becoming a lot more sophisticated.

OR

I disagree that we no longer need traditional entertainment
venues:

- Events at entertainment venues are memorable social
  occasions.
- Seeing performers live inspires young people.
- Home entertainment is controlled by large corporations.

UNIT 6 SPEAKING page 58 exercise 4

Two American researchers, James Kouzes and Barry Posner,
developed a survey that asks people about the characteristics
of leaders. According to over 75,000 people, the top five most
admired characteristics are: 1) honest, 2) forward-looking,
3) competent, 4) inspiring, 5) intelligent.

UNIT 6 LISTENING page 60 exercise 2

Students at Harvard University were asked to choose between a
job with a salary of $50,000 a year (option 1) or one with a salary
of $100,000 a year (option 2). The catch was that in option 1, the
students would get paid twice as much as everyone else, who
would only get $25,000. In option 2, they would get paid half as
much as everyone else, who would get $200,000. The majority of
people chose option 1. They preferred to do better than everyone
else, even if it meant getting less for themselves.

UNIT 6 EXAM CHALLENGE: WRITING
page 66 exercise 2

Possible answer

Plan:

Yes, I agree that job satisfaction is more important than high pay.

- Job satisfaction brings health benefits.
- Too much pay causes stress / anxiety and obsessional behaviour.
- Job satisfaction will lead to better home life.

Topic sentences:

The first reason why I think job satisfaction is more important than
high pay is that it brings health benefits that pay does not.

The second justification for my view is that too much pay causes
stress and obsessional behaviour.

The final advantage of job satisfaction over pay is that it is likely to
lead to a better home life.

UNIT 7 SPEAKING page 68 exercise 9

STUDENT A

1 Ask Student B the questions.

1 What's the weather like in your country at the moment?

2 Do you visit the coast much? Why / Why not?

3 Have you seen snow before? When?

4 Is the climate changing in your part of the world? How?

2 Answer Student B's questions.

UNIT 7 LISTENING page 71 exercise 10

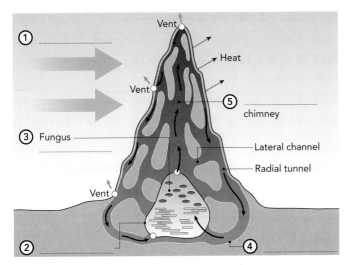

UNIT 7 WRITING page 72 exercises 2 and 3

Operation cat drop!

When the forces of nature threaten human life, authorities often fail to find an effective response. This was certainly true when the World Health Organization (WHO) tried to stop the spread of malaria in Borneo in the 1950s. It started when they sprayed the chemical DDT everywhere to kill the mosquitoes that carried the malaria. They succeeded, but the effects didn't stop there. The poisoned mosquitos were eaten by geckos, which were then eaten by cats. The cats started to die, the rats multiplied, and people were threatened by new diseases. To control the rats, the WHO then had to drop 14,000 live cats into Borneo by parachute!

UNIT 7 EXAM CHALLENGE: WRITING
page 76 exercise 2

Governments can now control the effects of extreme weather effectively. For example, if heavy snow is forecast they may put salt on the roads and tell drivers not to travel. This means that people can carry on their business as normal and schools remain open. If they do this, the economy does not suffer.

UNIT 8 SPEAKING page 79 exercise 12

STUDENT A

Ask Student B one set of questions below.

Set 1

1 Why do some people prefer not to use the internet for shopping?

2 When is it important to buy branded goods?

3 What might make people buy local products?

4 Is it better to get a recommendation from a friend or a shop assistant?

Set 2

1 Is it easier to buy electronic goods or clothes?

2 Why do some people spend more than others?

3 What are the most important qualities of a shop assistant?

4 Are there any types of shops that won't exist in the future?

Set 3

1 Will consumption levels continue to rise?

2 What's the most important thing to think about when you buy a car?

3 Why do some people write online reviews when they buy something new?

4 Is it better to give a gift or receive one?

UNIT 8 WRITING page 82 exercise 2

Researchers from Columbia University in the USA decided to do an experiment. They set up a tasting table in a supermarket. On one day, they put out six different flavours of jam; the next day, they put out 24 different flavours of jam. They were hoping to find the answers to two questions. First: 'In which situation were people more likely to stop and try some jam?' The result was that more people stopped, about 60%, when there were 24 flavours than when there were six flavours, about 40%. The second question they wanted to answer was: 'In which situation were people more likely to buy some jam?' Here, the researchers saw the opposite effect. Of the people who stopped when there were 24 flavours, only 3% of them actually bought some jam. Of the people who stopped when there were six flavours, 30% of them bought some jam. This meant that people were at least six times more likely to buy jam if they saw only six flavours than if they saw 24 flavours.

UNIT 8 WRITING page 83 exercise 10

Plan 1

Consumption is good:

● It creates jobs, e.g. in retail and factories.

● It increases levels of tax, e.g. in the UK, 20% of price goes to government.

● Large markets encourage new inventions, e.g. Apple and Samsung.

- Trade makes the world more peaceful, e.g. trade agreements.

Consumption is bad:
- It uses a lot of raw materials, e.g. oil and wood.
- Shopping isn't healthy, e.g. some people become addicted.
- Not everyone has money to shop, e.g. poor people are excluded.
- It creates waste, e.g. packaging.

Plan 2

The internet will replace shops:
- It's more convenient, e.g. you don't have to leave the house.
- It's cheaper, e.g. you can compare prices.
- There's more stock, e.g. more selection of colours.
- It's more informative, e.g. you can read other shoppers' comments and reviews.

The internet will not replace shops:
- It's not as much fun, e.g. you can't try on clothes.
- You can't inspect items, e.g. you can't touch them.
- It's unsociable, e.g. you don't talk to or interact with anyone.
- Delivery of orders can take time and isn't always guaranteed, e.g. if you need immediately or for a certain day.

Plan 3

Electricity is the greatest discovery:
- It has made modern factories possible, e.g. car plants.
- It has made digital technology possible, e.g. computers.
- It has made our lives more convenient, e.g. lighting.

Electricity is not the greatest discovery:
- The digital / machine age has brought problems too, e.g. overwork, unemployment.
- There have been negative effects on health, e.g. problems with sleep.
- Other major discoveries have been important, e.g. engines.

UNIT 8 EXAM CHALLENGE: WRITING
page 86 exercise 2

On the one hand, the giving of gifts brings a range of benefits. For example, the more we buy, the more economies are stimulated and this brings jobs and prosperity to many and a brighter future for the children themselves. Furthermore, it is clear that gifts do bring happiness to many children and give them something to look forward to. We should also remember that in the past most children didn't receive many gifts and our ability to give children many things indicates how much progress we have made.

On the other hand, the extent to which we now give gifts to children has surely led to a lack of appreciation for objects. Most presents are now used for a short while and then discarded. Furthermore, the disposal of packaging and of presents themselves places a huge strain on the environment, adding to the enormous piles of waste that have to be disposed of every day. Finally, some parents use gifts as an excuse for not building relationships with their children. Because their children ask for them, they believe they are good parents for buying them. In fact, psychologists would say that the sharing of time and conversation between parents and their children is far more important.

UNIT 9 WRITING page 92 exercise 2

Change of luck for homeless man

March 2013, Kansas City, USA. Sarah Darling accidentally dropped a diamond engagement ring in the cup of Billy Ray Harris, a homeless man. When he noticed the accident, Billy Ray Harris kept the ring safe until the woman came back two days later to claim it. News of Billy Ray Harris's action spread quickly via the media. Complete strangers who saw the news report went to find Harris to congratulate him and give him food. Sarah Darling's husband started an online campaign to collect money for him. It was so popular it went 'viral'. In twenty days the site collected more than 6,000 donations from all over the world and raised over $185,000. As a result of the media coverage, Harris was also reunited with his sister who he had lost contact with twenty years earlier.

UNIT 9 EXAM CHALLENGE: WRITING
page 96 exercise 2

In short, guidebooks still have a role to play. They are well written, easy to read, and offer a reliable resource for the traveller. Furthermore, access to digital media can be limited in some isolated areas. Guidebooks will no doubt continue to play a significant role alongside digital media long into the future.

UNIT 10 SPEAKING page 99 exercise 6

Country A: Ireland

Country B: Russia

Country C: South Korea

Country D: Mexico

UNIT 10 SPEAKING page 99 exercise 14

STUDENT A

1 **Read and check you understand questions 1–4. Then ask Student B. Use the paraphrase in *italics* below each question to help you to clarify.**

1 How have people's expenditure patterns changed in your country?
Do people spend their money on the same things now as they used to?

2 Do modern career paths differ wildly from those taken in the past?
Do people choose to do the same jobs now as they used to?

3 Is there a great deal more environmental degradation in today's world?
Is the environment today better or worse than it used to be?

4 Are communities as close-knit as they used to be?
Are people in communities as friendly and kind as they were before?

2 Listen to Student B's responses. Check that they:
- aren't too short
- aren't too personal
- respond to the question asked.

3 Listen to Student B's questions. Ask for clarification and answer the questions.

UNIT 10 LISTENING page 101 exercise 9

Describe each type of error the student has made in the answers below.

Example: 31 *The words don't fit in the gap.*

31	science experiment	✓ 31 ✗
32	is possible	✓ 32 ✗
33	small diner	✓ 33 ✗
34	tired in school	✓ 34 ✗
35	A	✓ 35 ✗
36	I	✓ 36 ✗
37	D/I	✓ 37 ✗
38	—	✓ 38 ✗
39	NC	✓ 39 ✗
40	no change	✓ 40 ✗

UNIT 10 LISTENING page 101 exercise 11

31		✓ 31 ✗
32		✓ 32 ✗
33		✓ 33 ✗
34		✓ 34 ✗
35		✓ 35 ✗
36		✓ 36 ✗
37		✓ 37 ✗
38		✓ 38 ✗
39		✓ 39 ✗
40		✓ 40 ✗

UNIT 10 WRITING page 103 exercise 11

First the room size and the time needed to clean are calculated. Next, the machine moves to middle of the room and begins moving around in a spiral pattern until it hits something when this happens, it reverses, rotates, and moves forward until finds a clear path. It avoids steps using four sensors on the bottom of the unit and if the battery power get low, the vacuum finds the charger and connects itself. Meanwhile, dirt removed from the floor by two spinning brush. At the same time, two dirt sensors check how much dirt is being kicked up and tell the cleaner to go back over durty areas again. At last, the dirt bin is automatic emptied into a large container.

UNIT 10 WRITING page 103 exercise 12

How a television works

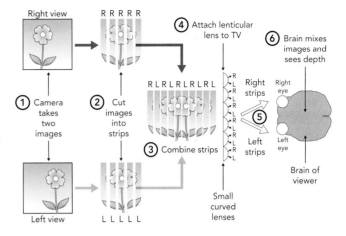

UNIT 10 EXAM CHALLENGE: WRITING
page 106 exercise 1

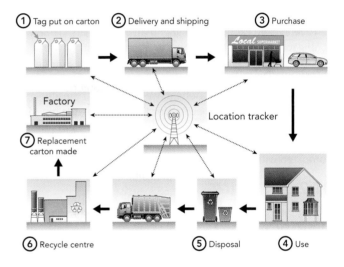

UNIT 1 SPEAKING page 9 exercise 15

STUDENT B

1 Answer Student A's questions. Try to speak for 15 seconds each time.

2 Ask Student A questions 1–3. Time the responses to make sure they speak for 15 seconds each time.

1 Who was your favourite teacher at school?

2 What subjects are you studying at the moment?

3 What subjects <u>don't</u> you want to study in the future?

UNIT 1 EXAM CHALLENGE: WRITING
page 16 exercise 2

The pie charts show the changes in undergraduate enrolment from 1995 to 2008 in five subject areas: medicine and biology, other sciences and technology, business, art and design, and humanities. They also include information about courses taken in more than one subject area. In general, we can see that trends in student enrolment varied considerably between subject areas.

The area with the sharpest rise was undoubtedly medical and life sciences, which grew markedly in popularity over the period shown, attracting over 13% of students in 1995 and just under 22% by 2008. In contrast, over the same period there was a notable fall in the percentage of students on other science and technology courses, from 26% to around 21%. The three remaining areas showed slight increases, with numbers rising from between 2% (business and humanities) and 4% (art). However, these increases may be explained by the decline in combined courses and so student numbers in these subject areas may be considered fairly stable. Only the science subjects therefore experienced considerable changes in popularity.

UNIT 2 EXAM CHALLENGE: WRITING
page 26 exercise 2

The table shows the life expectancy in ten countries of the world. In general, we can see that in many developed countries life expectancy is quite high, whereas in the less developed countries it is significantly lower.

Looking in more detail, we can see that three of the countries have an average life expectancy higher than eighty years, namely Japan, Singapore, and Sweden. These and other countries with a high life expectancy are all located in two main regions: Europe and the Far East. By contrast, when we look at data for countries in Africa and the Indian subcontinent, we can see that the life expectancy is significantly lower. In Africa in particular, the typical age someone can expect to live to is less than 50 years old. This is around 35 years lower than countries in the Far East and Europe, and compared with Japan, it is nearly half the number of years.

UNIT 7 SPEAKING page 68 exercise 9

STUDENT B

1 Answer Student A's questions.

2 Ask Student A the questions.

1 What's the weather like in your part of the world?

2 Do you prefer hot or cool weather? Why?

3 When was the last time you had very bad weather?

4 Does the weather change during the year where you live? How?

UNIT 10 SPEAKING page 99 exercise 14

STUDENT B

1 Listen to Student A's questions. Ask for clarification and answer the questions.

2 Read and check you understand questions 1–4. Then ask Student A. Use the paraphrase in italics below each question to help you to clarify.

1 How does your disposable income compare to your parents' generation?
Do people have more money to spend now than they did before?

2 Are contemporary educational standards higher than in the past?
Do people do better at school now than they used to?

3 Do we strike a better balance between work commitments and leisure than our ancestors did?
Is our work-life balance better now than it used to be?

4 Why are our health needs met more effectively now than they used to be?
Why have we become healthier these days?

3 Listen to Student A's responses. Check that they:

* aren't too short
* aren't too personal
* respond to the question asked.

UNIT 10 EXAM CHALLENGE: WRITING
page 106 exercise 2

The diagram shows the process of tracking a product from when it leaves the manufacturer to the point when it is recycled. In general, we can see how location tracking can be helpful for companies trying to keep track of their stock. The diagram shows the normal steps of the product life cycle. We see that first, a tag is placed on the milk carton at the factory. Then it is transported to the shop or supermarket. After that, the product is sold to a consumer and taken home to be drunk. Meanwhile, the manufacturer is continually tracking the progress of the carton and knows which stage of the product life-cycle the carton is at, and can plan or predict the need for new cartons. Finally, after the carton has been thrown away and taken to the recycling centre, the manufacturer can produce a replacement without needing to wait for an order.

GRAMMAR FILE

It and there

Empty subjects page 68

It is often used instead of a noun to describe the time, a place, a situation, or the weather. This is particularly common in spoken English.

It's late! (the time)

It's hot! (the temperature)

It is so crowded! (the streets)

Add extra information about the noun with an adverb or a prepositional phrase.

*It's hot **here**.*

*It is so crowded **in the city centre**.*

The extra information can also go at the beginning of the sentence.

***In my country** it is beautiful.*

When the extra information is at the beginning of the sentence, *it* cannot be removed.

NOT ~~In my country is beautiful.~~

To describe the *things* that exist in a place, replace *it* with *there*.

***There** is a shopping centre in my town.* NOT ~~It is a shopping centre in my town.~~

To say more than one thing exists, change *is* to *are*.

*There **is** a bank in my city.*

*There **are** several banks in my city.*

It for giving opinions page 29

It is often used (in spoken and written English) as a sentence subject to give opinions about an action. In these sentences, *it* always refers forwards to the action.

It is useful <u>to study</u> = *Studying is useful.*

Note that the infinitive with *to* is used after the adjective.

It is easy to play piano. NOT ~~It is easy play piano.~~

There for the existence of abstract nouns page 39

Use *there* to say that an idea (e.g. a reason or problem) exists.

There are many problems in my town.

There does not always refer to a specific place. It may be used to refer to a situation in general.

There are many reasons why we must protect the environment.

1A Choose the correct alternative for each sentence.

1 *There / It* is a big park near my house.

2 In the mountains, *there / it* is very beautiful in the summer.

3 *There / It* is more to do in the spring.

4 *There / It* is not enough time in my day.

5 Next month, *there / it* will be a carnival.

6 *There / It* is dangerous to walk on the ice.

7 *There / It* is my birthday soon.

1B Change one or two words in the sentences in exercise 1A. Make each sentence true for you.

Example: *There is a big school near my flat.*

2 Rewrite the sentences. Start with *it* or *there*.

1 Car ownership has many negative effects.
There _____.

2 Speaking English is easy.
It _____.

3 The climate is very dry in the south of the country.
It _____.

4 Not many people vote in local elections.
There _____.

5 Several cinemas can be found in larger towns.
There _____.

Pronoun referents page 75

Pronouns are used instead of repeating the same noun, and to help make writing more cohesive. They usually refer backwards.

*Fruit contains vitamins. **This** makes **it** an important part of our diet.*

However, they can sometimes refer forwards to an idea.

***It** is healthy to eat fruit.*

***Those** who eat fruit are often healthy.*

When reading, it is important to understand which idea the pronoun refers to in order to fully understand the text.

When writing, make sure an appropriate pronoun is selected for the idea it refers to. Below is a list of the most commonly used pronouns. (Note that pronouns *I*, *me*, and *you* are often avoided in academic writing.)

People

Subject (before verb):	I	he	she	we	they	you
Object (after verb):	me	him	her	us	them	you

Objects and ideas

It (singular objects), *they* (plural objects), *this* (whole idea / sentence), *there* (place), *those* (= the people)

113

1 What people or ideas in the text do words 1-6 in bold refer to?

The best people want to work for the best companies and the best companies want to keep ¹**them**. But what exactly is it that keeps people satisfied and motivated? There are many studies in this area and perhaps one of the most famous is by Frederik Herzberg. Herzberg interviewed 200 engineers and accountants about ²**their** experiences of work. The researchers first asked ³**these** people to recall a time when they felt exceptionally positive about their job and to think what had happened before ⁴**this**. Analysis showed that before the good times employees frequently mentioned one or more of the following: achievement, recognition, the work itself, responsibility, promotion. ⁵**They** then asked the employees to think of a time when ⁶**they** were particularly negative about their job. When talking about the bad times, employees regularly mentioned one of the following: company policy and administration, supervision, salary, interpersonal relations, working conditions.

2 Complete the paragraph with the words below.

> those   he   it   they (x2)   this (x2)

Although people in the western world have become much richer, there is evidence that ¹_____ are not happier. Psychologists have two main explanations for ²_____. The first one is that people often make comparisons between themselves and others. ³_____ is based on a psychological theory suggested by Leon Festinger. ⁴_____ proposed a theory in which people are happy if ⁵_____ have more than ⁶_____ who they usually compare themselves to. The result is that a person will usually be pleased with a new car – until a friend buys one just like ⁷_____!

Much / many / a lot of page 39

To use *much / many / a lot of* correctly, it is important to understand the difference between countable and uncountable nouns. Countable nouns are things we can count, e.g. *cities, people*. Uncountable nouns are things we cannot count, e.g. *information, data*.

Use *much* in questions and negatives with uncountable nouns. *Much* is used to mean a large quantity or to ask about quantity.

*There isn't **much** traffic in the city centre.*

*How **much** waste is produced?*

Use *many* in questions and negatives with countable nouns.

*There aren't **many** immigrants in our city.*

*How **many** people are out of work?*

Add *too* when there is a lot of something and it is a negative thing.

*There is **too** much traffic in the city.*

*There are **too** many people on the roads at rush hour.*

Use *a lot of / lots of* with both countable and uncountable nouns and in questions, negatives, and positive sentences.

*There isn't **a lot of** pollution in the river.*

1A Complete the sentences with *isn't much* or *aren't many*.

1 There _____ factories in my city.
2 There _____ traffic in my city.
3 There _____ pollution in my city.
4 There _____ people in my city.

1B Make the sentences in exercise 1A positive. Then add *too* if this is a problem where you live.

Example: *There are **too** many factories in my city.*

2 Change *much* to *a lot of* if it is used incorrectly in the sentences.

1 We didn't have much time.
2 She eats much food.
3 We create much waste.
4 It costs much money to maintain the roads.
5 It wouldn't cost much money.

Comparisons

Comparisons with *more / fewer / less* and *than*
page 22

More, *fewer*, and *less* are often used to compare the quantity of people or objects.

Use *more, less,* or *fewer* immediately before a noun.

More people are emigrating to live in other countries.

Use *less* with uncountable nouns and *fewer* with countable nouns.

*People do **fewer** hours of exercise nowadays.*

Use *more than, less than,* or *fewer than* immediately after a verb.

*Adults sleep **less than** children (do).*

Repeat the preposition with the second noun.

*More people go to the cinema than **to** restaurants.*
NOT *More people go to the cinema than restaurants.*

Comparative and superlative adjectives

For one-syllable adjectives, add *-er* or *-est* after the final consonant.

cheap ➔ *cheaper* ➔ *cheapest*

For a short adjective ending in a vowel and consonant, double the final consonant.

big ➔ *bigger* ➔ *biggest*

For two-syllable adjectives ending in *-y*, change the *-y* to an *-i* and add *-er* or *-est*.

busy ➔ *busier* ➔ *busiest*

For adjectives with two or more syllables not ending in -y, put *more* or *most* before the adjective.

interesting → *more interesting* → *most interesting*

Some adjectives are irregular, such as:

good → *better* → *best*

Add emphasis to a comparative adjective by adding *much*.

*The centre is **much** older than the rest of the town.*

Use *the* before superlative adjectives, e.g. *the funniest, the most boring*.

Use *as ... as* to show that two things are equal.

*London is **as** expensive **as** Tokyo.*

Use *not as ... as* to show two things are not the same.

*The internet here is **not as** fast **as** it is in my country.*

1A Complete the sentences with *less / fewer* or *less than / fewer than*.

1 People exercise _____ they used to.

2 People had _____ days holiday in the past.

3 People spend _____ time socializing with other people.

4 Most people make _____ effort _____ they think.

5 There are _____ people in this city _____ most people think.

1B Write new sentences with the same meaning as the first sentences in 1–5. Use *more, more than,* or *as ... as*.

1 I didn't think I weighed so much.
I weigh _____ .

2 I'm surprised how far my pedometer says I walked.
I walked _____ .

3 Every week I try to swim further.
I try to swim _____ .

4 I want to sleep over eight hours.
I want to _____ .

5 There are fewer people in the park on weekdays than there are at the weekends.
There aren't _____ .

2A Complete the sentences using a comparative form of the words below.

| happy   motivate   high   well   technological |

1 Psychologists understand depression _____ than they understand happiness.

2 Social networks make people _____ .

3 Many people are _____ by money than friendship.

4 Levels of happiness in Bhutan are _____ than levels of wealth.

5 With the arrival of more mobile devices, our lifestyles are becoming _____ .

2B Write the comparative and superlative forms of the adjectives below.

good _____   boring _____

busy _____   far _____

bad _____   small _____

excellent _____   long _____

little _____   different _____

Adverbs

Position of adverbs   page 48

The position of the adverb depends on the information it provides about:

1 actions (*quickly, slowly, well,* etc.)
Put the adverb after the main verb except when there is a direct object.
*I shut the door **quickly**. NOT ~~I shut quickly the door.~~*

2 feelings (*fortunately, hopefully, sadly,* etc.)
Put the adverb at the start of a sentence. Add a comma afterwards.
***Happily**, I passed my driving test.*

3 frequency (*often, usually, sometimes,* etc.)
Put the adverb just before the main verb, but always after the verb *be*.
*I **often** arrive **late**. NOT ~~I arrive often late.~~*
*I am **often** late. NOT ~~I often am late.~~*

4 possibility (*perhaps, definitely, probably,* etc.)
Put *maybe* and *perhaps* at the beginning of the sentence. Put *probably / definitely / certainly* immediately before the main verb in positive sentences (but after *be*). Put *probably / definitely / certainly* immediately before auxiliaries in negative sentences.
*They're **probably** right.*
*They **probably** aren't right.*
***Probably** they're right.*

Put phrases that are used like adverbs at the end of a sentence.

*I feel impatient **at times**.*

*I don't do it **at all**.*

*I swim **a lot**.*

Some adverbs give information about how strong a verb is: *very much* and *a lot* (positive); *at all* (negative). Put them at the end of sentences.

Adverbs of degree page 69

Some adverbs give extra information about how strong an adjective is. Put this type of adverb before the adjective.

◄─────────────────────────────────►

(weak) *quite / rather* *very / really* *extremely* (strong)

Before very strong adjectives, you often use *absolutely*.

Before adjectives that cannot be graded (e.g. *empty / full*, *dead / alive*), you often use *completely*.

A bit, *a little*, and *slightly* are usually used before adjectives with negative meanings.

*This talk is **a bit** boring.*

Really and *absolutely* are also used before emotion verbs to make the meaning stronger. Use *absolutely* with extreme verbs.

*I **absolutely** love cats.*

*I **really** dislike dogs.*

....

1 **Put the adverbs in brackets into the sentences in the correct places.**

1 I'll do a Master's degree. (maybe)

2 My family won't be happy. (certainly)

3 I like to do my homework. (well)

4 I find learning languages difficult. (really)

5 Some people are satisfied. (never)

6 I think private education is wrong. (personally)

7 I get up before my parents do. (often)

2 **Complete the sentences with the correct adverb below.**

| absolutely completely a little at all unfortunately |
| hopefully extremely from time to time |

1 _____, I'll see my best friend soon.

2 It's an _____ pretty town.

3 I feel _____ chilly.

4 I take the car _____ .

5 _____, I didn't enjoy the party.

6 We soon realized we were _____ lost.

7 Pancakes taste _____ wonderful with lemon.

8 I don't miss my country _____ .

Gerunds and infinitives page 9

When a phrase has two main verbs, you usually use the infinitive (e.g. *to be*) or the gerund (e.g. *being*) for the second verb.

Always use the infinitive after certain verbs. These include verbs for discussing the future.

*I hope **to go** ...*

Similar verbs include:

need want plan would like intend

Use the infinitive when the second verb indicates a purpose.

*I'm studying English **to get** a job.*

Always use the gerund after certain verbs. These include verbs for discussing likes and dislikes.

*I enjoy **going** ...*

*I don't mind **going** ...*

Use the gerund after *go* to refer to activities.

*I go **running** every week.*

Other uses

Use the infinitive after adjectives.

*It's fun **to study**.*

Use the gerund when the subject of the sentence is an action.

***Swimming** is fun.*

Use the gerund after a preposition.

*I'm interested in **travelling**.*

....

1A **Complete the sentences with the gerund or infinitive of the verbs in brackets.**

1 **A:** Where would you like to live in the future?
   B: I'd like _____ (live) by the sea. _____ (live) on an island would be wonderful.

2 **A:** What do you do to stay healthy?
   B: I really enjoy _____ (dance) but it's difficult _____ (find) time. I go _____ (cycle), too.

3 **A:** Why did you choose to learn English?
   B: _____ (get) a better job, really.

4 **A:** Are you going on holiday this year?
   B: Yes, I'm planning _____ (travel) to Austria because I love _____ (ski).

1B **Answer the questions in exercise 1A so they are true for you.**

─────────────────────────────────

Uses of *that*

Linkers: *that / is that* page 63

***That** can be used to connect two parts of a sentence when:*

1 **introducing a reason, effect, cause, or problem**
   *One effect of overpopulation **is that** roads become crowded.*

2 **reporting an opinion or statement**
   *Researchers have found **that** ...*

3 **introducing a hope, belief, or expectation.**
   *I hope **that** deforestation will stop.*

In these cases, a noun and verb is needed on both sides of the word *that*.

*The problem **is that** I can't swim. NOT ~~The problem that I can't swim.~~*

Relative pronoun

That can also be used to say which part(s) of a group is being referred to.

*The number of people **that** go to university is increasing.*

That can often be removed when it is followed by a new subject.

The hobby ~~that~~ I enjoy most is football.

Other uses

That may be used to refer to the words spoken by the other person in a conversation.

That's *true to some extent.*

That may also be used to refer to the consequence of a state or situation.

*I'm so tired at weekends **that** I stay in bed.*

....

1A Put *that* in the sentences where possible.

1 Many people believe war will end.

2 One benefit of consumerism is economies grow.

3 I hope to move house this year.

4 The subject I liked the most was art.

5 People play computer games become addicted easily.

6 One cause of crime is poverty.

7 I'm so hard-working I sometimes forget to have lunch.

1B Change the words after *that* in the sentences in exercise 1A to make new sentences.

Example: *Many people believe that money is the most important thing in life.*

'Real' conditionals and time clauses

Zero conditional for causes and effects page 73

The zero conditional is often used to talk about cause and effect relationships. Use the present simple in both clauses of the sentence after *if* or *when* in these cases.

*If / When sea levels **rise**, there **are** usually floods in coastal areas.*

First conditional page 16

The first conditional is often used to talk about future events that depend on something. Use the present simple after *if* in these cases.

*If I **go** to university next year, I ...*

The sentence is usually continued with a future form or a modal verb of possibility.

*If I go to university, I **will** / **'m going to** / **might** / **may** / **could** study law.*

Unless can be used to mean *except if* in all conditional sentences about the future or about general truths / habits.

Unless *I go to university, I'll get a full-time job.*

You do not need a comma when *if* or *unless* appear in the middle of the sentence.

*I won't be a doctor **if** I don't go to university.*

Time clauses page 19

To describe a habitual relationship between two events in time, replace *if* with adverbs like *after*, *before*, and the following:

as soon as = in exactly the same moment that
*I'll call **as soon as** I arrive.*

every time = is always true when sth happens
*We argue **every time** we meet.*

whenever = every time, often followed by a state rather than an action
*I sleep **whenever** I can.*

while = in another period of time
*I read **while** I'm on holiday.*

Future time clauses

As soon as, while, after, before, and when can also be used instead of *if* to indicate a future time relationship. In reference to the future, *when* and *if* have different meanings: *when* indicates certainty that the condition will happen.

....

1A Complete the sentences with the correct forms of the verbs in brackets.

1 **A:** What will happen if the population continues to grow?
  B: I think we _____ (have to) build more houses if that _____ (happen).

2 **A:** What do you do at the weekend?
  B: I _____ (have) a lie-in if I _____ (not have) any plans.

3 **A:** What will you study if you go to university?
  B: I haven't decided. If I _____ (pass) my maths exams, I _____ (study) engineering.

4 **A:** Do you often take photographs?
  B: I _____ (take) photographs whenever I _____ (be) on holiday.

5 **A:** Is tourism going to increase in the future?
  B: I don't think so, unless the economy _____ (grow).

6 **A:** Are you going on holiday soon?
  B: Yes. As soon as I _____ (have) enough money!

7 **A:** How do people react when there is unemployment?
  B: They _____ (become) angry.

1B Answer the questions in exercise 1A so they are true for you.

2A Choose the correct alternative for each sentence.

1 I won't learn to drive *if / unless* I get a car.

2 I'll move house *when / while* I get a good job.

3 Young people become obese *if / unless* they do exercise.

4 I'll get married *when* / *if* I'm 21.

5 I like to work *while* / *unless* I travel.

6 I see my family *whenever* / *every time* I can.

2B Rewrite sentences 1 and 3 in exercise 2A using the alternative you did not choose.

'Unreal' conditional

Second conditional page 59

The second conditional is used to express an unreal or imaginary situation and its possible result in the present or future.

The second conditional is normally formed with: *if* + 'past simple' form, *would* + infinitive without *to*. *Were* is often used instead of *was* in such sentences.

*If I **lived** in a city, my life **would be** more stressful.*

*If I **were** a senior manager, I **would receive** a higher salary.*

The position of the clauses can change without changing the meaning.

If we had more money, it wouldn't be a problem.

It wouldn't be a problem if we had more money.

You can also use *might* or *could* instead of *would* to indicate less certainty about the result.

*If we lived somewhere else, we **might** be happier.*

Could and would page 42

Could is used in the second conditional to talk about an unreal possibility.

*If I **could** meet anyone, it would be Rafael Nadal.*

Could is also used to propose solutions or make suggestions.

*We **could** use more renewable energy.*

Would can be used to talk about possible results when discussing a solution.

*Using renewable energy **would** cut pollution.*

1A Complete the sentences with the correct forms of the words in brackets.

1 If I _____ the president tomorrow, I _____ him to spend more money on poor people. (meet, tell)

2 If I _____ my job, I _____ happier. (change, not be)

3 If you _____ any amount of holiday per year, how many days _____ ? (take x2)

4 If I _____ the time, I _____ more. (have, travel)

5 If she _____ so unfit, she _____ taking exercise. (not be, enjoy)

6 If I _____ more money, I _____ happier. (have, be)

7 I _____ less stressed if we _____ fewer exams. (be, have)

8 If the government _____ taxes on junk food, it _____ obesity. (increase, reduce)

1B Why is *could* used in sentence 3 in exercise 1A? How does the meaning change if you add *could* to sentence 2 in exercise 1A?

2A Match 1–6 with a–f.

1 We could introduce …

2 Improved public transport would …

3 They could …

4 More recycling would …

5 Homes could …

6 Making homes more energy efficient would …

a mean that there were fewer cars on the road.

b reduce the amount of energy wasted.

c better public transport.

d result in less rubbish in landfill sites.

e be more energy-efficient.

f recycle more waste.

2B Complete the sentences with *could* or *would*.

1 I _____ speak to him if I were you.

2 If I _____ study anything, it _____ be psychology.

3 I _____ speak to him for you.

4 They _____ spend less money on military equipment so that they _____ have more to spend on education.

5 If I _____ solve one problem in my country, it _____ be the number of deaths from malaria.

Modal verbs

Ability in the past, present, and future page 85

Use *can* to talk about present ability.

*We **can** send messages instantly.*

Use *could* to talk about past ability and general ability.

*When I was a child, we **could** spend whole days doing nothing.*

Use *was able to* to talk about ability on one occasion.

*I **was able to** take some great photos.*

Use *will be able to* to talk about future ability.

*We **will be able to** work whenever we want.*

Can and may for possibility page 100

Can is used to talk about present or general possibility.

*I **can** meet you at two o'clock.*

May is used to talk about future possibility.

*I **may** go to Spain next year.*

Can cannot be used for future possibility.

I think shops may become larger in the future. NOT ~~I think they can become larger.~~

May cannot be used for general possibility.

You can watch the carnival if you go in February. NOT ~~You may watch the carnival if you go in February.~~

May and *might* can be used for future plans, but *could* cannot be used to mean *might* when talking about plans.

I could go to Spain next year. = it's a possibility but not likely

I may go to Spain next year. = it's a possibility I'm seriously considering

1 Complete the sentences with *can, could,* or *will be able to* in the positive or negative.

1 When I was young, I _____ play the piano really well.

2 I _____ speak three languages fluently.

3 In ten years, we _____ use oil more efficiently.

4 They _____ solve the problem without more money.

5 People _____ travel as easily in the past.

6 Children growing up in the digital era _____ focus on one task for long periods.

7 People type so much that in the future they _____ write by hand.

8 People _____ make simple changes to their lifestyles that will help the environment.

2A Complete the sentences with *can* or *may*.

1 I _____ study abroad next year.

2 I _____ work in any European country.

3 I _____ study three languages in my school.

4 I _____ travel around India in the summer.

5 I _____ change my job next month.

6 I _____ leave university in the summer.

7 I _____ change courses if I want to.

8 I _____ type very quickly.

2B In which sentences in exercise 2A can you change the modal verb for *might*?

Describing the past

Talking about past events page 89

Use the past simple to talk about events that happened in a period of time that is finished.

Some past simple verbs are regular. Make them by adding *-ed* to the verb.

In written English, if the verb ends in *-y*, change it to an *-i*. If the verb has a short vowel sound, double the last letter. If the verb ends in *-e*, add *-d*.

cry → *cried*

stop → *stopped*

enter → *entered*

Many verbs have irregular forms and it is important to learn them.

go → *went*

For negative sentences, use *didn't* + infinitive without *to*.

I didn't like broccoli as a child.

Use the past continuous tense to describe long actions that provide background information. Remember to use *was / were + -ing* form. In written English, if the verb has a short vowel sound, double the last letter to make the *-ing* form.

I once broke my leg. I was running on an icy road.

Do not use the past continuous for states.

I loved school. NOT ~~I was loving school.~~

You often connect past simple and past continuous sentences by inserting *while* before the past continuous part, or *when* before the past simple part.

While I was travelling, I suddenly became ill.

I was travelling when I suddenly became ill.

Used to page 99

To talk about past events you did regularly, use *used to* + the infinitive without *to*.

We used to have our family holidays on the Black Sea.

This form can also refer to past situations.

I used to play sport.

The negative form is *didn't use to*.

I didn't use to be tall.

Avoid *used to* if the action or situation still continues. In these cases, use the present perfect.

I have always loved going to the mountains. NOT ~~I used to love going to the mountains and I still love going there.~~

1A Find the past simple forms in the word string.

hididiedriedrankeptoldcutatendedrewon

1B Use some of the past forms in exercise 1A to complete the sentences below.

1 I _____ my homework but I _____ to make mistakes.

2 I _____ a goldfish in my bedroom but it _____ .

3 I always _____ the truth to my parents but they _____ the truth from me.

4 My football team was good – we usually _____ or _____ our matches.

5 I _____ a large slice of cake and _____ it quickly.

2 Choose the correct alternatives to complete the text.

We [1]used to go / went on camping holidays. We [2]used to put / were putting our tent next to rivers or lakes. I remember once we [3]were camping / used to camp by a river and the weather [4]used to be / was terrible. We [5]were sleeping / slept when the river level [6]started / was starting to rise. When we [7]were waking up / woke up, we [8]were realizing / realized that we [9]were being / were surrounded by water and all our clothes [10]were / used to be soaked!

The passive

The passive is formed with the verb *be* + past participle (*finished, sent, done,* etc.). The verb *be* can be used in most tenses.

*The product **is sold** all over the world.*

*The house **was destroyed**.*

In active sentences, the sentence topic (or subject) performs an action and there is often a direct object.

People (subject) speak (action) English (object) in Australia.

In passive sentences, the object of a verb is used as the sentence topic. The passive is therefore used to focus on <u>what</u> is done rather than who or what did it.

English (object) is spoken in Australia.

When there is a general topic like *people*, you do not need to add *by people* to the passive form. With a specific topic, you can add the information if it is important.

The building was constructed in 1901. (by workers)
*The building was designed **by Richard Rogers**.*

Use the passive infinitive (*be* + past participle) after a modal verb.

*Driving should **be banned** in the city centre.*
*The problem could **be solved** through co-operation.*

Passive for a process page 102

The passive is often used for describing processes because we are interested in what happens to objects during the process.

*First, the oranges **are picked**. Then, they **are taken** ...*

When describing processes, use the present simple tense.

---

1 Are the sentences active or passive? Write A (active) or P (passive).

1 A lot of tea is drunk in the UK.

2 Bikes are often stolen in the city centre.

3 The company delivers parcels every day.

4 The factory is cleaned twice a week.

5 Many people were rescued from the floods.

6 My brother took the photo.

2A Look at the information in the table. Then complete the text with the present simple active or passive of the verbs in brackets.

Typical monthly spending of teenagers		
	Male	Female
Clothes	£50	£80
Food	£30	£20
Computer games	£100	£50
Mobile phone	£30	£50
Total	£210	£200

An average of £210 [1]_____ (spend) by boys and an average of £200 [2]_____ (spend) by girls. Clothes [3]_____ (buy) most commonly by girls, whereas boys mostly [4]_____ (spend) money on computer games. The girls' mobile phones [5]_____ (cost) an average of £50 a month while the boys only [6]_____ (spend) an average of £30. A similar amount [7]_____ (spend) by both boys and girls on food.

2B Imagine the data in exercise 2A is for last month only instead of being typical over a longer period. How would this change the tense used?

2C Use the prompts to write sentences in the passive. Use the tenses shown in brackets.

1 My luggage / lose / on holiday. (past simple)

2 The streets / clean / every day. (present simple)

3 A lot of money / save. (future)

4 My wallet / steal. (past simple)

5 The parcels / deliver / at the end of the week. (present simple)

6 The carnival / hold / in March next year. (future)

VOCABULARY FILE

UNIT 1 EDUCATION & LEARNING

1 Complete the sentences with a school or university subject.

1 I enjoyed studying _science_. I liked studying the physical part – looking at volcanoes, rocks, and earthquakes. I didn't find the human side so interesting.

2 I'm hoping to study _physical_ at university. My uncle is a high court judge and I'd like to be a lawyer.

3 I'm taking _psychology_. I'm really interested in finding more out about how the mind works and to understand people's behaviour.

4 I'd like to study _mathematics_. I'm not sure my maths is good enough, but it's not just about structure, materials, and processes – it's also about design and I'm good at that.

5 I'm studying _____. I think I'm a natural leader and I have a good understanding of how organizations work.

6 I liked studying _____. I still love reading books now – especially thrillers and horror stories.

7 I want to be a doctor so I'm taking physics, chemistry, and _____. I like the human parts best rather than studying plants and animals.

8 I studied _____ for seven years. I want to be a doctor in the USA, a heart specialist, so I'm taking an English course.

2 Underline the words in exercise 1 related to each subject.

Example: *1 physical, volcanoes, rocks, earthquakes, human*

3 In your notebook, create a word family diagram for each subject from exercise 1. Add the words below to the diagrams. Some words can connect to more than one subject.

> legal hospital personality surgery poem natural
> charge organic bureaucratic biological geographical
> urban case author conscious relationships reader
> maintain authority build chairman rural

4 Add two more words of your own to each word family diagram.

5 Match the sentences in exercise 1 to questions a–c below. Each sentence can be used more than once.

a What subject would you like to study in the future?

b What was your favourite subject at school or university?

c What subjects are you studying at the moment?

6 Complete questions 1–7 with the phrases below.

> compulsory education   under pressure
> private school   school grades   ambition for
> levels of stress   greatest achievement

1 What's the _____ in your life so far?

2 Do you feel _____ in exams?

3 Do you think it's unfair that not everyone can go to a _____?

4 Are the _____ high in your school system or is it quite relaxed?

5 Are _____ important for future success?

6 When can you finish _____ in your country?

7 What's your academic _____ the future?

7 Ask and answer the questions in exercise 6 with a partner. Then write an extended response for each one.

8 Put the words into the correct columns of the table.

> rise increase significant fall slight
> dramatic minor major decline grow

Movement up	Movement down	Big change	Small change

9 Complete sentences 1–4 with the correct preposition.

> to (x2)   in   by   from

1 There was a significant increase _____ the number of people starting university.

2 The average grades fell _____ B _____ C in 2012.

3 The number of people studying engineering increased _____ 20% over the last five years.

4 The number of pupils in private education fell _____ under 100,000 during the recession.

UNIT 2 HEALTH & MEDICINE

1 Replace the words in bold in 1–9 with words of a similar meaning below. *(adj)* 的/科的の
繰返の いが立1む

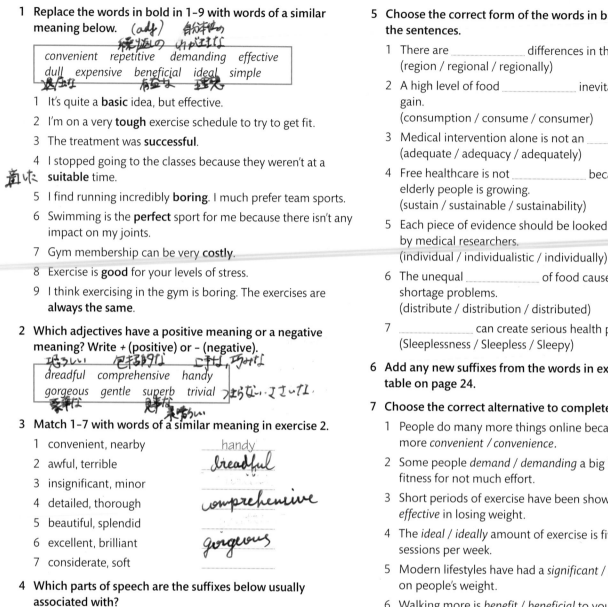

convenient	repetitive	demanding	effective	
dull	expensive	beneficial	ideal	simple

返/退は   有益な   理想

1 It's quite a **basic** idea, but effective.

2 I'm on a very **tough** exercise schedule to try to get fit.

3 The treatment was **successful**.

4 I stopped going to the classes because they weren't at a **suitable** time.   直た

5 I find running incredibly **boring**. I much prefer team sports.

6 Swimming is the **perfect** sport for me because there isn't any impact on my joints.

7 Gym membership can be very **costly**.

8 Exercise is **good** for your levels of stress.

9 I think exercising in the gym is boring. The exercises are **always the same**.

2 Which adjectives have a positive meaning or a negative meaning? Write + (positive) or – (negative).

恐ろしい   包括的な   口ましい、便わしい
dreadful	comprehensive	handy
gorgeous	gentle	superb	trivial

些細な・ささいな

豪華な   素晴な
素晴らしい

3 Match 1–7 with words of a similar meaning in exercise 2.

1 convenient, nearby — *handy*

2 awful, terrible — *dreadful*

3 insignificant, minor

4 detailed, thorough — *comprehensive*

5 beautiful, splendid

6 excellent, brilliant — *gorgeous*

7 considerate, soft

4 Which parts of speech are the suffixes below usually associated with?

-ate (x2)	-ive	-ful	-ment	-ic	-ly	-al
-able	-ed (x2)	-es (x2)	-y	-ness	-tion	

5 Choose the correct form of the words in brackets to complete the sentences.

1 There are _____ differences in the levels of obesity.
(region / regional / regionally)

2 A high level of food _____ inevitably leads to weight gain.
(consumption / consume / consumer)

3 Medical intervention alone is not an _____ solution.
(adequate / adequacy / adequately)

4 Free healthcare is not _____ because the number of elderly people is growing.
(sustain / sustainable / sustainability)

5 Each piece of evidence should be looked at _____ by medical researchers.
(individual / individualistic / individually)

6 The unequal _____ of food causes many of the food shortage problems.
(distribute / distribution / distributed)

7 _____ can create serious health problems.
(Sleeplessness / Sleepless / Sleepy)

6 Add any new suffixes from the words in exercise 5 to the table on page 24.

7 Choose the correct alternative to complete the sentences.

1 People do many more things online because they find it more *convenient / convenience*.

2 Some people *demand / demanding* a big improvement in fitness for not much effort.

3 Short periods of exercise have been shown to be *effect / effective* in losing weight.

4 The *ideal / ideally* amount of exercise is five 30-minute sessions per week.

5 Modern lifestyles have had a *significant / significance* impact on people's weight.

6 Walking more is *benefit / beneficial* to your health.

7 I read the instructions *thorough / thoroughly* but I still can't use it.

8 I need to *consider / considerate* all the options before I decide.

8 Choose four words from this page. Use them in four different sentences about your diet, health, and exercise routine.

Example: *Ideally, I'd like to do some exercise every day.*

UNIT 3 SOCIETY & FAMILY

1 Put the verbs in the correct column of the table.

> account   associate sth   benefit
> react   lead   search   convince sb

for sth	from sth	of sth	to sth	with sth

2 Match the expressions with prepositions from exercise 1 to definitions 1–7.

1 persuade sb of sth

2 look for sth

3 result in sth

4 be the explanation or cause of sth

5 connect sth to sb or sth

6 gain sth positive from a situation

7 respond to sth

3 Choose the correct alternatives to complete the sentences.

1 Birth order is *associated with / convinced of* success. Older siblings and only children are usually the most successful.

2 The increased number of elderly people *benefit from / account for* the higher proportion of private pensions.

3 Some people still need to be *led to / convinced of* the need for equal opportunities.

4 China has *benefited from / associated with* having a large population.

5 Many people *react to / benefit from* news by posting comments in message boards.

6 Living alone has *convinced of / led to* increased levels of consumption.

7 People often *react to / search for* reasons to explain why something happens.

4 Complete sentences 1–8 with the words below.

> housework   responsibility   well-being   opportunities
> customs   income   immigration   laws

1 Is it the _____ of the government or individuals to promote exercise and healthy diets?

2 Should _____ be introduced to ban unhealthy food?

3 Who should do the _____ at home?

4 Is it important to protect the _____ and traditions of a culture?

5 Is it important for a country to control _____ or should people be able to come and go as they please?

6 Should the government provide job _____ for young people?

7 Should there be a limit to the _____ an individual can receive?

8 Is your _____ or money more important to you in your life?

5 Think about your answers to the questions in exercise 4. Then choose three questions and write your answers as complete sentences.

6 Correct the mistakes with prepositions in sentences 1–6.

1 Looking closely at the results leads of some surprising conclusions.

2 I read an article into the effects of old age on family members.

3 Her motivation about returning to work was linked to gender equality.

4 The rationale into living together was the fact that people were financially dependent on each other.

5 The analysis about behaviour is often carried out using studies of twins.

6 Research for living alone often focuses on the psychological impact of living alone.

7 Write sentences about society and families in your country. Use some of the expressions in exercises 1–3.

Example: *In my country, the high cost of housing has led to young people living at home for longer.*

8 Match adjectives 1–8 to a–h with the opposite meaning.

1	adventurous	a	lazy
2	caring	b	serious
3	creative	c	unimaginative
4	clever	d	cautious
5	easy-going	e	unintelligent
6	hard-working	f	cold
7	sociable	g	inflexible
8	fun-loving	h	shy

9 Write sentences about someone you know. Describe them using some of the adjectives in exercise 8.

Example: *My older brother is very sociable and easy-going.*

UNIT 4 POPULATION & THE ENVIRONMENT

1 **What types of area do the problems below mostly affect? Write _U_ (urban), _R_ (rural), or _B_ (both urban and rural).**

overcrowding _____	_exhaust emissions_ _____
depopulation _____	_poor public transport_ _____
lack of green spaces _____	_uncontrolled migration_ _____
congestion _____	_unemployment_ _____
lack of facilities _____	_household waste_ _____

2 **Which problems in exercise 1 are sentences 1–10 about?**

1 People don't have access to doctors, hospitals, or schools.

2 The flats are very small and there are too many people using things like public transport.

3 Slums appear with poor sanitation facilities because the government doesn't control who can move to cities.

4 If you haven't got a car, you have to walk or cycle everywhere.

5 The air pollution is really high in some of the country's bigger cities.

6 We need to recycle more of the waste we produce at home.

7 The traffic jams are so bad it can take several hours to travel a few kilometres.

8 With fewer people living there, the government has stopped investing money in supporting these regions.

9 Many people leave rural areas because there isn't enough work, but some also fail to find good jobs in cities when they move there.

10 The city has so many big buildings everywhere. There are hardly any parks or open areas.

3 **Underline the words in exercise 2 that helped you to match the sentences with the problems in exercise 1.**

4 **Complete the causes and effects in 1–4 with the words or phrases below.**

climate change _flood_ _desertification_ _extinction of species_

1 Chopping down trees → loss of natural barriers →
_____

2 Food shortages → over-farming → loss of nutrients in the soil → _____

3 Burning of fossil fuels → increased pollution →
_____

4 Increasing population → increasing consumption → deforestation → loss of natural habitats → _____

5 **Complete sentences 1–4 with words or phrases from exercise 4.**

1 An _____ is a fairly recent problem. Since the industrial revolution it has risen from under 1 billion to over 7 billion.

2 _____ are a concern for nearly 1 billion people, while at the same time there are over 1 billion obese people in the world.

3 An increase in the standard of living is also linked to _____ of goods and services.

4 The _____ is a growing concern. Of the 44,838 identified worldwide, 905 have already disappeared and 16,928 are listed as endangered.

6 **Match words 1–8 with definitions a–h.**

1 decrease / reduce _____   5 modify _____

2 develop _____   6 limit _____

3 construct _____   7 introduce _____

4 improve _____   8 adapt _____

a to form something by putting different things together

b to become better than before; to make sth / sb better than before

c to make sth less or smaller in size, quantity, price, etc.

d to stop sth from increasing beyond a particular amount or level

e to make sth available for use, discussion, etc., for the first time

f to change sth in order to make it suitable for a new situation

g to change something slightly

h to gradually grow or become bigger, more advanced, stronger, etc.; to make sth do this

UNIT 5 CULTURE & ENTERTAINMENT

1 Put the words and phrases into the correct columns of the table. Some words can go in more than one column.

> police   fact   life events   crime   psychology
> space   extra-terrestrials   planets   creatures
> imaginary lands and species   relationships   betrayal
> monsters   murder   real events   frightening   love

Biography	
Detective story	
Fantasy	
Horror story	
Romance	
Sci-fi	

2 Use the words in exercise 1 to write a description of each type of book. Change the form of the words if necessary.

Example: *A biography is a factual story about the real events in a person's life.*

3 Cross out the places where you would <u>not</u> expect to find entertainment facilities 1–6.

1 VIP box   plane, nightclub, stadium
2 aisle   plane, theatre, nightclub
3 snack bar   theatre, cinema, hotel
4 screen   cinema, stadium, theatre
5 balcony   theatre, cinema, opera house
6 stage   theatre, opera house, stadium

4 Decide if the words in groups 1–3 introduce examples, reasons, or effects.

1 since, due to, because, as ....
2 for instance, such as, in particular, for example ....
3 consequently, outcome, resulting in, as a result ....

5 Add the words to each group in exercise 4.

> illustrates   therefore   hence   in the case of
> so   origin   including   root   owing to

6 Complete the sentences with words from exercises 4 and 5.

1 The .... of the review was major changes to the education system.
2 .... films, people can post reviews for others to read online.
3 The .... of film criticism was nearly 100 years ago in the USA.
4 .... the positive impact that artistic activities can have, many people would like to see them taught more widely in schools.
5 Playing music has many benefits, ... improving reading and maths skills.

7 Add the words to groups 1–3 below.

> upgrade   attain   raise   contribute   present   fulfil

1 accomplish, achieve, gain, ..., ...
2 develop, enhance, improve, ..., ...
3 create, give, provide, ..., ...

8 Which words from exercise 7 collocate with words 1–3?

1 opportunities
2 standards
3 goals

9 Use collocations from exercise 8 to write sentences about artistic activities.

Example: *Increased government spending has created opportunities for more people to take part.*

UNIT 6 CAREERS & SUCCESS

1 Choose words to describe people who typically follow careers 1–3. Some words can be used more than once.

> inspiring   intelligent   fair   determined   imaginative
> passionate   ambitious   courageous   forward-looking
> honest   supportive   dependable   extroverted
> sociable   competent

1 teacher
2 politician
3 sportsperson

2 Complete the sentences with the correct form of the words in brackets.

1 My father was my .... (inspire) for becoming a doctor.

2 A successful team .... (dependable) on each other to succeed.

3 It's my .... (ambition) to become a successful lawyer.

4 I am .... (passion) about studying literature, but not because it will lead to a career.

5 .... (competent) in a foreign language is expected for many different jobs.

6 A good manager is .... (support) of all their staff equally.

7 It's important for companies to treat employees .... (fair).

8 .... (determine) is essential for people who want to start their own business.

3 Choose the correct alternative to complete the sentences.

1 Many people work *full time / part time* because of family commitments such as taking children to school.

2 I get an annual *salary / bonus* on top of my basic pay.

3 I pay 8% of my salary into my *pension / pay rise* fund.

4 My company allows *overtime / flexitime* so I start at 7 a.m. and finish at 3 p.m.

5 My company has an extensive *promotion / training* programme. I've learnt a lot since starting here.

6 The attractive *location / holiday* allowance is one of the main benefits of working in the public sector.

7 My *colleague / boss* doesn't delegate enough work. He tries to do too much himself.

8 We get five *sick leave / public holidays* in this country.

9 *Commission / Praise* is more motivating over a longer period than money.

4 Replace the words in bold in sentences 1–5 with a phrase below with a similar meaning.

> drawback of   advantage of   consequence of
> reason for   way to   explanation for

1 Many people hope that the **result of** going to university is a better career.

2 One **good effect** of living in a city is the wider employment opportunities.

3 One **disadvantage of** being successful can be the stress that comes with it.

4 The **solution to** reduce unemployment is to make people relocate.

5 The **cause of** the company collapse was the risks taken by the directors.

6 The **justification for** their failure was the low level of staff skills.

5 Complete opinions 1–7 about success with the words below.

> looks   dress   intelligence   drive   curiosity
> family background   educational background

1 Appearance in an interview is very important. The way people .... can have a real impact on what other people think.

2 A lot of people have natural talent, but to reach the top you need the .... to get there.

3 To be successful in science you should have .... about the world around you.

4 Your .... can affect your success because in some professions such as law, for example, you need to go to a top university.

5 .... often has a major impact on educational success. If a child's parents didn't do well at school, often the child also does poorly.

6 Good .... help a lot in this profession. Most people working in this sector are attractive.

7 You don't necessarily have to be well qualified, but you do need to have a high level of ....

6 Write three sentences using the words in exercise 5. Say how you feel each factor does / doesn't influence success.

Example: *Good looks can help you to meet people more easily.*

UNIT 7 NATURE & BIOLOGY

1 Complete the words about weather.

1 ch_____geab_____   7 c_____l
2 st_____y   8 dr_____
3 p_____as_____t   9 w_____dy
4 ch_____y   10 o_____rcas
5 s_____y   11 w_____t
6 mi_____   12 hum_____

2 Write the words in exercise 1 along the line according to whether they describe good weather or bad weather.

good weather ◄————————————► bad weather

3 What types of weather are the words in *italics*? Write R (rain), S (sun), or S/I (snow/ice).

1 The skiers were warned about a possible *avalanche*.
2 The *flood* was so bad we had to go up to the top floor.
3 The airplane couldn't take off because of the *blizzard*.
4 It was *boiling* so we spent most of the time swimming.
5 You shouldn't drive tonight – it's going to be *freezing* and the roads will be dangerous.
6 The *hailstones* were so big they damaged lots of cars.
7 During the *heatwave* we cooled ourselves down with ice packs.
8 Only light *showers* are forecast for tomorrow.

4 Complete statements 1–8 with the information below.

> *Angel Falls   half the size   Canada*
> *the Netherlands   almost non-existent*
> *9.3 metres   Victoria Falls   11 kilometres*

1 The Marianas Trench is the deepest point in the Earth's seabed, located _____ below the surface.
2 Cherrapunji in India holds the world record for the most rainfall in a single month at _____ .
3 _____ has the world's longest coastline at over 200,000 kilometres.
4 At the top of _____ you can swim right to the edge in some of the highest rock pools in the world.
5 The Arctic ice cap is shrinking and is now _____ it was 30 years ago.
6 _____ is the highest waterfall in the world.
7 50% of _____ is just 1 metre above sea level.
8 Felix Baumgartner jumped from a balloon at 38,969 metres where the air pressure is _____ .

5 Match the words in groups 1–3 with possible solutions a–c.

1

flood	a dams and canals
food shortage	b relocation
volcano	c redistributing supplies

2

asteroid	a reservoirs
drought	b specially constructed buildings
earthquake	c missiles

3

disease	a renewable energy
erosion	b vaccinations
climate change	c sea barrier

6 Write sentences explaining the solutions to problems in exercise 5.

Example: *A vaccination for malaria could save hundreds of thousands of lives.*

impulse (心の)衝動、一時の感情   ※白物家電・掃除機、洗濯機、冷蔵庫、エアコン

UNIT 8 PRODUCERS & CONSUMERS

1 Complete sentences 1–6 with the words below.

*白物
家電*

> impulse buys   ~~branded goods~~   ~~services~~   ~~electronic goods~~
> white goods   ~~gifts~~   chewing gum   clothes   perfume
> chocolate   ~~laptop~~   ~~washing machines~~   shoes   ~~toys~~
> ~~financial advice~~   ~~dishwashers~~   ~~tablet~~

1 You always see _impulse buys_ placed near the checkout in a shop. They include things like _chocolate_ and _chewing gum_

2 _white goods_ such as _washing machines_ and _dish washers_ are some of the most expensive things you can buy for the home.

3 The _gifts_ I buy aren't very original. I usually get _toys_ for my children and _perfume_ for my wife.

4 I love _branded goods_, especially designer labels. I like having a style and image, so I always buy particular _clothes_ and _shoes_

5 I love to have up-to-date _electronic goods_. I get a new phone every year and a new _washing machines_ or _dishwashers_ every two years.

6 I have my own business so I use _services_ such as _financial advice_ to help me to run the company.

2 Choose the correct alternatives to complete the sentences.

1 To me, this watch is (priceless) / worthless. My grandfather left it to me after he died.

2 Most people think of my country as (wealthy) / good value, but there are actually a lot of poor people there.

3 It's my aim to be valuable / (rich.) I don't care how I make the money – I just want plenty of it!

4 This part of the city is (very poor) / a waste of money.

5 I don't agree with buying a new phone every year – it's really (wasteful) / pricey.

3 Write sentences to describe things you buy / don't buy using words from exercise 2.

Example: *I don't buy branded clothes because I think they're a waste of money.*

4 Match words from exercise 2 to groups 1–5 below.

1 fake jewels, some currencies _worthless_

2 antiques, jewellery, property

3 air conditioning in cold climates, clothes you never wear

4 designer clothes, sports cars, luxury holidays

5 sales, bargains, discounts

5 Put the linking words below into groups 1–5 with words of a similar meaning.

> such as   lastly   additionally   moreover   first   whereas

1 finally, _lastly_

2 secondly, furthermore, _additionally_ , _moreover_

3 firstly, to begin with, _first_

4 on the other hand, however, _whereas_

5 for example, for instance, as a case in point, _such as_

6 Complete sentences 1–5 with words you added to the groups in exercise 5.

1 Crime statistics have a number of uses, _____ governments being able to show that there has been a reduction in the levels of crime committed.

2 This essay will look at three main points. _____ it will look at consumer behaviour online.

3 Some people buy new products very quickly, _____ others wait for a product to become established.

4 Buying a new phone every year causes a lot of waste. _____, many now use certain metals that are limited in supply.

5 _____, the essay will conclude by offering a prediction about the future.

---

priceless 貴重な
worthless 役に立たない
wealthy 裕福な
good value 価値がある
valuable 高価な
aim to 心掛ける
plenty of 充分な
(n.) waste 浪費する
(adj) wasteful 浪費的、不経済

UNIT 9 MEDIA & TRAVEL

1 Replace the words and phrases in bold in sentences 1–8 with the phrasal verbs below. Use the past tense of the verbs.

> break out   break into sth   take place   run over sb
> go off   run off   come across sth   crash into sth

1 Police say the gun **was fired** by accident.
2 The thief **escaped** before the shop assistant could call the police.
3 The violence **started** around 8 p.m. last night.
4 The criminals **illegally entered** the offices during the night.
5 The royal wedding **happened** last April.
6 The driver **knocked over** a pedestrian.
7 Scientists **found** a potential cure for the disease from a plant in the Amazon.
8 The driver **hit** the side of the building.

2 Match the words below to groups of people 1–3.

> robbery   speeding   discovery   blackmail
> breakthrough   murder   invention   jam
> innovation   congestion   hacking   motorway

1 scientists
2 drivers
3 criminals

3 Complete sentences 1–8 with the words below.

> street market   harbour   monument   mall
> art gallery   fountain   cathedral   mosque
> main square   city wall   public gardens   statue

1 The _____ is full of ships, and lots of tourists visit the surrounding fish restaurants.
2 The _____ is dedicated to the memory of those who died in the Second World War.
3 The _____ has more shops, stores, and square metres of space than any other in the world.
4 The _____ give the city a lot of open, green space.

5 At the _____ you can buy local food, snacks, clothing, and souvenirs.
6 The _____ contains sculptures, paintings, and other priceless artefacts.
7 It was so hot that children were splashing each other with the water of the _____.
8 The _____ is over 500 years old and stretches for nearly 4 kilometres.

4 Underline the words in exercise 3 that helped you to choose the answers.

5 Write a short description of a place you know well using words from exercise 3.

6 Match words 1–8 with definitions a–h.

1 media profile ____
2 media event ____
3 news broadcast ____
4 social media ____
5 television network ____
6 mass media ____
7 new media ____
8 media coverage ____

a a company that has many channels and programmes
b things watched or read by large numbers of people, such as TV programmes, newspapers, and magazines
c the reputation sb or sth has in the media
d the internet rather than TV and newspapers
e sth such as an important interview and press conference
f the amount of time or space given to a story or event
g a TV programme that reports the events of the day
h websites and computer programmes that allow people to communicate

7 Cross out the words that do not fit in each of groups 1–4.

1 media   advert, newspaper, magazine, TV
2 social media   (hash)tag, network, broadcast, trending list
3 advert   brand, logo, slogan, programme
4 broadcast   programme, news, search engine ranking, documentary

UNIT 10 SCIENCE & PROGRESS

1 Complete sentences 1–10 with the words and phrases below.

> education   housing   safety   jobs
> work-life balance   health   communities
> environment   civic engagement   incomes

1   The _____ in some cities lacks basic facilities such as clean water and a sewage system.

2   _____ is good in my country. Most people have a good quality of life.

3   _____ have fallen since the recession started.

4   Improved levels of _____ have helped the global average for life expectancy to reach just over 70 years.

5   In my opinion, _____ isn't as important as most people think. It's all about personal connections.

6   Crime is a problem in this area because so many young people don't have _____ .

7   _____ have broken down because people move around so much.

8   Traffic levels have dramatically increased damage to the _____ .

9   _____ is fairly low in my country. Very few people vote in elections, for example.

10   _____ is a concern in some parts of the city at night.

2 Match the words and phrases below to the sentences in exercise 1 with a similar topic.

> employment   grades   public concern   violence   sanitation
> earnings   elderly   neighbourhood   pollution   leisure time

3 Write sentences about progress in your country. Use words and phrases from exercises 1 and 2.

Example: *There are high levels of pollution in most of our main cities.*

4 Complete the sentences with the correct form of the words in brackets.

1   The _____ (design) is one of the main selling points.

2   The _____ (discover) of antibiotics is one of the greatest medical breakthroughs.

3   Many _____ (experiment) were performed to test patient responses.

4   The smartphone is perhaps one of the world's greatest _____ (invent).

5   When do you _____ (predict) there will be a cure for cancer?

6   There doesn't seem to be much scientific _____ (prove).

7   Further _____ (research) is needed.

8   It was just one of many _____ (test) that were performed.

5 Complete the sentences with a word from exercise 4. You may need to change the form of the word.

1   It is _____ that nano-robots will be able to deliver drugs to specific parts of the body.

2   There are ways to change our DNA before we are born but some people are worried that parents will want _____ babies. In other words, they might choose things like their hair and eye colour.

3   _____ on animals for medical purposes is less controversial than for products such as make-up.

4   Researchers have _____ that a single form of cancer is actually made up of many different types of cancer.

5   Pharmaceutical companies have to _____ that their drugs are safe before they can be sold.

6   _____ on animals can help us to understand the effect of a disease on humans.

7   Surprisingly, a car mechanic has _____ a device that is likely to make childbirth easier.

8   _____ and development is expensive so companies will only do it if they think they can make a profit.

6 Choose one of the topics below to write a short paragraph about. Try to include at least three words from exercise 5 in your paragraph.

- Animal testing should be banned.

- Pharmaceutical companies should not be allowed to make a profit.

- People should only be allowed to control DNA for medical reasons.

STUDY SKILLS FILE

Vocabulary

1 Which item of research 1-4 is the most surprising? Why?

1 Teaching does not necessarily lead to learning. File & Adams (2010) found that less than half of the words that are taught by teachers are actually learnt by students.

2 Students have to read or hear a word 10–30 times or sometimes up to 50 times before they can connect the form, i.e. spelling or sound, with the meaning (Waring, 2009).

3 Wide reading of graded readers is a very useful way for students to learn common vocabulary (Nation, 2011).

4 Using 'word cards' can speed up students' progress. Self-testing on the words with longer intervals between each test is an effective way of learning (Pyc & Rawson, 2007).

2 Read student comments A–D about learning vocabulary. Which comment(s) describe how you feel? Which item(s) of research from exercise 1, if any, would you tell the students?

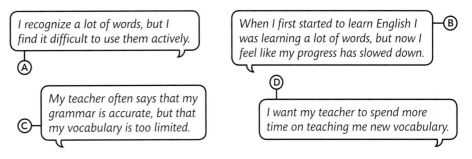

A *I recognize a lot of words, but I find it difficult to use them actively.*

B *When I first started to learn English I was learning a lot of words, but now I feel like my progress has slowed down.*

C *My teacher often says that my grammar is accurate, but that my vocabulary is too limited.*

D *I want my teacher to spend more time on teaching me new vocabulary.*

3 Look at the ideas for learning vocabulary. Which idea is best for each student in exercise 2?

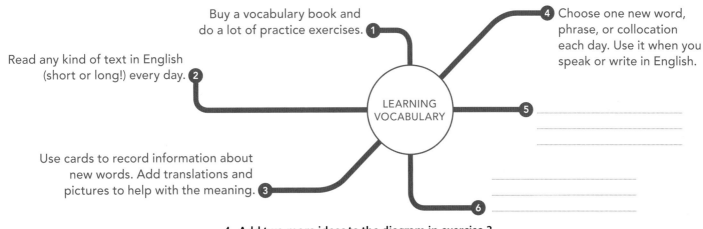

1 Buy a vocabulary book and do a lot of practice exercises.

2 Read any kind of text in English (short or long!) every day.

3 Use cards to record information about new words. Add translations and pictures to help with the meaning.

4 Choose one new word, phrase, or collocation each day. Use it when you speak or write in English.

LEARNING VOCABULARY

5 ....

6 ....

4 Add two more ideas to the diagram in exercise 3.

5 Which three ideas from exercise 3 would be most helpful for <u>you</u>? Which one idea can you do today?

Speaking

1 **Which item of research 1–4 is the most surprising? Why?**

1 The amount that students read has a significant impact on how fluently they speak (Stanovich & Cunningham, 1998).

2 Preparing a four-minute talk and then giving it in three minutes to one person and then in two minutes to a different person helps to improve students' fluency (Nation, 1989).

3 Communicating in real-time conversations on a computer can improve students' spoken fluency (Razagifard, 2012).

4 When students learn how to provide feedback to other students it has a positive effect on their grammatical accuracy (Sato & Lyster, 2012).

2 **Read student comments A–D about speaking in English. Which comment(s) describe how you feel? Which item(s) of research from exercise 1, if any, would you tell the students?**

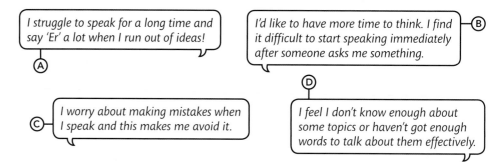

A *I struggle to speak for a long time and say 'Er' a lot when I run out of ideas!*

B *I'd like to have more time to think. I find it difficult to start speaking immediately after someone asks me something.*

C *I worry about making mistakes when I speak and this makes me avoid it.*

D *I feel I don't know enough about some topics or haven't got enough words to talk about them effectively.*

3 **Look at the ideas for improving speaking. Which idea is best for each student in exercise 2?**

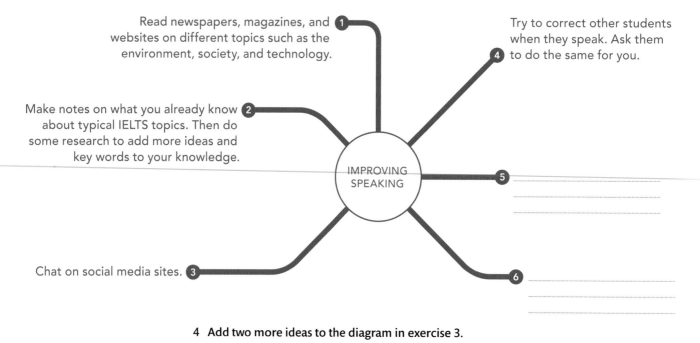

1 Read newspapers, magazines, and websites on different topics such as the environment, society, and technology.

2 Make notes on what you already know about typical IELTS topics. Then do some research to add more ideas and key words to your knowledge.

3 Chat on social media sites.

4 Try to correct other students when they speak. Ask them to do the same for you.

IMPROVING SPEAKING

5

6

4 **Add two more ideas to the diagram in exercise 3.**

5 **Which three ideas from exercise 3 would be most helpful for <u>you</u>? Which one idea can you do today?**

Listening

1 **Which item of research 1–4 is the most surprising? Why?**

1 Individual sounds are unreliable, so students need to rely on words or groups of words (Field, 2008).

2 It is better for students to practise listening to short texts regularly (30 seconds–2 minutes) than longer texts (Thompson & Rubin, 1996).

3 Learning how to pronounce English naturally improves students' listening (Ghorbani, 2011).

4 When students practise writing the exact words they hear, it can improve their listening ability and confidence (Seigel & Seigel, 2013).

2 **Read student comments A–D about listening in English. Which comments describe how you feel? Which item(s) of research from exercise 1, if any, would you tell the students?**

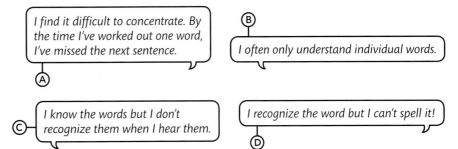

A *I find it difficult to concentrate. By the time I've worked out one word, I've missed the next sentence.*

B *I often only understand individual words.*

C *I know the words but I don't recognize them when I hear them.*

D *I recognize the word but I can't spell it!*

3 **Look at the ideas for improving listening. Which idea is best for each student in exercise 2?**

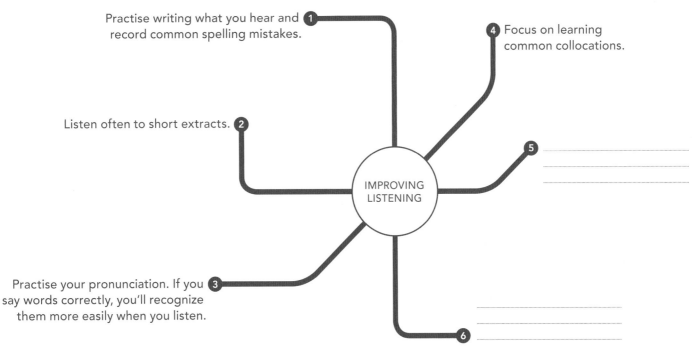

1 Practise writing what you hear and record common spelling mistakes.

4 Focus on learning common collocations.

2 Listen often to short extracts.

3 Practise your pronunciation. If you say words correctly, you'll recognize them more easily when you listen.

IMPROVING LISTENING

5

6

4 **Add two more ideas to the diagram in exercise 3.**

5 **Which three ideas from exercise 3 would be most helpful for you? Which one idea can you do today?**

Writing

1 Which item of research 1–4 is the most surprising? Why?

❶ Practising connecting sentences improves 60% of students' writing (Hillocks, 1986).

❷ Reading helps to build fluency in writing and understanding of connections between words (Horst, Cobb & Meara, 1998).

❸ Learning how to write in steps or stages significantly improves writing. Skilled writers spend more time organizing and planning what they are going to write (Hillocks, 1986).

❹ Writing immediately after vocabulary learning improves students' writing (Lee, 2003).

2 Read student comments A–D about writing in English. Which comments describe how you feel? Which item(s) of research from exercise 1, if any, would you tell the students?

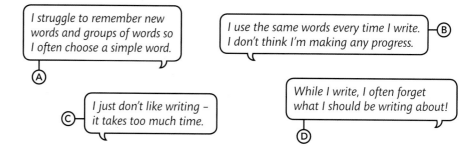

I struggle to remember new words and groups of words so I often choose a simple word. Ⓐ

I use the same words every time I write. I don't think I'm making any progress. Ⓑ

Ⓒ *I just don't like writing – it takes too much time.*

While I write, I often forget what I should be writing about! Ⓓ

3 Look at the ideas for improving writing. Which idea is best for each student in exercise 2?

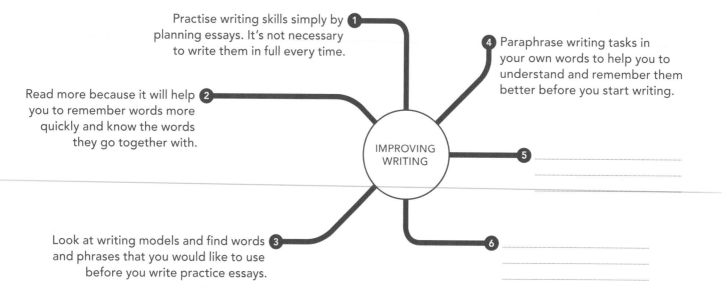

❶ Practise writing skills simply by planning essays. It's not necessary to write them in full every time.

❷ Read more because it will help you to remember words more quickly and know the words they go together with.

❸ Look at writing models and find words and phrases that you would like to use before you write practice essays.

❹ Paraphrase writing tasks in your own words to help you to understand and remember them better before you start writing.

IMPROVING WRITING

❺ ....

❻ ....

4 Add two more ideas to the diagram in exercise 3.

5 Which three ideas from exercise 3 would be most helpful for <u>you</u>? Which one idea can you do today?

Reading

1 **Which item of research 1–4 is the most surprising? Why?**

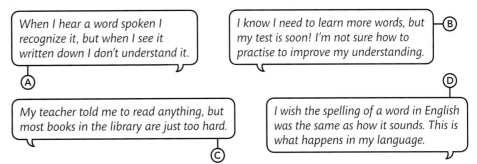

1 Understanding the sounds of a language can help students improve their reading comprehension (Walter, 2008).

2 Reading materials that are too difficult will make students avoid reading more and reduce the rate by which they improve their reading (Stanovich & Cunningham, 1998).

3 Reading aloud helps students to recognize the connections between written and spoken forms and can improve reading speeds (Stanovich, 1991).

4 Reading quickly can improve students' comprehension (Breznitz, 1997).

2 **Read student comments A–D about reading in English. Which comment(s) describe how you feel? Which item(s) of research from exercise 1, if any, would you tell the students?**

(A) *When I hear a word spoken I recognize it, but when I see it written down I don't understand it.*

(B) *I know I need to learn more words, but my test is soon! I'm not sure how to practise to improve my understanding.*

(C) *My teacher told me to read anything, but most books in the library are just too hard.*

(D) *I wish the spelling of a word in English was the same as how it sounds. This is what happens in my language.*

3 **Look at the ideas for improving reading. Which idea is best for each student in exercise 2?**

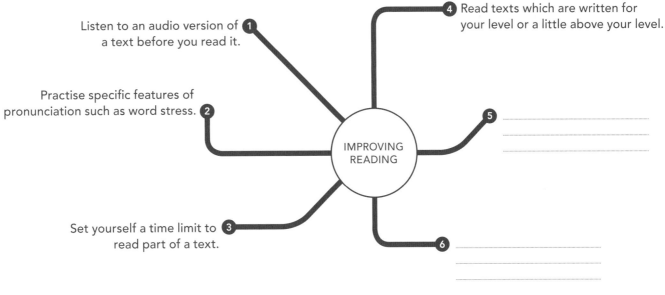

1 Listen to an audio version of a text before you read it.

2 Practise specific features of pronunciation such as word stress.

3 Set yourself a time limit to read part of a text.

4 Read texts which are written for your level or a little above your level.

5 ....

6 ....

IMPROVING READING

4 **Add two more ideas to the diagram in exercise 3.**

5 **Which three ideas from exercise 3 would be most helpful for <u>you</u>? Which one idea can you do today?**

WRITING FILE

Writing tasks: Summary of types

Task 1 types	Key language	Important information	See pages
Description of trends	Trend verbs	Describe the key trend before the detail.	137
Comparison	Comparative structures	Describe key similarities and differences between categories.	138
Description of a process	Present tenses and the passive	Include an overview statement on the process as a whole.	139
Description of a diagram / illustration	Prepositions of place and movement	Include a general statement which compares the features.	140

Task 2 types	Common instructions / questions	Important information	See pages
Personal opinion essay	Give your opinion and support it. Do you agree or disagree? To what extent do you agree or disagree?	Give your own opinion.	141 & 143
Discussion essay	Discuss both views. What are the advantages and disadvantages ...?	Discuss both sides of the argument.	142
Explanation essay	What problems are associated with ...? What can governments do to ...?	Give and explain your ideas. Don't give your own opinion.	144

Note: In Task 2, you may be asked to do a combination of two types of essay. In this case, make sure you do both parts of the task.

Task 1: Description of trends

1 Look at the Exam practice task on page 13.

2 Now read the model answer below. Look carefully at the underlined features 1–10.

> The bar chart shows how long, on average, schoolchildren remained at school in five regions of the world from 1970 to 2009[1]. In general[2], we can see that there was an increase in the length of time that children stayed at school in all regions. Looking in more detail[3], the bar chart illustrates that this increase was particularly large in both the Arab states and Latin American countries[4]. In the former, the number of years spent in education rose by 5 years, from under 6 years to around 11 years, while in the latter the increase was slightly greater still, from 8 to 14 years[5]. This rise was especially great in the 1970s but growth remained steady throughout the period shown. By contrast[6], the increase in the number of years spent at school in the wealthier[7] nations was of around 3 years over the 40-year period. Although the rate of increase was relatively modest[8] here, the length of time children remained at school still remained higher than in other parts of the world[9], at around 16 years.
>
> In conclusion[10], it could be said that the traditionally richer nations are being 'caught up' by the rest of the world in terms of duration of schooling.

Features of the model answer

1 Definition of bar chart.
2 Overview statement gives general picture of data.
3 Important information is selected and described first.
4 Regions are grouped according to common features.
5 Statement is supported with specific data.
6 Relationship between ideas is clearly marked by linking phrase.
7 New label shows relationship between regions in this category.
8 Avoids repetition with synonym.
9 Complex grammar structure is attempted.
10 Concluding comment adds additional interpretation of data.

3 Look at the task, the chart, and the sample answer below. Which of features 1–10 in exercise 2 are missing?

The chart below shows information about the proportion of female teachers in primary education in various regions of the world between 1990 and 2009.

Summarize the information by selecting and reporting the main features, and make comparisons where relevant.

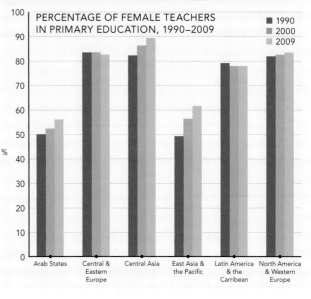

> The bar chart shows the percentage of female teachers in primary education from 1990 to 2009 in various regions. First, we can see that in the Arab states the proportion of female teachers rose a little. A similar pattern can be seen in three of the other regions: Central Asia, East Asia and the Pacific, and North America and Western Europe. The increase was particularly notable in East Asia and the Pacific. However, there was a sizeable drop in Central and Eastern Europe, and in Latin America and the Caribbean.
>
> In conclusion, it seems that primary education is becoming an increasingly common career for female workers.

Task 1: Comparison

1 Look at the Exam practice task on page 23.

2 Now read the model answer below. Look carefully at features 1–10.

> The bar chart shows how common sleep problems were between 2006 and 2007 in eight different countries. In general, we can see that women reported sleep problems more than men did in all countries, though the difference between genders ranges from a single percentage point in some countries to 20% in others.[1]
>
> In terms of the overall levels of sleeplessness, it is difficult to establish patterns between countries. The three countries with the most reported sleep problems are South Africa, Vietnam, and Bangladesh, where one in three adults had these concerns[2]. In contrast, far fewer[3] people in other African and Asian countries[4] reported problems: around one in twenty adults in Indonesia, India, and only a little more in other African nations.[5]
>
> In Bangladesh[6], the difference between the number of men and women[7] who couldn't sleep well is also great. To be specific, just under half of women reported suffering from sleep problems while just under a quarter of men stated that they had similar difficulties. However[8], the difference between genders is greatest in Kenya where, despite there being fewer sleep problems overall, women reported twice the number of problems than men did.[9] [10]

Features of the model answer

1 General statement presents key differences early in description.

2 Avoids repeating language by using synonym references.

3 Comparative form is used to maintain connection between ideas.

4 Groups data and creates categories.

5 All observations are supported by data.

6 Paragraphs are connected by topic so description flows nicely.

7 Description is clearly organized, reporting first national differences and then gender difference.

8 Relationship between ideas is clearly marked by linking phrase.

9 Conclusion omitted in this answer to avoid repetition.

10 Avoids giving explanations for data trends.

3 Look at the task, the chart, and the sample answer below. Which of features 1–10 in exercise 2 are missing?

> The chart below shows information about the use of complementary and alternative medicines (CAM) by age in one Western country in 2007.
>
> Summarize the information by selecting and reporting the main features, and make comparisons where relevant.

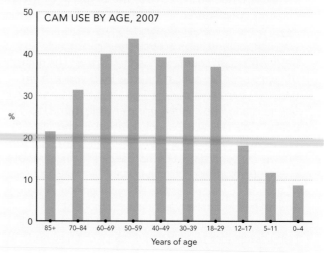

> The data reveals how much of the population used complementary and alternative medicines (CAM) in one Western country in 2007. We can see a rise in usage of CAM towards mid-life, when around 40% of the population used CAM, before the figures declined again towards old age.
>
> Only 20% of people over 85 years of age used CAM. This surprises me because I thought older people were more traditional. People in their fifties used CAM the most, with around 43% of people in that age group using CAM. The 0–4 year group used CAM the least (only 10% of them did), though the younger categories contain a narrower range of ages and, proportionally, young people's use of CAM was similar to that of the elderly. The fact there were fewer young people using CAM may be because parents are scared to give treatments that are not tested scientifically to their children.
>
> In conclusion, we can see that middle-aged people used CAM the most.

Task 1: Description of a process

1 Look at the Exam practice task on page 103.

2 Read the model answer below. Look carefully at features 1–8.

> <u>The diagram shows one process by which 3D (three-dimensional) TV images are created</u>[1]. <u>In general, we can see that the process is very complex and involves tricking the brain into seeing depth.</u>[2]
>
> [3]At the beginning of the process, two images <u>are recorded</u>[4] by the camera. One is for the right eye and the other for the left. The image is <u>then</u>[5] cut into vertical strips, which are combined and shown on TV. <u>After that</u>[5], the combined image passes through a device called a lenticular lens. This is made up of <u>a set of small, curved lenses that send the strips in two directions</u>[6]. As the images leave the lens, the right image strips are sent to the right eye <u>while</u>[7] the left image strips are sent to the left eye. <u>Next</u>[5], the two images are combined in the human brain as one single image, creating an illusion of a three-dimensional object.[8]

Features of the model answer

1 Opening statement defines type of data that is presented.

2 Overview statement comments on feature of process as a whole.

3 New paragraph separates general and detailed information.

4 Passive is used to maintain focus on object of description.

5 Order of actions clearly marked by variety of sequencing phrases.

6 Technical language from diagram is explained in simpler terms.

7 Two actions that occur together are indicated with a linking phrase.

8 Conclusion unnecessary in Task 1 descriptions.

3 Look at the task, the diagram, and the sample answer below. Which of features 1–8 in exercise 1 are missing?

The chart below illustrates the scientific method.

Summarize the information by selecting and reporting the main features, and make comparisons where relevant.

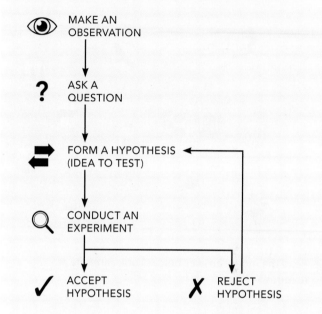

> In general, we can see that despite the complexity of science, the method behind it is very simple, consisting of just five steps. First of all, scientists make observations about the world around them. Then they ask questions about things that they are unable to explain or which they haven't understood clearly.
>
> Then they create a hypothesis, which is a type of guess that they need to prove. To see if their ideas are correct, scientists must then carefully design and carry out experimental work, usually in a special laboratory. If the experiments eventually prove that the hypothesis is correct, then scientists accept the idea and it becomes a scientific fact. If the experiment suggests the hypothesis is not correct, then scientists will have to rethink their hypothesis and conduct further experiments.

Task 1: Description of a diagram

1 Look at the task and the diagram below.

The diagram shows a model of land use and conservation strategies in a coastal area.

Summarize the information by selecting and reporting the main features and make comparisons where relevant.

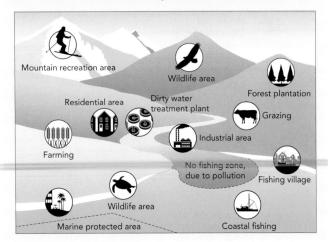

2 Read the model answer below. Look carefully at features 1–10.

> This diagram represents how land could be used in a mountainous coastal region. In the model, planners have carefully <u>arranged</u>[1] developments to create a balance between human activities and conservation.
>
> We can see a range of human activities represented, mostly <u>located close to the river and sea</u>[2]. These include <u>developed areas dedicated to traditional industrial activity</u>[3], such as a <u>fishing community</u>[4], a <u>relatively small</u>[5] industrial zone, and areas for leisure and tourism, both on the coast and in the mountains. <u>There is</u>[6] also a small residential area, <u>which has its own treatment plant for dirty water nearby.</u>[7]
>
> <u>Between</u>[8] these developed areas are areas of nature – either farmland or zones designed for wildlife to be protected. The aquatic areas are also <u>divided</u>[9], with parts dedicated to fishing and marine conservation. <u>In general, we can see that the conservation areas and farmland cover a greater area than the developed environment, which is far smaller in area than one might expect.</u>[10]

Features of the model answer

1 If diagram doesn't refer to a time, present perfect tense can be used for completed actions.

2 No data or sequence to describe but writer may give details of location.

3 Features of diagram are still grouped where possible.

4 Labels are paraphrased where possible.

5 Size of comparable features is compared.

6 Used to refer to existence of features in diagram.

7 Relative clauses add information about features in diagram.

8 Prepositions are used frequently to indicate location.

9 Passive is used frequently to avoid referring to unknown agents.

10 General statement focuses on comparisons between features, even if less clear than in a data graphic.

3 Look at the task, the diagram, and the sample answer below. Which of features 1–10 in exercise 2 are missing?

The diagram shows details of a street improvement project in a city.

Summarize the information by selecting and reporting the main features and making comparisons where relevant.

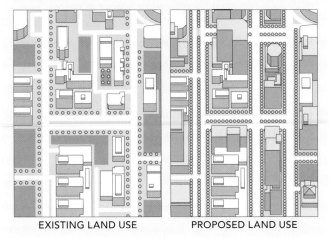

EXISTING LAND USE   PROPOSED LAND USE

> The diagrams show existing land use in an urban area and the proposal for changing it. In the image for existing land use, we can see two parallel streets. One large street connects these streets. The buildings on the map are fairly low. We also have many green spaces and trees along the road.
>
> In the proposed street plan, we can see that the number of parallel streets increases to three and an additional connecting street now exists. The number of buildings planned has increased dramatically and the new ones are a lot higher. Consequently, under the proposal, far fewer green spaces exist. However, a far larger number of trees replace these spaces to some extent. The trees have been planted along the centre of the main roads, too.

Task 2: Personal opinion essay (1)

1 Look at the Exam practice task question 1 on page 33.

2 Read the model answer below. Look carefully at features 1–12.

> In many countries, the last few decades have seen a rise both in wealth and the number of single people[1]. Both these trends have contributed to a rise in the numbers of individuals who are choosing to live alone. This essay will argue that this is a negative development and that the government needs to act to place limits on it.[2]
>
> [3]Of course, there are many reasons why governments have not acted to stop this trend. Many[4] would argue that we should be free to choose our own living arrangements and that government interference in such personal matters would be unwelcome. Clearly, governments would run the risk of making themselves unpopular if they were to restrict our choices.
>
> However[5], no modern government can be blind to the environmental damage that living alone is causing.[6] By living independently, we use heating and lighting that we would otherwise share with others[7]. This makes it much more difficult for governments to meet their CO_2 emissions targets.[8]
>
> Furthermore[9], governments must act to avoid a crisis in housing supply. The global population continues to grow quickly and we cannot continue to build new houses to meet the demand because we need to protect green spaces. It is therefore necessary that we find alternative solutions and encouraging people to live in larger households[10] would certainly help.
>
> To conclude, our current living habits need to be changed and we must take sensible steps to make better use of housing resources[11]. It may not be appropriate for governments to ban independent living, but taxation changes and publicity campaigns to promote living with others would be welcome.[12]

Features of the model answer

1 Background statement introduces essay topic and links it to real world events.

2 Task requires writer's opinion so this is made clear in introduction.

3 *To what extent* in essay question invites consideration of both viewpoints. This paragraph considers the opposing argument.

4 Confirms this is not writer's opinion.

5 Change in direction of argument clearly indicated by linking word.

6 First reason for writer's view is given clearly in topic sentence.

7 Main idea in topic sentence is explained in detail.

8 Paragraph concludes with consideration of wider implications.

9 Linking word shows writer continues to build argument.

10 Avoids repetition with synonym phrase.

11 Conclusion begins with clear summary of argument.

12 Concluding comment offers suggestion for future action.

3 Read the essay question and sample essay below. Which of features 1–12 in exercise 2 are missing?

> It is the responsibility of everyone in society to help parents make sure that children are raised well. To what extent do you agree or disagree?

> When the misbehaviour of young people appears in the news, we often hear criticism of parents. But should we not all take responsibility for the lives of our young people? This essay will discuss whether society as a whole needs to take more responsibility for raising our young.
>
> Of course, the main responsibility for raising children should remain with the parents. They usually understand their children's needs the best and are most likely to have their best interests at heart, so it is therefore right that the majority of decisions about their education or punishment should remain with them.
>
> Other members of society can offer important advice and guidance to children. Parents cannot see how children behave with school friends and it is important that teachers feel able to offer guidance and punishment in school as well. Similarly, when children play in parks or in the streets, parents are often not there to teach them how to respect neighbours. Older people or local residents should be free to criticize poor behaviour.
>
> Not all parents have the ability to look after their children well. Being a parent can be a stressful experience and often families break down, leaving the children in an unhealthy home environment where they might not feel protected. In such cases, it is clearly right that teachers, neighbours, or family members intervene to protect or offer additional support.
>
> Unless we create a strong network of support for all children, we may not be able to ensure that all receive a minimum standard of care, or that there are adequate levels of guidance for the young.

Task 2: Discussion essay

1 **Look at the Exam practice task on page 43.**

2 **Read the model answer below. Look carefully at features 1–11.**

> Ever since the arrival of cheap air travel, the numbers of visitors to countries has increased dramatically and many argue that high levels of tourism are damaging the environment[1]. This essay will discuss whether we should allow tourism to grow without limitation.[2]
>
> The kind of damage that tourism brings is well-known[3]. Environmentalists[4] often point to the level of CO_2 emissions from airplanes, adding that they also create a great deal of noise, too. Though tourists are not the only people who travel by plane, they represent a large proportion of air travellers. In addition, the environmental problems of tourism may continue when tourists arrive. Large hotels and resorts are sometimes[5] built in the middle of areas of great natural beauty, destroying natural habitats and landscape. Furthermore, leisure activities, like hiking or biking, can erode the landscape and visitors frequently leave litter behind them.
>
> However[6], the tourism industry often points out that not all tourism has a negative effect on the environment. Most tourists are keen to conserve nature[7] and some authorities have been able to construct accommodation and facilities that respect local populations and ecosystems. Furthermore[8], the income from tourism can be spent on measures to protect the environment[9], such as hiring rangers or monitoring pollution.[10] As regards air travel, there is also hope that in the future airplanes may use greener technology and be far less damaging to the environment.
>
> In conclusion, it is perhaps not so much the quantity of tourism that should be reduced. Rather it is the way that tourism is managed that needs our careful attention. Governments must allow both tourism and nature to coexist and thrive.[11]

Features of the model answer

1 Background statement introduces essay topic and links it to real world events.

2 Views of writer not required so states an intention to discuss others' views.

3 Topic sentence indicates negative effects will be discussed first.

4 Neutral word confirms writer is reporting view without bias.

5 Cautious language confirms that writer is neutral.

6 Linking word emphasizes that contrasting view is presented.

7 Avoids repetition with synonym.

8 Linking words within each paragraph show writer continues to build argument.

9 Varied range of points is used to support each side of argument.

10 Point is supported with quick examples.

11 Conclusion states thoughtful position between two views.

3 **Read the task and sample essay below. Which of features 1–11 in exercise 2 are missing?**

> Environmental problems in cities can be resolved most effectively through improvements in public transport. Discuss the arguments for and against this view.

> This essay will discuss whether improving public transport is the answer to urban environmental problems, considering both sides of the issue.
>
> On the one hand, I think it is important to improve public transport. The addition of tramways and extended bus networks will encourage people to leave cars at home, which will have a range of positive effects. Air quality will be improved, as levels of other exhaust emissions are reduced. Congestion will be reduced, creating more peaceful and safer streets for all to enjoy.
>
> On the other hand, I think we must also consider the alternatives to public transport. Buses are always noisy and dangerous, especially for cyclists, and so they are a terrible solution. By comparison, improving cycle networks and expanding green spaces and areas where people can walk would definitely have a more positive effect on our health and well-being. It would also create quiet areas for relaxation, and habitats for creatures like birds and butterflies.
>
> To conclude, there are valid arguments on both sides of the debate, but personally I think governments would be better off investing in projects that contribute to public health, and not in public transport infrastructure.

Task 2: Personal opinion essay (2)

1 Look at the Exam practice task on page 53.

2 Read the model answer below. Look carefully at features 1–10.

> The effects of technology on our ability to communicate are well known, but we rarely consider how the performing arts have benefited in our high-tech age. <u>I believe passionately that we should celebrate the contribution of technology to the performing arts and will outline reasons below.</u>[1]
>
> First, we <u>must</u>[2] consider how online media have brought the performing arts to a far larger audience than, for example, Mozart or Shakespeare could have dreamed possible. <u>Of course, there are issues with how artists should be paid when content is viewed online,</u>[3] but thanks to technology their work is now enjoyed by millions, even billions, of people across the globe, and this must be the priority for any self-respecting artist.
>
> Secondly, technology has made it possible for the <u>great</u>[4] performances of the past to be preserved and adapted for future generations. For example, we can still hear <u>Elvis Presley</u> or listen to <u>Jacqueline du Pré</u>[5] in high-quality, digital sound. True, we can still enjoy live performance – recorded music simply ensures that great music remains available for all.
>
> <u>Finally</u>[6], we must consider the wonderful sounds that digital technology has created. <u>Where would we be without the emotional power of the electric guitar or the atmospheric tones of the keyboard?</u>[7] If people want to learn the violin or flute, they still can, but we should celebrate the additional range of expression that these <u>electronic instruments</u>[8] allow us to have.
>
> <u>In conclusion, technology has enriched the performing arts and enabled them to reach an audience of millions</u>[9]. <u>We should welcome it without reservation.</u>[10]

Features of the model answer

1 Writer has decided to take strong stance, which task allows.

2 Language is strengthened with imperatives and modals of strong obligation.

3 Considering an opposing view makes writer seem more persuasive and authoritative.

4 Emotional language and adjectives persuade reader.

5 Examples from writer's experience.

6 All paragraphs support stance of writer, in line with strong stance taken.

7 Rhetorical question as a persuasive technique.

8 Substitute words are used throughout paragraph.

9 Main ideas are summarized neatly in one sentence.

10 Views of author are stated again in conclusion.

3 Read the sample essay below. Which of features 1–10 in exercise 1 are missing?

> The arts – like music, painting, literature, and film – have the power to bring people from different nations and cultures together. To what extent do you agree or disagree?

> In today's globalized world, there are very few forms of art that are known only in one country or region. The music of the Andes can be sold in the street markets of Calcutta and the works of authors can be translated into English and distributed online to millions. Exhibitions frequently tour the globe, too.
>
> First, art forms can often overcome language boundaries. Admittedly, the English language is slowly uniting the globe, but it is spoken in accents and varieties that are often associated with particular places. Music and painting, on the other hand, do not seem so connected to place and we often enjoy a tune or painting without much knowledge of who wrote it or where it came from.
>
> Perhaps most importantly, forms of art may teach us about the lives of others. When we enjoy a book or film by a foreign artist, we can learn what it means to have a different religion, to be of a different race, or to live under a different political system, and this helps us to respect and appreciate different views and perspectives on life.
>
> However, art forms can be misunderstood or viewed very differently by people in different cultures. For example, a play that features political material or naked actors may be considered interesting in one society, but confusing or even insulting in another. Consequently, some forms of art can have the effect of emphasizing differences between countries and cultures.
>
> In conclusion, I believe art forms can unite people from around the world and governments should invest in developing artistic endeavour as much as possible in the interests of peace and global unity.

Task 2: Explanation essay

1 Look at the Exam practice task question 2 on page 63.

2 Read the model answer below. Look carefully at features 1–11.

> The question of motivation is a never-ending issue for employers, and the health of economies all over the world depends on it[1]. Given this, what can be done to motivate employees?[2]
>
> One traditional method is to offer rewards[3]. Bosses have long believed that the promise of a bonus or a company car or a bigger office will drive people to dedicate themselves to their company. However, there is nothing to stop other companies offering similar rewards, and an employee may not be motivated by improved pay if there is the sense that it is an expected or normal condition of employment.[4]
>
> An alternative is to punish workers who do not perform well[5]. Employers can threaten to take away certain expected benefits, such as a staff party, if certain conditions are not met[6]. Alternatively, they may even threaten to demote a member of staff. However, this approach may have the effect of making staff members disloyal to companies or encourage them to do only the minimum needed to protect their benefits.
>
> A third way is perhaps to make sure that staff members are happy in their jobs[7]. This[8] can be done by ensuring staff can contribute to decision-making or that they have some control over the projects they undertake. It may also be achieved by allowing them to have flexible working hours or by trying to stop bullying. This might encourage many workers to fully dedicate themselves to their work.[9]
>
> In conclusion, there are a variety of tools that managers can use to motivate staff members, the best of which is perhaps to create a happy workforce[10]. However, it should be remembered that all people are different and will respond differently to various methods of motivation, and bosses should remain open to all techniques.[11]

Features of the model answer

1 Background statement establishes topic and connects essay to the real world.

2 Thesis statement may be replaced by question in this type of essay.

3 Ideas that are weaker, more obvious, or more accepted are mentioned first.

4 Early ideas are criticized to give sense of progression towards better ideas.

5 Each paragraph contains new idea that supports the thesis statement.

6 Idea in topic sentence is explained fully.

7 Third idea adds sense of progression and range in response.

8 Used to refer back to idea in topic sentence.

9 Language remains neutral and objective throughout.

10 Summary and evaluation of ideas are offered in conclusion.

11 Final comment provides additional level of analysis.

3 Read the sample essay below. Which of features 1–11 in exercise 2 are missing?

> What effects does having a large supply of graduate students have on a country?

> University enrolments have risen dramatically in many countries over the last half-century and ever higher numbers are entering adulthood with a university degree. This essay will outline the effects that this has on the economic and social life of a country.
>
> Perhaps the main impact is on a nation's economy and this effect may be two-fold. There will, of course, be a greater supply of highly trained talent available to businesses and so more innovation within the workplace. On the negative side, competition for graduate jobs will increase and lead to some unemployment unless the number of jobs available grows at the same pace. It may also result in a lack of supply for sectors of the economy that do not require graduates, and therefore an increased need for migrant labour.
>
> Secondly, a large number of graduates may have a significant and broadly positive impact on society. Higher levels of education should result in a larger number of people who participate in politics. Also, graduates are likely to marry and settle down later in life, resulting in a lower number of births overall. University also puts young people in contact with people from other backgrounds and the result may be greater familiarity and openness towards other cultures.
>
> In conclusion, governments should continue to make university education an attractive option for students, provided there are an adequate number of graduate jobs available.

EXAM TIPS

EXAM TIPS: SPEAKING

Part 1 questions page 9

Speaking Part 1 lasts 4 to 5 minutes and the examiner asks you questions about a range of personal topics, such as your family, hobbies, work or education, and holidays. Listen carefully for the question word – *where, when, who, how, how often* – and try to respond in a conversational way. It's important that you understand the question, and give a full response to show that you can use a variety of language. Try to add some extra information that gives the examiner something more than a basic response. Each response should be about 15 seconds.

Part 2 preparation time page 19

In Speaking Part 2, it's difficult to remember everything you want to say but the 1 minute of preparation time can help. Writing notes on the topic during this time is useful or, if you prefer, close your eyes and try to imagine the things you're going to describe. You could also set yourself different objectives for each stage of the extended speaking. Your first objective could be to speak for 25 seconds about the first prompt on the card. If you can do this, you should be able to speak for more than 1 minute in total. Then, for the next stages, focus on demonstrating your grammar, vocabulary, and pronunciation in turn.

Sounding enthusiastic page 29

Sounding enthusiastic can help you to get a better mark for pronunciation because your intonation and word stress will be more varied. However, it's not always easy to do this, especially when the examiner is looking down and taking notes. Try to imagine you're talking with a friend instead!

Talking about problems page 39

In Speaking Part 2, you may have to talk about a problem you have experienced, and what the causes and effects of this problem are. Also, you'll probably be asked to say what you have done to resolve it. For example, when talking about the causes and effects of problems in the environment (such as too much household waste), you might be asked to say what you personally do or could do to help the situation (such as recycle more efficiently).

Using adverbs page 48

Using adverbs correctly can really improve your grammar and vocabulary. In Speaking Part 1, you can add adverbs like *sometimes* and *usually* to say how often you personally do something. In Speaking Part 3 – where the ideas discussed are more complicated – you can use adverbs like *maybe* or *perhaps* to show you're not certain about something. In all parts of the Speaking test, you can put adverbs like *actually* or *generally* at the beginning of sentences to make your ideas seem clearer and more natural.

Varying language page 59

Varying your language helps you to get a higher mark for vocabulary and grammar. In Speaking Parts 1 and 3, the different questions you're asked usually give you the chance to demonstrate different language. However, during the 2 minutes of Part 2 it's less easy to keep your language varied because there aren't as many questions. Try to show variety by using different parts of speech or grammar structures, like a passive or conditional sentence.

'The four Ss' page 68

In Speaking Part 2, you'll be asked to describe something, for example a place, for 2 minutes. When you're feeling nervous or under pressure, it can be difficult to think of details to talk about. Use the preparation time to try to remember things that could extend your talk. One way you could do this is to use 'The four Ss': sights, sounds, smells, and sensations. These four categories should help you to think of some interesting details.

Part 3 questions page 79

In Speaking Part 3, you can be asked a wide range of question types related to the topic in Part 2. For example, you may be asked to predict, evaluate, speculate, or compare. Other questions may require you to talk about change, give opinions, explain, or hypothesize. The different questions will give you the opportunity to show you can use different grammar structures, vocabulary, and phrases. This is why you need to practise listening for certain types of question and prepare phrases that you could use for each type.

Part 2 description page 89

In Speaking Part 2, you may be asked to describe a series of events or, in other words, to 'narrate'. For example, you may be asked to describe something that happened to you or something that you saw. This provides a good opportunity to use a range of regular and irregular past tenses. A good way to give background to your narrative is by using the past continuous tense, as in *I was walking down the street near my home when* … You can then continue with the past simple tense to describe what happened.

Clarifying part 3 questions page 99

In Speaking Part 3, the questions are sometimes complicated so it's important you listen carefully and answer the question you're actually asked. Unlike in Part 1, you can ask the examiner for clarification if you don't understand. Try to remember some phrases to help you, and begin your question with *Sorry* or *Sorry, but* to sound more natural.

EXAM TIPS: LISTENING

Section 1 numbers and names page 10

In Listening Section 1, candidates often make mistakes writing down details such as numbers and names. With numbers, think about what would be realistic in each gap because this will help you to understand the number correctly. It's also a good idea to practise listening to longer numbers, like telephone numbers, which are often said quickly. With names, candidates often misspell them because they confuse how each letter is said – particularly the vowels: *a, e, i, o, u*. The main thing is to read the instructions and look at the information carefully to find out if names or numbers are required ... or both!

Section 2 tables page 20

In Listening Section 2, you may have to complete a table with information – numbers or individual words. Candidates often hear the information that's needed but then write it down incorrectly by failing to add articles (*a* or *the*) or the right endings. This will lose you marks in the exam. Make sure you look carefully at the forms of other words in the same column of the table, as these can help you to decide the type of word or number you need.

Section 3 dialogues page 30

In Listening Section 3, you hear two or three speakers. The conversation takes place in an academic environment – for example, a university classroom or lecture hall. But it can also take place anywhere on 'campus' – that means the university grounds – such as in a sports centre or student café. The speakers often express different opinions and you may be tested on how well you understand any disagreements.

Key words page 40

When you're preparing to listen, it helps to underline 'key words' in the questions and sentences. Key words are basically the words with the most meaning, so usually nouns and verbs rather than 'small' words like prepositions and articles. You can also quickly try to think of similar words or synonyms that might be used to describe the same thing. This can help you to notice when a topic is mentioned in a listening.

Plans and maps page 50

On plans and maps, there's a lot to look at and it's sometimes difficult to find all the question numbers. As well as making sure you find the gaps for all the questions, check the instructions to see if you have to write a letter or a word. Then, in the 30 seconds you have to prepare, use your knowledge of similar places to predict the ones on the plan or map.

Completing notes page 60

When you complete notes from a recording, make sure you read the notes before you listen. While you read them, think about possible answers and possible types of words that could fill each gap. It's very important that you do this before the recording starts, because it's hard to read, listen, and write at the same time! The sentences that you hear will be different from the sentences that you read, so don't listen for the exact sentences on your paper.

Section 4 labelling diagrams page 71

In Listening Section 4, you have to label diagrams and you'll hear a lot of technical words. Quite often you'll hear words that you haven't heard before. If this happens, don't panic! Many of the words will be compound nouns – words made from two (or more) other words. Even if you don't understand the meaning of a particular compound noun, you should know the individual words that make it up. Listen carefully to the whole word and try to recognize smaller, individual words, using the context to help you to guess. The words in less common compound nouns are usually written separately.

Multiple-choice options page 81

In addition to basic multiple-choice questions, you may have to choose more than one option from a list. This can be difficult because sometimes the answers may not be mentioned in order. For this reason, you should consider all the options on the list as you listen. As usual, preparation is important. Make sure you read all the options before the recording starts and underline key words that you should listen for.

Recognizing individual words page 90

In the Listening test, you often have to write down individual words that you hear. This is difficult because, in natural spoken English, the words in a sentence often seem 'connected' together. You can't easily hear where one word ends and another begins! Also, the sound of the individual words sometimes changes when they're spoken with others. This means you might not recognize them. With practice, however, you can improve your ability to recognize individual words and work out which are important.

Avoiding common errors page 101

A few simple steps can help you to avoid common errors in the Listening test. First, it's important to read the instructions carefully so that you answer in the correct way. Make sure you know how many answers will be given in each recording, as sometimes you'll hear the answers to more than one set or you may have to turn the page to find some of the questions. At the end of the test, you'll have time to transfer your answers to the answer sheet. Use this time to make sure that your answers fit the gaps grammatically and to check that they are spelt correctly. You can also guess any answers you weren't sure about!

EXAM TIPS: WRITING

Context and key trend page 12

When you write a report about a chart or a graph, don't focus on the detail straight away. Take a step back and make sure you see the context or 'bigger picture'. Start by defining what the graphic shows. The next thing you should do is to write a sentence that describes the key trend. Did the numbers rise or fall? If they didn't rise or fall, you can say that there's no clear trend. Even after you've given the key trend, don't try to describe everything in detail!

Key similarities and differences page 23

In Writing Task 1, when you write about tables (and also bar charts or pie charts), look for key similarities and differences between the categories. You should then compare and contrast these pieces of information. Remember that you don't have to write about why the data shows what it does, though you may add some interpretation of the data in your conclusion.

Parts of an essay question page 33

There are three main parts to an essay question – each of which has a different function. First, the main topic gives the general area to discuss. Second, the issue tells you how you should discuss it, for example, looking at what should be done. Third and probably most important, the instruction tells you what type of essay you actually need to write, for example, to show agreement or disagreement. If you ignore or misunderstand the instruction, then you won't answer the question properly and you'll get a low mark.

Brainstorming essay ideas page 43

Always brainstorm ideas or reasons before you start writing an essay. If you don't, you may find you'll repeat the same points or think of extra, better ideas when you have no time left to write them! Of course, you don't have long to brainstorm in the test so you don't need to produce a long list. For example, for a discussion essay, try to think of three reasons for each opposing view. For a personal opinion essay, save time by deciding whether you agree or disagree before you start brainstorming! Then, try to brainstorm about five or six reasons for your view.

Paragraph topics page 52

Before you start writing your essay, it's important to write a plan with paragraph topics. Choosing good paragraph topics will help you to organize your ideas clearly and avoid repetition. Each topic you choose must be different from the others but general enough for you to add examples and explanations in the paragraph. Look for points in your brainstorm that you could group together in one category and try to think of labels like *social*, *economic*, or *cultural* that connect them.

Topic sentences page 62

The first sentence in each paragraph of an essay is often a topic sentence. It contains the main idea of the paragraph and should connect to your thesis statement. For example, if you give your opinion in the thesis statement, each topic sentence should give a reason for this opinion. Or, if you say you're going to discuss an argument, each topic sentence should introduce one side of the argument. If you say you're going to explain causes or effects, each topic sentence should state a cause or effect. Note that each point in your plan should become a topic sentence.

Paragraph structure page 73

Make sure your paragraphs are well structured. What this means is that the sentences are all connected logically. A main idea is given first in the topic sentence, and then other sentences in the paragraph support the idea of the topic sentence, providing explanation or examples. Your examples might include causes and effects, depending on the essay question. Make sure everything is directly related to the topic sentence and doesn't go too far from the main point of the paragraph.

Discussion or personal opinion essay page 82

If a Task 2 essay question asks about opinions, check whether you have to write a discussion essay or personal opinion essay. This is important because they require different approaches. In a discussion essay, you should give a balanced response by giving one view and then the opposite view. You can give your own personal opinion in the conclusion but it's not required by the task. In a personal opinion essay, on the other hand, you must make your own opinion clear, right from the introduction. Then, in the body section, you focus on giving reasons for your opinion and, perhaps, reasons why the opposite view is wrong.

Essay conclusion page 93

In a conclusion, you should include a summary of your main points and a sentence that directly answers the question – even if you've already stated this in the thesis statement. You may also wish to include a personal comment that's not connected to the essay question but which is relevant to the essay topic. This could be a prediction about the future – in an essay about energy use, for example, you could predict how people's lives might change.

Overview statement for a process page 103

When you describe a process, try to include an 'overview statement'. This is difficult because it requires a different approach to how you write an overview statement for describing data. With a process, there's no mention of trends, numbers, or possibly no comparisons. Instead, try to comment on a feature of the process as a whole that makes it interesting. For example, it may be particularly complex or have a surprisingly large number of stages.

EXAM TIPS: READING

Multiple-choice options page 14

Multiple-choice questions with four options often feature in the Reading test. As you read the options, underline key words or make a quick note next to any options which you think are possible answers. Of course, you then have to decide which option the passage actually agrees with. The 'stems' are useful because they give you an idea of where to look for the information in the passage.

New or difficult words page 24

You won't know the meaning of every word in the passages in the Reading test. If you think a new or difficult word is necessary to answer a question, try to guess its meaning. First, start by deciding what part of speech it is: a noun or a verb, for example. Then use clues in the surrounding text (this is called the 'context') to help you to guess the meaning. Finally, as a check, think of an easier word with the same meaning and see if it makes sense in the sentence.

Scanning page 34

Scanning is a reading strategy you can use when looking for specific information such as a word, number, or name. It's common in real life – think about how you scan a TV guide to see what's on at a certain time, the sports results to look for your favourite team, or a timetable to see when a train or bus is due to leave. It's also useful for questions requiring short answers in the Reading test.

Organization of passages page 44

In the test, there are many different types of passage. Three common types are problem–solution, information, and discussion, which gives an author's opinion. The first paragraph often tells you the type of passage because key words or phrases show that a problem, some information, or a discussion and opinion are going to be described. If you know the type of passage, you should be able to predict its organization and, as a result, find information more quickly. For example, if a question about an information passage refers to the future, this information is usually found at the end of the passage – you can then start your search in the final paragraph.

Matching questions page 54

Some matching questions in the Reading test ask you to look for specific information. To do this, you'll need to scan the passage to identify which paragraph contains the information. Before you actually start looking, underline all the key words in the questions and then decide which key word to look for first in the passage. Proper nouns, like people's names, and dates are usually easiest to find. Once you've located the word or idea you're looking for, read that part of the passage carefully to make sure that there are synonyms for all the key language in the question.

Finding topic sentences page 64

Finding topic sentences is a very important skill. They're usually located near the beginning of each paragraph. If you just read the topic sentences, you'll be able to understand the main ideas of the passage and, more importantly, the information that each paragraph contains.

True / False / Not Given questions page 74

In *True / False / Not Given* questions, you have to compare several statements with information in the reading passage. The *Not Given* option can make this type of question confusing. This is because *Not Given* doesn't mean *Not True* – instead, it means that a statement could be *True* or *False*. Also, *Not Given* doesn't always mean that the information is not mentioned. Information related to *Not Given* options may sometimes be in the passage but it won't be similar enough to decide if the answer is *True* or *False*.

Using topic sentences page 84

In order to understand the main idea of a passage, you don't always need to read the complete passage. Often, you need to read just the topic sentences of each paragraph. This strategy is particularly useful for questions where you choose the best heading, or questions where you complete a summary. But it can also help you to predict the missing word for a gap or help you to find the paragraph of a passage that contains the most useful information.

Yes / No / Not Given questions page 94

Yes / No / Not Given questions are different to *True / False / Not Given* questions. *Yes / No / Not Given* questions test your ability to identify opinions rather than facts. You can often find the author's main opinion in the final paragraph. Understanding this can help you to predict or guess whether they agree with the statements in *Yes / No / Not Given* questions.

Labelling graphics page 105

You may be given a series of two or more graphics and be asked to complete labels for them or to choose the correct graphic. The first thing you should do in these cases is consider how they're different. For example, one may point to a square object and another to a round object, or one will refer to a certain century and another to a different century. If you have to complete labels, first study the visual information to help you to predict answers. The missing labels will quickly tell you the type of information you need – often a number or a name. You can then scan the passage and underline sentences which contain possible answers.

LISTENING

Section 1

Questions 1–7

🔊 2.39 *Complete the form below.*

Write NO MORE THAN TWO WORDS AND/OR A NUMBER for each answer.

Temporary Employment Registration Form	
Category:	**0** <u>full-time</u> employment
Name:	**1** ....
Address:	**2** .... Avenue
Postcode:	**3** ....
Contact number:	**4** ....
Current situation:	studying **5** .... at university
Availability:	July–September
Experience:	retail: assistant in a **6** .... catering: worked as a **7** ....

Questions 8–10

🔊 2.40 *Complete the notes below.*

Write NO MORE THAN TWO WORDS for each answer.

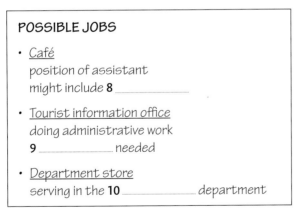

POSSIBLE JOBS

- <u>Café</u>
  position of assistant
  might include **8** ....

- <u>Tourist information office</u>
  doing administrative work
  9 .... needed

- <u>Department store</u>
  serving in the **10** .... department

Section 2

Questions 11–15

🔊 **2.41** *Complete the table below.*

Write NO MORE THAN TWO WORDS for each answer.

Parents' Evening – Talks		
Time	**Speaker**	**Topics**
7.00–7.30	head teacher	– tests in the future – the latest **11** ....
7.30–7.45	deputy head teacher	– changes at **12** .... – new rules for **13** ....
7.45–8.00	a **14**	– school trips during the year – **15** .... the children will use

Questions 16–20

🔊 **2.42** *Label the plan of part of the school below.*

Write the correct letter, A–H, next to questions 16–20.

AREA OF SCHOOL USED FOR PARENTS' EVENING

16 healthy eating scheme ....

17 refreshments ....

18 parents' association ....

19 maths teachers ....

20 head teacher ....

Section 3

Questions 21–24

🔊 **2.43** *What surprised the speakers when they were doing their research?*

Write the correct letter, L, H, B or N next to questions 21–25.

Write

L *if Liam only was surprised*

H *if Holly only was surprised*

B *if Both of them were surprised*

N *if Neither of them was surprised*

21   the paper's sales figures

22   the paper's response to the arrival of the internet

23   the amount of influence the paper has had

24   the cartoons in the paper in the past

Questions 25–27

🔊 **2.44** *Choose THREE letters, A–F.*

Which THREE features of the paper have stayed the same according to the speakers?

A   its political views

B   its weather reports

C   its coverage of famous people

D   its sports section

E   its handling of social issues

F   its appearance

Questions 28–30

🔊 **2.45** *Choose the correct letter, A, B or C.*

28   In the general section, Liam is going to focus on

    A   why British people choose to read a particular newspaper.

    B   how British people judge other readers of newspapers.

    C   what gives each newspaper its reputation.

29   In the general section, Holly is going to discuss

    A   why someone stops reading a particular newspaper.

    B   reasons for a decline in loyalty to newspapers.

    C   how newspapers change to appeal to new readers.

30   One reason why both speakers have enjoyed doing the project is that

    A   they could choose what to focus on.

    B   it has involved less work than other projects.

    C   they have learnt a lot about a single topic.

Section 4

Questions 31–34

🔊 **2.46** *Complete the summary below.*

Write NO MORE THAN TWO WORDS for each answer.

Short history of Tower Bridge

Before Tower Bridge was built, the only way to cross the river in that area was through Tower Subway, which was built in 1870. At first, Tower Subway had an **31** _____ but after three months it became a tunnel for people to walk through. To meet the demand for a new crossing, a committee was formed, and they used a **32** _____ to find the best design. A fixed bridge could not be used because **33** _____ ships had to go through it, so a bridge was created with 'bascules'. These were two sections that would separate when they were **34** _____ so the ships could pass.

Questions 35–37

🔊 **2.47** *Label the diagram below.*

Write NO MORE THAN TWO WORDS for each answer.

HOW TOWER BRIDGE WAS RAISED

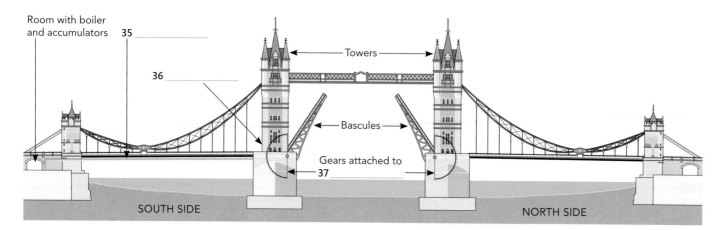

Room with boiler and accumulators **35** ....

36 ....

Towers

Bascules

Gears attached to **37** ....

SOUTH SIDE

NORTH SIDE

Questions 38–40

🔊 **2.48** *Complete the sentences below.*

Write NO MORE THAN TWO WORDS AND/OR A NUMBER for each answer.

38 During the day, _____ were placed on the bridge to signal to ships.

39 During the day, ships were required to have a _____ in a high position.

40 Nowadays, ships have to notify the bridge _____ before they want to pass through it.

Reading passage 1

*Read Passage 1 and answer **Questions 1–13**.*

The birth of the child detective

Emil and the Detectives, by Erich Kästner, was an instant hit when it was published in 1928. Just three years later it was adapted into a film and the book and its sequel, *Emil and the Three Twins*, have since been translated and adapted many times. But the book is not simply notable for its success; it also brought a great deal of innovation to the world of children's literature.

The hero of the book, Emil Tischbein, is a boy who is set a task: to take some money by train to his grandmother, who lives in the big city, Berlin. Money is a big deal as he is being brought up by a single mother. We hear that his father was a plumber but died, and his mother has to work as a hairdresser. With a touch of realism that is the flavour of the book as a whole, we learn that, 'Sometimes she is ill, and then Emil fries eggs for her and for himself'. So, Emil is anxious about the money in his pocket on the train. He is also anxious about a crime he has committed: together with his friends, he has drawn a moustache on the face of the town statue of the Grand Duke Charles.

On the way to Berlin, Emil sits in a carriage with an odd gentleman, Herr Grundeis, and though he tries to avoid it happening, Emil falls asleep. When he wakes up, his money has gone and so has Herr Grundeis. This occurs not long after a quarter of the way through the book, so for the rest of the story we live with Emil's swirling emotions, his meetings with a group of boys in Berlin, and the eventual capture of Grundeis. The reason why Emil doesn't involve the police is because he fears exposure as the criminal who daubed the Grand Duke's statue. The word 'detectives' is in the title, but in a way the book is a detective novel in reverse, as it requires Emil and the boys to first catch the criminal and only then prove his guilt to unbelieving adults.

The secret to the book's popularity may be lost on many adults, who may doubt the likelihood of children taking such control of events. After all, the detective in most fiction is usually a clever adult who will make the world safer for us ordinary mortals. Perhaps it is even a contradiction that children, who are the symbols of innocence, can be as clever as their fictional adult counterparts. But that, of course, is the point of the book: real children, with flaws (they might fall asleep on the train, or lie to their parents), manage a very difficult job. We should remember that children's fiction often appeals to a child's desire for power and independence. As smaller, un-powerful members of the human race, they are greatly attracted by heroes that are capable of acts beyond a child's usual capabilities.

When *Emil and the Detectives* first appeared, it broke new ground in many ways at once. It is probably the first of the 'child detective' books, a genre taken up so successfully by other authors. It is also one of the first books for children that gives us a full picture of a child in a single-parent family of very little means, and one of the first which treats the city as a place of excitement. And it appears to approve of the actions of children working together for a common purpose without the guidance of adults.

As if this wasn't enough, there are many more technical innovations, too. The book breaks from the usual format of a single line of narrative told to us in the third person by a knowing narrator, and adds witty one-page commentaries on people appearing in the story. These are written in the first person as if the narrator is thinking aloud for our benefit and talking directly to us. The dialogues, too, are innovative since in the original German, the boys whom Emil meets talk with a Berlin slang. Whereas in most children's books of the time urban speech told the reader that that person was bad or stupid, in *Emil and the Detectives* the local dialect seems to confirm the resourcefulness of the boys. Even the film adaptation was innovative in the realistic acting of child actors and the use of 'synch' sound on location on the streets of Berlin.

The original context for the story stemmed partly from Kästner's own life. He was born in 1899 and grew up in a small town rather like Emil's home town, and like Emil he lost his father when he was young. He, too, then made his way to Berlin, where he worked as a writer. But we should note that not all the credit for the story can go to Kästner, for it was the head of a Berlin publishing house, Edith Jacobsen, that approached him, and she who suggested the idea of a children's detective novel.

Questions 1–4

Complete the summary below.

Choose NO MORE THAN TWO WORDS from the passage for each answer.

Write your answers in boxes 1–4 on your answer sheet. (page 163)

Story of *Emil and the Detectives*

The story concerns a boy called Emil who has to deliver money to **1** _____ in Berlin. He lives with his mother, who is a hairdresser and not well-off. On the journey, he meets someone who he thinks is strange, and while Emil is **2** _____ , the money disappears. When he gets to Berlin, he meets some **3** _____ and they help him to find the person who took the money. He does not want to report this theft because he is worried about some damage that he did to a **4** _____ and thinks he will get into trouble for that.

Questions 5–7

*Choose the correct letter, **A**, **B**, **C** or **D**.*

Write the correct letters in boxes 5–7 on your answer sheet. (page 163)

5 What point does the writer make about *Emil and the Detectives* in the fourth paragraph?

    A It says something important about adult behaviour.

    B It has a different outcome from most detective fiction.

    C The children are different from most real children.

    D The children are like the adults in other detective fiction.

6 The writer says that children particularly like fiction which

    A describes children being in control of events.

    B presents situations they are personally familiar with.

    C is read to them by adults in an enthusiastic way.

    D includes a large number of surprising events.

7 The writer says that a feature of the book that was new at the time was

    A its focus on children's opposition to adults.

    B its use of a city as the main setting for much of the action.

    C its portrayal of a child growing up in difficult circumstances.

    D its inclusion of more than one child detective.

Do the following statements agree with the information given in Reading passage 1?

In boxes 8–13 on your answer sheet (page 163), write

TRUE   *if the statement agrees with the information*

FALSE   *if the statement contradicts the information*

NOT GIVEN   *if there is no information on this*

  8 The book is unusual because it has more than one narrator.

  9 Some readers found it hard to understand the slang used by some characters.

10 Local dialect is a positive feature of some of the characters.

11 The film of the book had features that were unusual at the time.

12 Kästner based the whole story on real events in his life.

13 Kästner wrote the story and then sent it to a publisher.

Reading passage 2

*Read Passage 2 and answer **Questions 14–26**.*

The Park Hill housing development

A   The huge Park Hill housing development in Sheffield is a Brutalist masterpiece, widely praised by architects, and it has been admired by many in the media, too, since its recent redevelopment. But it has had a controversial past. Jack Lynn, one of a pair of idealistic young architects leading the project, designed Park Hill when there was a major post-war shortage of housing in the city. In December 1940, two nights of bombing had brought devastation to the area, destroying many of the Victorian terraced streets. The city was left with a major homelessness problem, which became even worse when the remaining Victorian housing was judged unsuitable for living in. Land was also in short supply as much of it was 'green belt'.

B   In a desperate effort to solve the problem, Sheffield City Council sent a group of experts to look at housing projects in Europe. They returned full of enthusiasm for the modernist developments they had seen. The inspiration for Jack Lynn, his colleague Ivor Smith, and the city architect Lewis Womersley, was the work of Le Corbusier, whose concrete 'streets in the sky' were very popular in France. The idea was to replace Sheffield's slums with ultra-modern flats and facilities, recreating the communities that had flourished in the pre-war housing developments. The new development was also designed as a response to what were considered, even in the 1950s, to be modern architecture's failures: empty spaces, isolation, a lack of street life, and a middle-class 'we know what's good for you' ethos.

C   When the estate was formally opened in 1961, Park Hill was intended to be a perfect vision of social housing. Conceived as a town within a town, it consisted of 996 flats that would house almost 3,000 people and was equipped with every sort of public facility – shops, a doctors' surgery, dentist, clinic, nursery, school, four pubs, and a police station. While most tower blocks of the era had flats built around narrow, dark corridors, Park Hill's flats had interlinked 'street-decks' – communal areas running along each storey where children could play and families socialise. The decks were as broad as real streets and wide enough for a milk float to pass along. The blocks of flats themselves were connected by walkways, and their height varied, from four storeys to thirteen, in order to maintain a roof line that remained level across the development.

D   Motivated by a deep social commitment, Jack Lynn and his colleagues did everything they could to ensure that the new residents felt at home in their new environment. Cobblestones from the old terraced streets surrounded the flats and paved the pathways down the hill to Sheffield station; brick infill panels were made of the same material as the houses they replaced, and the flats all had traditional front doorsteps. Each floor was given an old street name and neighbours were rehoused together.

E A survey of residents conducted by the housing department a year after the flats had been officially opened was overwhelmingly positive, and awards were heaped on the designers. 'When one looks out from some part of it and sees another of its limbs swinging across the view,' enthused the architectural critic Reyner Banham, 'the effect is like that of suddenly realising that the railway lines on the other side of some valley in Switzerland are the same that one's own train has just traversed a few moments before.' The vision of Park Hill as a living community also seemed justified. Of the walkways, Banham wrote: 'Toddlers play on them, teens mend bikes and swap gossip, and grannies stand at their doors …'

F But Park Hill did not age as well as its admirers hoped. The concrete in which it was built proved less suited to the damp climate of Sheffield than the dry heat of the south of France, and as the years passed it became damaged. By the 1970s problems were accumulating. Cockroaches invaded the estate and a series of violent attacks led to headlines in the papers. In the 1980s, as unemployment soared, social problems multiplied. There were burnt-out cars, boarded-up shops, rubbish, and graffiti. The council was accused of dumping problem families there, while the 'streets in the sky' proved an ideal place for gangs to hide from police. Deliverymen found that they often had to dodge milk bottles and other missiles, while older inhabitants who had once chatted and gossiped with their neighbours began locking their doors. The cost of refurbishing the flats and of maintenance was also getting too high as councils struggled to deal with the many problems. By the 1980s, Park Hill had come to be regarded as a dangerous no-go area, an embarrassing blot on the face of the city.

Questions 14–19

*Reading passage 2 has six paragraphs, **A-F**.*

Choose the correct heading for each paragraph from the list of headings below.

*Write the correct number **i-ix** in boxes 14–19 on your answer sheet. (page 163)*

List of headings

i	A massive decline
ii	Including familiar elements in the development
iii	Problems with the development predicted
iv	Meeting a need at the time
v	Various opinions on the new development
vi	An initial response to the housing problem
vii	A change of plan for the development
viii	Influences on the design
ix	What the development offered residents

---

14 Paragraph A
15 Paragraph B
16 Paragraph C
17 Paragraph D
18 Paragraph E
19 Paragraph F

Questions 20-22

Label the diagram below.

Choose NO MORE THAN TWO WORDS from the passage for each answer.

Write your answers in boxes 20-22 on your answer sheet. (page 163)

FEATURES OF THE PREVIOUS HOUSING USED FOR PARK HILL

Brick panels

22 Level ....

20 ....

21 ....

Public facilities

Cobble stones

Questions 23-26

Answer the questions below.

Choose NO MORE THAN TWO WORDS from the passage for each answer.

Write your answers in boxes 23-26 on your answer sheet. (page 163)

23 What showed that residents liked the development at first?
24 What was badly affected by the weather in Sheffield?
25 According to some, what kind of people did councils put in Park Hill in the 1980s?
26 Which visitors were attacked when visiting Park Hill?

Reading passage 3

*Read Passage 3 and answer **Questions 27–40**.*

Human distrust of robots that look like us

A   We humans have evolved to relate emotionally to non-living objects, which is strange when you think about it. Children play with dolls and toy soldiers as if they were people. Adults talk to their cars. As long as they are robot-like and 'mechanical', we are comfortable around them, and can display affection (as for an old car). But when it comes to human-like robots, something different happens. As they become more human-like, our affection disappears and we begin to feel less comfortable. Our liking turns to revulsion. Androids that look too human freak us out.

B   This odd phenomenon is called the 'uncanny valley', a term coined by robotics professor Masahiro Mori. But the effect has particularly confused and puzzled engineers and scientists who design robots and interactive software. The term comes from the dip in a graph with two parameters: affection and human likeness. As human likeness increases, so does our affection. As soon as the resemblance becomes too great, though, affection drops below zero – hence the 'valley'. The effect was highlighted by studies of machines such as the Geminoid F robot, created by Professor Hiroshi Ishiguro of Kyoto University. His robots have human-like bodies but their movements, although impressively human-like, show something of the mechanism beneath their 'skin' and people didn't respond well to them. Making robots look human is a major goal of robotic engineers and scientific writers have long dreamt of androids, so the 'uncanny valley' could potentially spell the end to their dream.

C   Researchers have tried to find the cause of the 'uncanny valley'. One of the most interesting insights has come from an international team led by Ayse Pinar Saygin of the University of California, San Diego (UCSD). Saygin and her team conducted an experiment scanning the brains of twenty subjects aged 20–36 while they were looking at three different things: a human, a mechanical-looking robot, and a human-like robot. Interpreting the results from the fMRI scans, the researchers suggested that the cause for the valley is a conflict in perception between two processes in the brain: that of recognising a human-like face and that of recognising different kinds of movement.

D   These processes, or pathways, meet in an area of the brain called the parietal cortex. There, information from the visual cortex relating to bodily movement is integrated with information from the motor cortex that contains mirror neurons, the brain cells that register that what we are seeing is 'one of us'. Alarm bells go off in the brain when there is a conflict between the human-like features of the robot and its inhuman movement. This mismatch creates a feeling of revulsion similar to what we feel when looking at a movie zombie. We instinctively expect human-like creatures to have human-like movements. As Saygin says: 'The brain … look(s) for its expectations to be met – for appearance and motion to (match).'

E   The discomfort we feel is not logical and has its roots in our evolutionary past. Researchers believe that the modern mind came into being between 60,000 and 40,000 years ago when pathways in the brain became connected, probably thanks to the evolution of language. The way we understand our world then emerged from these new connections. Robotic evolution challenges this mental 'software' of ours. The 'uncanny valley' seems to represent the point at which logic stops and our instincts start to react.

F   Despite such studies, many (e.g. MacDorman et al) believe that cultural factors also contribute to the effect, and researchers have pointed to the fact that young people who are used to technology seem less affected by the effect. Furthermore, the 'uncanny valley' effect has been observed in our response to still photographs of humans that have been altered slightly with Photoshop software. Even as far back as the 19th century, the great naturalist Charles Darwin noticed that we react most adversely to species with eyes, nose and mouth arranged like our own. The phenomenon may therefore be more complex than Saygin's research suggests.

G   So is this the end of robots as we have dreamt them? Are our brains unable to cope with mechanical doubles? Perhaps not. It may just be a temporary phenomenon. The positive response to recent androids shows that once the design and movements of robots become even more human-like, the affection graph rises again from the 'uncanny valley'; acceptability returns steeply to normal. We seem to be at ease with androids that have human bodies and human movements, even if we know they are not human. As we cross the 'uncanny valley' another basic instinct comes into play: empathy. It is possible to mix human and mechanical characteristics without getting trapped in 'uncanny valley'. Eventually, human-like robots will make us love them, too.

Questions 27–30

*Reading Passage 3 has seven paragraphs, **A–G**.*

Which paragraph contains the following information?

*Write the correct letter, **A–G**, in boxes 27–30 on your answer sheet. (page 163)*

27 a belief that we may have strong, positive feelings for robots in the future

28 a description of how the human brain developed over time

29 a contrast between our reaction to various objects and our reaction to robots

30 an example of robots which people have a very negative reaction to

Questions 31–33

Look at the following statements and the list of scientists below.

*Match each statement to the correct scientist, **A–E**.*

*Write the correct letter, **A–E**, in boxes 31–33 on your answer sheet. (page 163)*

31 We feel disgusted when things don't move as we think they will.

32 We feel visual disgust when animal faces appear similar to human faces

33 The causes of the 'Uncanny Valley' effect are not just biological.

List of scientists
A MacDorman
B Professor Hiroshi Ishiguro
C Charles Darwin
D Ayse Pinar Saygin
E Masahiro Mori

Questions 34–36

Complete the sentences below.

Choose ONE WORD ONLY from the passage for each answer.

Write your answers in boxes 34–36 on your answer sheet. (page 163)

34 The 'uncanny valley' concerns the relationship between how much a robot looks like a human and the amount of .... people feel.

35 Scientists think that the development of .... played an important part in the development of the modern mind.

36 The 'uncanny valley' reaction is also seen when people look at .... which have been changed a little.

Questions 37–40

Do the following statements agree with the views of the author in Reading Passage 3?

In boxes 37–40 on your answer sheet (page 163), write

YES   *if the statement agrees with the views of the author*

NO   *if the statement contradicts the views of the author*

NOT GIVEN   *if it is impossible to say what the author thinks about this*

37 It is surprising that people can have strong emotional feelings for objects.

38 The term 'uncanny valley' is very difficult for many people to understand.

39 The research in California adequately explains the 'uncanny valley' effect.

40 Researchers will probably learn to overcome the 'uncanny valley' effect.

WRITING

Writing task 1

You should spend about 20 minutes on this task.

> **The chart below shows the number of openings and closures in the UK by shop category in the first six months of 2013.**
>
> **Summarize the information by selecting and reporting the main features, and make comparisons where relevant.**

Write at least 150 words.

SHOP OPENINGS AND CLOSURES IN THE UK, FIRST SIX MONTHS OF 2013

Writing task 2

You should spend about 40 minutes on this task.

Write about the following topic:

> **In recent times and in many countries, schools that achieve good exam results in maths, literacy, and science are being considered 'good schools' while schools that do well in other subjects like art or music are not receiving high ratings. This is a negative development.**
>
> **To what extent do you agree or disagree with this opinion?**

Give reasons for your answer and include any relevant examples from your own knowledge or experience.

Write at least 250 words.

SPEAKING

Part 1

Sports
- What sports have you played?
- What are the most popular sports in your country? Why?
- Do you go to sports events and/or watch them on TV? When / Why?
- Would you like to try any sports in the future? Why?

Food
- Who prepares the food where you are living?
- What was the first meal you learnt to cook?
- Do you prefer to eat in a restaurant or at home?
- How are eating habits changing in your country?

Part 2

You will have to talk about the topic for one to two minutes.

You have one minute to think about what you are going to say.

You can make some notes to help you if you wish.

> **Describe a city that you enjoyed visiting.**
> **You should say:**
> > **why you went there**
> > **what you did while you were there**
> > **what you liked about the place**
> **and explain why you would or wouldn't like to live there.**

Part 3

City life
- What kinds of people most enjoy living in a big city?
- Why do some people find life in cities hard?
- Are more people likely to live in cities in the future?

Problems in cities
- Do modern cities have more or fewer problems than cities 100 years ago?
- What can we do to make cities more attractive places?
- Should we destroy old housing where possible to create modern apartments?

Listening and Reading answer sheet

LISTENING

1		✓ 1 ✗	
2		✓ 2 ✗	
3		✓ 3 ✗	
4		✓ 4 ✗	
5		✓ 5 ✗	
6		✓ 6 ✗	
7		✓ 7 ✗	
8		✓ 8 ✗	
9		✓ 9 ✗	
10		✓ 10 ✗	
11		✓ 11 ✗	
12		✓ 12 ✗	
13		✓ 13 ✗	
14		✓ 14 ✗	
15		✓ 15 ✗	
16		✓ 16 ✗	
17		✓ 17 ✗	
18		✓ 18 ✗	
19		✓ 19 ✗	
20		✓ 20 ✗	

21		✓ 21 ✗	
22		✓ 22 ✗	
23		✓ 23 ✗	
24		✓ 24 ✗	
25		✓ 25 ✗	
26		✓ 26 ✗	
27		✓ 27 ✗	
28		✓ 28 ✗	
29		✓ 29 ✗	
30		✓ 30 ✗	
31		✓ 31 ✗	
32		✓ 32 ✗	
33		✓ 33 ✗	
34		✓ 34 ✗	
35		✓ 35 ✗	
36		✓ 36 ✗	
37		✓ 37 ✗	
38		✓ 38 ✗	
39		✓ 39 ✗	
40		✓ 40 ✗	

READING

1		✓ 1 ✗	
2		✓ 2 ✗	
3		✓ 3 ✗	
4		✓ 4 ✗	
5		✓ 5 ✗	
6		✓ 6 ✗	
7		✓ 7 ✗	
8		✓ 8 ✗	
9		✓ 9 ✗	
10		✓ 10 ✗	
11		✓ 11 ✗	
12		✓ 12 ✗	
13		✓ 13 ✗	
14		✓ 14 ✗	
15		✓ 15 ✗	
16		✓ 16 ✗	
17		✓ 17 ✗	
18		✓ 18 ✗	
19		✓ 19 ✗	
20		✓ 20 ✗	

21		✓ 21 ✗	
22		✓ 22 ✗	
23		✓ 23 ✗	
24		✓ 24 ✗	
25		✓ 25 ✗	
26		✓ 26 ✗	
27		✓ 27 ✗	
28		✓ 28 ✗	
29		✓ 29 ✗	
30		✓ 30 ✗	
31		✓ 31 ✗	
32		✓ 32 ✗	
33		✓ 33 ✗	
34		✓ 34 ✗	
35		✓ 35 ✗	
36		✓ 36 ✗	
37		✓ 37 ✗	
38		✓ 38 ✗	
39		✓ 39 ✗	
40		✓ 40 ✗	

AUDIOSCRIPT

◀)) 1.1, 1.2 page 8 exercises 6 and 7

1 At school, I hated studying sciences, especially biology and chemistry. However, now I'd like to study medicine!

2 I prefer studying vocational subjects connected to my chosen career. I hope to go into business, so economics and management are particularly important.

3 I enjoy studying psychology at university, but at school I didn't like studying in general because most subjects we learnt, like history and geography, were compulsory.

◀)) 1.3, 1.4 page 9 exercises 9 and 10

1 I hated studying sciences.
2 I'd like to study medicine.
3 I prefer studying vocational subjects.
4 I hope to go into business.
5 I enjoy studying psychology.
6 I didn't like studying in general.

◀)) 1.5 page 9 Exam tip

Speaking Part 1 lasts 4 to 5 minutes and the examiner asks you questions about a range of personal topics, such as your family, hobbies, work or education, and holidays. Listen carefully for the question word – where, when, who, how, how often – and try to respond in a conversational way. It's important that you understand the question, and give a full response to show that you can use a variety of language. Try to add some extra information that gives the examiner something more than a basic response. Each response should be about 15 seconds.

◀)) 1.6, 1.7 page 10 exercises 3 and 4

Globally and on average, 25% of students attend additional courses outside school. More than 75% of students in Colombia, Latvia, the Slovak Republic, the Philippines, and South Africa have private tuition in mathematics. In Japan and South Korea respectively, the figures are 71% and 64%, while in the UK, 20% of students attend extra courses. In general, the levels of tuition are especially high in East Asian countries where over 70% of students receive extra tuition at some point in their school careers. Levels of tuition are lower in European countries, for example in Germany, where recent surveys indicate that around 16–20% of students receive tuition, usually in mathematics.

◀)) 1.8 page 10 Exam tip

In Listening Section 1, candidates often make mistakes writing down details such as numbers and names. With numbers, think about what would be realistic in each gap because this will help you to understand the number correctly. It's also a good idea to practise listening to longer numbers, like telephone numbers, which are often said quickly. With names, candidates often misspell them because they confuse how each letter is said – particularly the vowels: a, e, i, o, u. The main thing is to read the instructions and look at the information carefully to find out if names or numbers are required ... or both!

◀)) 1.9 page 11 exercise 9

a Pablo Hernandez – P-a-b-l-o H-e-r-n-a-n-d-e-z
b 115
c Irene Allegri – I-r-e-n-e A-l-l-e-g-r-i
d 8th
e Mohammed Bagabas – M-o-h-a-m-m-e-d B-a-g-a-b-a-s
f 772289
g 86 kilograms
h 07789 471147

◀)) 1.10 page 11 exercise 11

Receptionist: Foxhill House College. Hello?

Caller: Hi, I'm calling about the International Law course. Could you give me some more details?

Receptionist: Certainly, what would you like to know?

Caller: Er, what time do the classes start?

Receptionist: They run from 7 p.m. till 9 every Monday ... for 10 weeks.

Caller: OK. And how much does the course actually cost?

Receptionist: It's £500, but there are discounts available.

Caller: Right. What do we look at in the class?

Receptionist: You look at how international law developed and how it works.

Caller: OK. And where does the course take place?

Receptionist: It's in Nottingham and the next one starts on the ... let's have a look ... on the 31st of May.

Caller: Great. Er, what other courses do you have that are international?

Receptionist: Well, there's 'Intercultural communication'.

Caller: OK. How long is that?

Receptionist: It's a twelve-week course ... and it's earlier, too – from 6.30 p.m. till 8 p.m.

Caller: And how much does it cost?

Receptionist: Hold on ... Ah, here we are. It's £1,200 for the three months.

Caller: OK. What's covered?

Receptionist: In the first month, you study language and culture. In the second month, you look at dealing with cultural change, in other words, cultural training methods ... and in the third month, you study culture and business.

Caller: OK – sounds useful. Where does it take place? In Nottingham, too?

Receptionist: No, it's in Derby.

Caller: Right. And when does it start?

Receptionist: You can start on the 25th of April or ... one moment ... on the 2nd of September.

Caller: Great. Er, could you possibly send me information about how to book and register – a full brochure or something?

Receptionist: Of course. What's your name?

Caller: It's Claire Kuhles. That's C-l-a-i-r-e ... and family name, K-u-h-l-e-s.

Receptionist: OK ... And where do you live?

Caller: 20 College Street, Oxford, OX1 5NP.

Receptionist: OK. And what's your email address?

Caller: It's c-dot-kuhles at lastmail dot com.

Receptionist: ... at lastmail dot com. OK, I'll put the information in the post to you today.

Caller: Fantastic – thanks a lot!

◀)) 1.11 page 12 Exam tip

When you write a report about a chart or a graph, don't focus on the detail straight away. Take a step back and make sure you see the context or 'bigger picture'. Start by defining what the graphic shows. The next thing you should do is to write a sentence that describes the key trend. Did the numbers rise or fall? If they didn't rise or fall, you can say that there's no clear trend. Even after you've given the key trend, don't try to describe everything in detail!

◀)) 1.12 page 14 Exam tip

Multiple-choice questions with four options often feature in the Reading test. As you read the options, underline key words or make a quick note next to any options which you think are possible answers. Of course, you then have to decide which option the passage actually agrees with. The 'stems' are useful because they give you an idea of where to look for the information in the passage.

◀)) 1.13 page 18 exercise 2

1 It was a Swiss doctor called Susanne Klein-Vogelbach who first suggested that giant plastic balls could be used for health purposes and 'Swiss balls', as they became known, soon became very popular. Many people believe that sitting on a Swiss ball is an effective way of building your muscles. These days, you'll see them used for general fitness training when you go to a gym. They're also ideal for doing yoga and Pilates.

2 The Wii Balance Board arrived with Nintendo's *Wii Fit* in 2007. It's a convenient way of exercising because you can use it whenever you're at home. It's also simple to use because it actually remembers your exercise programmes for you. Obviously, you need a Wii and the *Wii Fit* game to use the Balance Board, which are all quite expensive, but it's worth the money.

3 Sports watches measure how far and how fast you walk or run. Most can also measure your heart rate and how many calories you burn. They're really beneficial as they encourage people to be as active as possible. As soon as you turn the watch on, it starts working and can tell you how far you've walked or run. You can wear it wherever you are. For some people, jogging can be a bit dull, but with a sports watch you have something to focus on.

4 Exercise bikes are a common sight in gyms everywhere and are used by a wide range of people. Parents can even buy exercise bikes that rock a baby to sleep while they use them. They have a variety of programmes to make the exercise as easy or as demanding as you want and they tell you how far you cycle as well as how many calories you burn. However, some people find doing the same exercise programmes a little repetitive and they prefer to use a normal bike outside.

🔊 1.14 page 18 exercise 5

1 Sitting on a Swiss ball is an effective way of building your muscles.

2 They're also ideal for doing yoga and Pilates.

3 It's a convenient way of exercising because you can use it whenever you're at home.

4 It's also simple to use because it actually remembers your exercise programmes for you.

5 You need a Wii and the *Wii Fit* game to use the Balance Board, which are all quite expensive.

6 They're really beneficial as they encourage people to be as active as possible.

7 For some people, jogging can be a bit dull.

8 They have a variety of programmes to make the exercise as easy or as demanding as you want.

9 Some people find doing the same exercise programmes a little repetitive.

🔊 1.15 page 19 exercise 9

1 A I listen to music while I'm running.
  B I listen to music while I'm running.

2 A I go to the gym after 9 a.m. when it's less crowded.
  B I go to the gym after 9 a.m. when it's less crowded.

3 A Whenever I can, I try to do yoga.
  B Whenever I can, I try to do yoga.

4 A I have a shower as soon as I finish running.
  B I have a shower as soon as I finish running.

5 A I don't exercise indoors when it's warm and sunny.
  B I don't exercise indoors when it's warm and sunny.

🔊 1.16 page 19 Exam tip

In Speaking Part 2, it's difficult to remember everything you want to say but the 1 minute of preparation time can help. Writing notes on the topic during this time is useful or, if you prefer, close your eyes and try to imagine the things you're going to describe. You could also set yourself different objectives for each stage of the extended speaking. Your first objective could be to speak for 25 seconds about the first prompt on the card. If you can do this, you should be able to speak for more than 1 minute in total. Then, for the next stages, focus on demonstrating your grammar, vocabulary, and pronunciation in turn.

🔊 1.17 page 19 exercise 12

OK, I'd like to talk about a friend of mine, called Ann. She's an old friend – she's in her thirties now and has a child, but she's really active. Actually, she's played sports for as long as I've known her. She always wears a tracksuit and trainers, even when she's shopping or going out! Er, her favourite activity is definitely yoga. She goes to the gym to do classes whenever she can and as soon as she gets home she does extra exercises, too. I think she probably does it in her dreams! She gets into all sorts of strange positions which I could never do. I don't know how she does it. OK. The good thing about yoga is that you don't need a lot of equipment. Ann uses a long plastic mat – there's always one on the floor of her living room. It's green and looks very soft and comfortable. You have to have loose clothing, too, but she always wears this anyway, as I said before. And there are probably things you can buy if you want, but nothing important. I think what she does is great and I wish I was more like her. She seems very calm and cheerful. But I'm not sure that kind of lifestyle is good for everyone. Personally, I think I'd probably find it a bit dull and repetitive; I need more variety. I'm quite different from Ann, I think!

🔊 1.18 page 20 Exam tip

In Listening Section 2, you may have to complete a table with information – numbers or individual words. Candidates often hear the information that's needed but then write it down incorrectly by failing to add articles (*a* or *the*) or the right endings. This will lose you marks in the exam. Make sure you look carefully at the forms of other words in the same column of the table, as these can help you to decide the type of word or number you need.

🔊 1.19 page 20 exercise 3

Perhaps you're one of those people who don't actually like taking exercise? Well, the good news is that you don't necessarily need to work too hard to keep fit. Of course, there are some demanding forms of exercise that are good for you. Running, for example, can burn 1,267 calories if you run at 17.5 kilometres per hour. Almost as useful are other forms of physical, outdoor work. Chopping wood, for example, can really build stomach muscles. If you're worried about injuries, then swimming is an ideal activity because it's a low impact form of exercise but still burns the same number of calories as martial arts! Scuba-diving is particularly useful because it helps to reduce stress. And there are some things we might not think of as 'proper' exercise but which can still help. Playing the drums, for example, is great for releasing tension in the body and just walking the dog or playing with pets in the garden can help you to burn calories, about 281 per hour, and also exposes you to fresh air. Even riding a motorbike is better than sitting in a car because it can help strengthen knees and thighs. So, there you go – no excuses – if you stay active, then you can also keep fit!

🔊 1.20 page 21 exercise 7

Hi, everyone. Can I just have your attention? Thanks. Well, first of all, welcome to Ab-Solutions Gym. We're going to start this introductory session with a quick look at our timetable. Has everyone got one? Good. As you can see, the group exercise classes are all in the evenings. On weekdays, you can do Spinning with Deborah from 7 o'clock – that's a 45-minute session. After that, we have Abs blast and Core blast – both are pretty hard-core sessions and not ones I'd really recommend for complete beginners! They're a bit demanding so both last for about half an hour, but if you want something more relaxing then I do recommend Aerobics at quarter past nine. This usually attracts the ladies but if any guys want to have a go, then they're also welcome! At the weekend, things change around. We start with our very popular Beach body workout – that's with Paul – before we do Aerobics with Moira. Two great sessions for general fitness. Following that, we have Boxercise, though I'm afraid the timetable is wrong there and, in fact, Gary will be leading that session instead of Paul. Don't forget that at the end of the day on Saturday we have Advanced yoga, too. Finally, on Sunday it's all change again. We have an energetic session of Ladies' fitness with Moira for 45 minutes, then if you haven't tried martial arts before, we have a visiting instructor coming in to take a karate class. It's beginner level, so I'd give it a go. That's then followed by Zumba, and Pilates on Sunday evening.

🔊 1.21 page 21 exercise 8

OK, so if you follow me, I'll show you the main room of the gym. To get in, you have to pass your identity card over the scanner here. Look after your card carefully, because you also need it to use the equipment. Anyway, I'll let us all in for now … There we go. OK. Over here, there are several computer screens. I should say these aren't for checking emails! The idea is that you can type in your unique personal code – you get this when you arrive – and then download an exercise programme that matches your level. Now for the equipment itself. OK, first of all, it's very important to leave the equipment clean for the next user, so we expect everyone to wipe down the machines after use with the spray provided and a paper towel. When using all machines, please remember to wear clean shoes that haven't been worn outdoors and to wear loose, comfortable clothes. You should also bring plenty of fluid so that you don't become dehydrated. All of the exercise machines have an audio socket so you can plug in your own headphones, or you can buy a pair of them at reception. The machines all allow you to choose from a selection of music and videos so there's no reason to get bored! OK? Great. If you have any questions, please ask a member of staff – there's someone here at the gym all the time and happy to help. So, if you come this way, I'll show you some of the most popular machines …

🔊 **1.22** page 23 Exam tip

In Writing Task 1, when you write about tables (and also bar charts or pie charts), look for key similarities and differences between the categories. You should then compare and contrast these pieces of information. Remember that you don't have to write about why the data shows what it does, though you may add some interpretation of the data in your conclusion.

🔊 **1.23** page 24 Exam tip

You won't know the meaning of every word in the passages in the Reading test. If you think a new or difficult word is necessary to answer a question, try to guess its meaning. First, start by deciding what part of speech it is: a noun or a verb, for example. Then use clues in the surrounding text (this is called the 'context') to help you to guess the meaning. Finally, as a check, think of an easier word with the same meaning and see if it makes sense in the sentence.

🔊 **1.24** page 28 exercise 4

Interviewer: Right, I'd like you to say whether you agree with these statements. Here's the first one: Men shouldn't do housework. Do you agree?

Respondent: No, absolutely not. I think it's important to share housework. If men don't help, women won't be able to go to work.

Interviewer: OK. And here's the next statement: Women should be prepared to stop paid work because of family responsibilities. Do you agree with that?

Respondent: Well, it depends. It's right for women to have freedom of choice. Of course, that puts more pressure on the man to earn enough to support the family.

Interviewer: OK, fine. The next statement: People should care for the well-being of everyone in society. Do you agree?

Respondent: Yes, definitely. It's necessary to protect everyone in society. If we don't, then some people might lose their homes and possessions and commit crimes.

Interviewer: OK. So here's the next one. Should the government reduce differences in income?

Respondent: No, I don't think so. Because it's wrong to take money away from people who have worked hard. If we do, rich people might move to a different country.

Interviewer: OK. Almost there. Should there be more controls on immigration?

Respondent: Yes, to some extent. It's necessary to welcome people from all countries nowadays, but for immigrants it's difficult to be part of a society that looks very different from theirs. If we

welcome a lot of immigrants, we have to help them to integrate.

Interviewer: OK. Here's the last statement: People should never break the law. Do you agree?

Respondent: Yes, of course I do! What kind of society would we have if we allowed people to break the law whenever they wanted to?

🔊 **1.25** page 29 exercise 10

Interviewer: Do you think the government should reduce differences in income?

A: Well, it depends. It's important to be fair, but I think it's difficult to have complete income equality.

B: Well, it depends. It's important to be fair, but I think it's difficult to have complete income equality.

🔊 **1.26** page 29 exercise 11

Well, it depends. It's important to be fair, but I think it's difficult to have complete income equality.

🔊 **1.27** page 29 Exam tip

Sounding enthusiastic can help you to get a better mark for pronunciation because your intonation and word stress will be more varied. However, it's not always easy to do this, especially when the examiner is looking down and taking notes. Try to imagine you're talking with a friend instead!

🔊 **1.28, 1.29** page 30 exercises 2 and 3

A: I think older siblings have more fun.

B: I don't know about that. They often have to help look after younger children.

A: That's true, so I suppose that makes them a bit more responsible.

B: Definitely!

A: Er, OK. I also think older siblings tend to be brighter – you know, more clever academically.

B: I agree to some extent. Apparently, Einstein was the oldest child! But I think younger siblings are probably more creative.

A: Yes, I think so, too. And more adventurous, perhaps.

B: Really? I disagree. I think older siblings are better at leading and doing more courageous things.

A: Hmm, that's partly right but then I think sometimes parents are usually more relaxed about second children and let them go out more.

🔊 **1.30** page 30 Exam tip

In Listening Section 3, you hear two or three speakers. The conversation takes place in an academic environment – for example, a university classroom or lecture hall. But it can also take place anywhere on 'campus' – that means the university grounds – such as in a sports centre or student café. The speakers often express different opinions and you may be tested on how well you understand any disagreements.

🔊 **1.31** page 30 exercise 6

Isabella: I thought Professor Greene's lecture today was interesting.

Simon: Yes. I don't think I've ever really thought about why me and my older brothers are different.

Isabella: Hmm. The new research he mentioned into older siblings was really fascinating.

Simon: Yeah, but I'm not sure I understood the idea. I thought that part of the lecture was very difficult. He said that babies who are born first are cleverer, didn't he?

Isabella: I don't think so. They achieve higher scores in intelligence tests than their younger siblings, but only when they're eighteen, so they seem to become cleverer later.

Simon: Hmm. So is that because they get all the attention from their parents before their brother or sister is born?

Isabella: No, Professor Greene said that can't be right, because at twelve years of age the younger siblings do better in intelligence tests. So that means that younger siblings …

🔊 **1.32** page 31 exercise 8

Simon: Oh, right. So what was the reason, then?

Isabella: Well, he thinks it's because older children teach their brothers and sisters.

Simon: But I don't get it. Shouldn't the youngest learn more, then?

Isabella: No, because when you teach something, it improves your thinking. It's good for your brain.

Simon: Right. OK. I think I need to go and look at the research! Did Professor Greene say there were copies of the report available in the library?

Isabella: Yes. There's a copy of the research in the social sciences section, I think.

Simon: What, in the main library?

Isabella: No, in the faculty library, next door.

Simon: Everyone'll try to borrow that copy!

Isabella: Well, don't forget you can access an electronic copy online. Have you registered with the journals website?

Simon: Yeah. Hope I can remember my password!

Isabella: You have to look in a journal called Science.

Simon: OK, I'll make a note of that, but did he say it's available in Intelligence, too?

Isabella: Oh, yes. I think so.

Simon: OK. So, are you going to Wednesday's lecture on attachment theory?

Isabella: Definitely, but first there's the lecture tomorrow on infant development. We have to attend that for our research.

Simon: You're right, I forgot. What time's that lecture?

Isabella: Oh, I can't remember. Eleven, perhaps?

Simon: Hold on. I'll check in the timetable. Yeah, you're right … and it finishes at twelve fifteen.

🔊 1.33 page 31 exercise 10

Simon: So, Isabella, you're the oldest child in your family. Would you say you're more intelligent than your brother?

Isabella: Well, me and my brother are both students, but ... he went to a better university so I think he's cleverer.

Simon: Really? I don't think you can say that. Perhaps he's at a better university because he studies harder ...

🔊 1.34 page 31 exercise 12

Simon: So, Isabella, you're the oldest child in your family. Would you say you're more intelligent than your brother?

Isabella: Well, me and my brother are both students, but ... he went to a better university so I think he's cleverer.

Simon: Really? I don't think you can say that. Perhaps he's at a better university because he studies harder.

Isabella: Yes, but I think you can become more intelligent if you study hard, like the research said.

Simon: Yes, that's true. Anyway, I think you're probably as clever as him, but you're intelligent in different ways.

Isabella: I don't think so, but I'm definitely better at choosing clothes!

Simon: So why don't you study as hard as him?

Isabella: I think it's because I'm just not that interested in studying, and my family don't expect me to be successful.

Simon: I have a different theory. I think younger children choose to do different things from their siblings because they don't want to compete with them.

Isabella: Hmm. Maybe that's true for a few people, but I know lots of siblings who do similar hobbies. Anyway, I think there are other things that affect your behaviour a lot more – parents, for example. I think if your parents go to a good university, you will, too.

Simon: OK. I think I agree with you there. Oh, by the way, I meant to ask you about your notes from last week's lecture ...

🔊 1.35 page 33 Exam tip

There are three main parts to an essay question – each of which has a different function. First, the main topic gives the general area to discuss. Second, the issue tells you how you should discuss it, for example, looking at what should be done. Third and probably most important, the instruction tells you what type of essay you actually need to write, for example, to show agreement or disagreement. If you ignore or misunderstand the instruction, then you won't answer the question properly and you'll get a low mark.

🔊 1.36 page 34 Exam tip

Scanning is a reading strategy you can use when looking for specific information such as a word, number, or name. It's common in real life – think about how you scan a TV guide to see what's on at a certain time, the sports results to look for your favourite team, or a timetable to see when a train or bus is due to leave. It's also useful for questions requiring short answers in the Reading test.

🔊 1.37 page 39 exercise 8

There is a lot of household waste.
There are a lot of traffic jams.

🔊 1.38 page 39 Exam tip

In Speaking Part 2, you may have to talk about a problem you have experienced, and what the causes and effects of this problem are. Also, you'll probably be asked to say what you have done to resolve it. For example, when talking about the causes and effects of problems in the environment (such as too much household waste), you might be asked to say what you personally do or could do to help the situation (such as recycle more efficiently).

🔊 1.39 page 40 Exam tip

When you're preparing to listen, it helps to underline 'key words' in the questions and sentences. Key words are basically the words with the most meaning, so usually nouns and verbs rather than 'small' words like prepositions and articles. You can also quickly try to think of similar words or synonyms that might be used to describe the same thing. This can help you to notice when a topic is mentioned in a listening.

🔊 1.40 page 40 exercise 6

Part 1

OK, so in today's lecture we're going to look at the causes and effects of deforestation. Well, we all know what deforestation is ... but why does it happen? Well, firstly, trees are cut down for a variety of purposes, but generally it's because people need to earn money or to grow food for their family. Typically, farmers take a small area to produce plants or to feed their animals. The number of these small areas combined is what has such a negative impact on the forest itself. The main reason for deforestation, therefore, is the need for agricultural land and not because companies take trees for wood, as is often thought. But this does not mean that logging companies don't play a part. They provide the world's wood and paper products, and cut down large numbers of trees each year. Loggers, some of them acting illegally, also build roads to access remote forests – which leads to, well, further deforestation. Not only that but forests are also cut down as a result of expanding towns and cities. I should add, however, that not all deforestation is intentional – it's also caused by chance when fires destroy vegetation. I'm sure you've heard about examples of destructive forest fires that happen every summer all round the world ...

🔊 1.41 page 41 exercise 7

Part 2

Right, before we look at the effects of deforestation on wildlife, let's consider why wildlife is so important to us. So firstly, how many species of wildlife are there on Earth? Well, it's difficult to say exactly. Scientists have already identified nearly 2 million individual species, and even conservative estimates suggest that more than 9 million remain undiscovered! But the planet's amazing variety of life is more than just something for academics to study; humans depend on it. For example, farmers rely on worms, bacteria, and other organisms to break down organic waste and keep soil high in nitrogen levels – processes that are important to agriculture. Pharmaceutical companies use a wide range of different species to create medication ... and many more breakthroughs could still be undiscovered in Earth's unknown species. However, a stable food supply and a source for pharmaceuticals are only a couple of the benefits that Earth's biodiversity provides. The next point I'd like to make connects biodiversity to the planet as a whole. It does this by, well, Earth's plant life reduces the effect of global warming by absorbing carbon dioxide, yet 90% of those plants depend on the nearly 190,000 species of insects to keep them alive. Scientists from Cornell University in the US actually calculated the value of the different services that Earth's plants and animals provide. They arrived at a grand total of $2.9 trillion – and that was back in 1997. So, what issues does the threat to biodiversity cause? Well, global warming is increasingly forcing species away from their natural environment in search of better, er, more suitable temperatures, and scientists fear that not all species will survive climate change. Overhunting, which famously led to the extinction of the dodo, of course, and the passenger pigeon, continues to endanger larger animals like the rhino. Species like kudzu and the brown tree snake, introduced by humans to other environments, can also rapidly force native species to become extinct. In the US, invasive species cause between 125 billion and 140 billion dollars in damage every year, and are thought to have played a part in nearly half of all extinctions worldwide since the 1600s. Forests are particularly important to wildlife ...

🔊 1.42 page 41 exercise 8

Part 3

So, back to the main theme of the lecture. The greatest threat to Earth's biodiversity is deforestation. While deforestation threatens ecosystems across the globe, it's particularly destructive to tropical rainforests. In terms of Earth's biodiversity, rainforests are hugely important; though they cover only 7% of the Earth's surface, they are home to more than half the world's species. Through logging, mining, and farming, humans destroy approximately 2% of the Earth's rainforests every year, often damaging the soil so badly in the process that the forest has a difficult time recovering. OK. As their habitats disappear, plants and animals are forced to compete with one another for the remaining space – those that can't compete become extinct. In recent history, deforestation has led to approximately 36% of all extinctions. So, how can it be stopped? Well, deforestation is particularly difficult to stop because it has so many causes. While it's easy to blame irresponsible logging and mining companies for the destruction, their practices are in some ways a symptom of larger problems. For instance, many rainforests are located in developing countries that don't have enough resources to enforce environmental regulations. These countries also benefit greatly from the economic activity that the companies produce, making them even less likely to stop deforestation. Fortunately, hope remains for the Earth's rainforests …

◄)) 1.43 page 43 Exam tip

Always brainstorm ideas or reasons before you start writing an essay. If you don't, you may find you'll repeat the same points or think of extra, better ideas when you have no time left to write them! Of course, you don't have long to brainstorm in the test so you don't need to produce a long list. For example, for a discussion essay, try to think of three reasons for each opposing view. For a personal opinion essay, save time by deciding whether you agree or disagree before you start brainstorming! Then, try to brainstorm about five or six reasons for your view.

◄)) 1.44 page 44 Exam tip

In the test, there are many different types of passage. Three common types are problem-solution, information, and discussion, which give an author's opinion. The first paragraph often tells you the type of passage because key words or phrases show that a problem, some information, or a discussion and opinion are going to be described. If you know the type of passage, you should be able to predict its organization and, as a result, find information more quickly. For example, if a question about an information passage refers to the future, this information is usually found at the end of the passage – you can then start your search in the final paragraph.

◄)) 1.45, 1.46 page 48 exercises 2 and 3

1 Actually, I have a confession to make. I recently bought an e-reader and I soon realized that nobody can see what I'm reading. So now, I occasionally read celebrity biographies! Maybe other people do the same – who knows?

2 I often buy two or three books a day for my e-reader. Generally, if I see an advert, read a good review or a friend recommends a book, I just buy it. Sometimes the books are good; sometimes they're terrible! I know I spend a lot of money, but perhaps because they're only e-books it doesn't feel that bad.

3 Basically, I'm happy with my e-reader, but I still love my local bookshop. I regularly spend hours there at the weekend looking at all the covers. Possibly, I'll read for a while, too. But then if I like a book, I don't buy it at the shop – I just go to the shop's café and download a cheap, digital copy.

◄)) 1.47 page 48 Exam tip

Using adverbs correctly can really improve your grammar and vocabulary. In Speaking Part 1, you can add adverbs like *sometimes* and *usually* to say how often you personally do something. In Speaking Part 3 – where the ideas discussed are more complicated – you can use adverbs like *maybe* or *perhaps* to show you're not certain about something. In all parts of the Speaking test, you can put adverbs like *actually* or *generally* at the beginning of sentences to make your ideas seem clearer and more natural.

◄)) 1.48 page 49 exercise 10

1 I often drink coffee when I read.

2 I often drink coffee when I read.

◄)) 1.49 page 50 Exam tip

On plans and maps, there's a lot to look at and it's sometimes difficult to find all the question numbers. As well as making sure you find the gaps for all the questions, check the instructions to see if you have to write a letter or a word. Then, in the 30 seconds you have to prepare, use your knowledge of similar places to predict the ones on the plan or map.

◄)) 1.50 page 50 exercise 6

Welcome to the Pitt Lane Theatre. Here we are outside the main entrance. To the right, you can see the ticket office. As we enter the theatre, on your right you'll see a cloakroom and in the middle of the foyer there's a snack bar. If you need the toilets, they're on the left. When you're ready, go straight on, across the foyer and opposite you'll see a door into the main auditorium. Through this and in front of you there's the stage. Turn to your left and you'll see the seating area and on the other side you'll see the fire exit.

◄)) 1.51 page 51 exercise 8

OK, so let's look at the map. Er … The Other Stage is at the far side of the festival area. Now we're camping in Spring Field, here, so we're lucky because that's right next to the pedestrian gate. You need to go through that and then straight on down the track. OK? On your right, you'll pass a property locker if that's useful to you for storing your stuff. There are also a couple of ATMs – erm, here they are. Then eventually you'll come to the market area – that's the big square section in the middle of the map, just here. It's really easy to get lost because there are so many stalls and things to look at, but don't worry because there's a meeting point just to the right of it. Can you see? OK, so you need to continue to the opposite corner of this area, around the track past the main arena. There you'll find the charging tent – useful if your mobile battery dies. Anyway, just behind that you'll see The Other Stage, though you'll probably hear it first! We'll be there all afternoon so come and find us. We usually sit somewhere near the back of the field, sort of here, away from the stage and close to the medical centre. Call or text me once you get there! OK?

◄)) 1.52 page 52 Exam tip

Before you start writing your essay, it's important to write a plan with paragraph topics. Choosing good paragraph topics will help you to organize your ideas clearly and avoid repetition. Each topic you choose must be different from the others, but general enough for you to add examples and explanations in the paragraph. Look for points in your brainstorm that you could group together in one category and try to think of labels like 'social', 'economic', or 'cultural' that connect them.

◄)) 1.53 page 54 Exam tip

Some matching questions in the Reading test ask you to look for specific information. To do this, you'll need to scan the passage to identify which paragraph contains the information. Before you actually start looking, underline all the key words in the questions and then decide which key word to look for first in the passage. Proper nouns, like people's names, and dates are usually easiest to find. Once you've located the word or idea you're looking for, read that part of the passage carefully to make sure that there are synonyms for all the key language in the question.

◄)) 1.54 page 59 Exam tip

Varying your language helps you to get a higher mark for vocabulary and grammar. In Speaking Parts 1 and 3, the different questions you're asked usually give you the chance to demonstrate different language. However, during the 2 minutes of Part 2 it's less easy to keep your language varied because there aren't as many questions. Try to show variety by using different parts of speech or grammar structures, like a passive or conditional sentence.

◄)) 1.55 page 60 exercise 5

Anna: Sam, hi. How's it going?

Sam: Good. Anna, guess what! I've been offered that job!

Anna: Congratulations! Great news!

Sam: I know, I know. But I haven't accepted it yet.

Anna: Oh. Why not?

Sam: Well, actually … I just wanted to ask what you think about conditions.

Anna: OK. So what are they offering?

Sam: Well, it's a full-time position – working 40 hours a week – but they say I'll be expected to do a couple of hours' overtime most days, which isn't paid.

Anna: Mmm, that doesn't sound so good.

Sam: I know, but the salary is quite good. I get £25,000 a year and there's a profit-related bonus of up to £5,000. After one year, I'll get a 10% pay rise, too.

Anna: That is good. What about the other conditions? How much responsibility will you have?

Sam: Well, at first I won't be in charge of anyone. But if things go well and I get a promotion, I'll be responsible for a team of six people.

Anna: Wow! Great!

Sam: Yes, but some of the other benefits don't seem so great. I only get 20 days' holiday and there are no flexitime arrangements – we have to be in the office from 9.00 to 5.00 every day. I'd like to be able to finish early some days, say at 3.00.

Anna: Hmm. OK.

Sam: So, do you think I should take it?

Anna: Well, it's a difficult one. I think it depends on whether time or money is more important to you at the moment. You know, if I were you …

🔊 1.56 page 60 exercise 7

1 Forms have to be filled in.

2 Earning money is a priority for most students when their courses finish.

3 The hard-working employees have free use of a lovely gym and a subsidized restaurant.

🔊 1.57 page 60 Exam tip

When you complete notes from a recording, make sure you read the notes before you listen. While you read them, think about possible answers and possible types of words that could fill each gap. It's very important that you do this before the recording starts, because it's hard to read, listen, and write at the same time! The sentences that you hear will be different from the sentences that you read, so don't listen for the exact sentences on your paper.

🔊 1.58 page 60 exercise 9

Student: Hi. I'm interested in graduate places at Sterne Consulting. Can I ask you some questions?

Representative: Sure. Are you graduating this year?

Student: That's right. I'm graduating in Business and Management.

Representative: OK – excellent. What grade do you think you'll get?

Student: Well, what grade do I need to apply to your company?

Representative: You need at least 65% when you come to do your final exams.

Student: OK, that should be fine. I hope I'm going to get a first-class honours, which is over 70%. Is there anything else that can help my application?

Representative: It's always an advantage to do a part-time graduate course. It helps if you've already booked or started one before you apply.

Student: OK, I'll look into that. How many positions do you have?

Representative: Quite a lot. We have twenty-five positions available but we actually get over 500 applications.

Student: I know it's a trainee position but could I ask some questions about basic conditions?

Representative: Of course.

Student: Do trainees work full-time or do we go to college as well?

Representative: It's full-time, so you have to work quite hard. Any extra study is done in your own time.

Student: Can I ask about conditions now? What's the starting pay like?

Representative: The basic salary is quite high at £30,000, but we don't pay a bonus or commission at first. You may not be interested in this yet, but there's also a good company pension scheme.

Student: How many days off do employees get?

Representative: Usually twenty days' holiday a year.

Student: And what other benefits do you provide?

Representative: Well, it depends on the office you work in. There's a staff restaurant in all our office locations and an onsite gym that you pay nothing for.

Student: Great. What training do you provide?

Representative: Well, for graduate places there's an extensive training programme in your first year. We train you to use a range of computer software and we teach you a range of skills from time management to negotiating.

Student: OK, great. So what should I do next?

Representative: Well, the best thing is to leave us your email and I'll send you a link to our online application …

🔊 1.59 page 61 exercise 10

Representative: So you're thinking of becoming a teacher?

Student: Yes, but I'd like to find out a bit more about the training course and the long-term job prospects first.

Representative: OK. So what would you like to know?

Student: Well, firstly, what happens on the training course?

Representative: It's a mixture of learning theory at college, but for a lot of the time you'll have to go out of college and teach in real classrooms. In fact, you'll work in four during the year.

Student: How long do you work in each classroom?

Representative: It varies, but generally it's between two and six weeks.

Student: What happens afterwards?

Representative: You go back to college, reflect on the experience, and continue your theory work.

Student: How are we assessed during the course?

Representative: Some of the grades come from watching you teach and the other half are based on essays you write.

Student: What do people find the hardest?

Representative: It's different for everyone, but for most people it's controlling the children. They can be quite unkind to new teachers.

Student: What are the benefits like?

Representative: The salary isn't high compared to other postgraduate positions but you do get twelve weeks holiday every year, including six weeks in the summer, and a good pension when you finish.

Student: OK, thank you. Could I take a brochure?

Representative: Of course. Please do.

🔊 1.60 page 62 Exam tip

The first sentence in each paragraph of an essay is often a topic sentence. It contains the main idea of the paragraph and should connect to your thesis statement. For example, if you give your opinion in the thesis statement, each topic sentence should give a reason for this opinion. Or, if you say you're going to discuss an argument, each topic sentence should introduce one side of the argument. If you say you're going to explain causes or effects, each topic sentence should state a cause or effect. Note that each point in your plan should become a topic sentence.

🔊 1.61 page 64 Exam tip

Finding topic sentences is a very important skill. They're usually located near the beginning of each paragraph. If you just read the topic sentences, you'll be able to understand the main ideas of the passage and, more importantly, the information that each paragraph contains.

🔊 1.62, 1.63 page 68 exercises 3 and 4

1 The weather in my part of the world is quite varied. It's humid and wet by the sea but as you move away from the coast it becomes very dry and chilly in the winter. It also changes a lot during the year. In the summer months it's really wet but then it won't rain again for the rest of the year.

2 Where I'm from, the weather is less extreme than in many parts of the world. Winters are not very cold, quite mild in fact, and summers can be relatively cool. The weather can be changeable, too – overcast and cloudy one day, with sunshine the next. It's best to be prepared. Carry an umbrella in the summer and watch out for icy roads in the winter!

3 Generally speaking, the weather where I'm from is pleasant and it's sunny all year round. There's a rainy season, but rainfall varies depending which side of the island you're on. The most dangerous time is the hurricane season when it gets stormy and extremely windy in some areas.

🔊 1.64 page 68 Exam tip

In Speaking Part 2, you'll be asked to describe something, for example a place, for 2 minutes. When you're feeling nervous or under pressure, it can be difficult to think of details to talk about. Use the preparation time to try to remember things that could extend your talk. One way you could do this is to use 'The four Ss': sights, sounds, smells, and sensations. These four categories should help you to think of some interesting details.

🔊 1.65, 1.66 page 69 exercises 11 and 12

I'm going to tell you about Mount Etna in Sicily near my home town of Caltagirone. A lot of tourists go there in the summer so it can be a little chaotic then. There are always a lot of noisy tour buses taking visitors to and from the main attractions and families with children shouting, but it's a really peaceful place at other times of the year. The easiest place for tourists to travel from is one of the popular towns on the coast such as Taormina, which is an absolutely lovely resort with lots of scenic beaches and rocky bays. It takes about an hour to get to Etna from there. Anyway, when you get to the volcano, you can go right to the top if you have a guide. I recommend taking warm clothing even in the summer because it's often fairly chilly and cloudy near the top. In fact, it can be a bit disappointing if you can't see the views because of the mist, so it's worth taking a lot of photos as you walk up. You can take a cable car when you're near the top, which children love, although you see a few worried faces when the passengers go over some old, burnt cars. The volcano is still active and there can be a disgusting smell of sulphur but it's still worth going up. It sometimes erupts, too. You obviously can't climb it when that happens, but it makes the sky look colourful. It's amazing to see, especially at night, and even at a distance it makes you feel quite scared at the power of nature.

🔊 2.1 page 70 exercise 3

Part 1

Good morning. Good morning and welcome to this lecture on applied biology. Ever since the industrial revolution, people have turned away from nature in an effort to make progress. We have learnt how to burn and destroy things in nature to create energy or to engineer new materials like concrete, asphalt, and glass, with which we've covered the natural landscape. But with this violence towards nature, have we perhaps overlooked the benefits of working with nature to solve our problems? Today we'll be looking at ways in which humans are increasingly turning towards nature for a range of solutions to our everyday problems …

🔊 2.2, 2.4 pages 70 and 71 exercises 6 and 9

Part 2

OK, so I want to start by showing a good example of how we can use natural processes to replace processes that we once used chemicals for. The slide shows a diagram of a natural pool. In the centre, you can see the main swimming area. To the left of this, we have the filter zone, which is separated from the swimming area by a dividing wall. In the filter zone, the water is naturally cleaned and impurities are removed. It consists of silver or copper beads and rocks, with water plants above them on the surface. A pump, seen on the right of the diagram, draws water in a circular motion around the pool. It first flows to the left, then downwards through the filter zone, and then back to the right below the pool bottom. It is then pumped into a UV filter, seen in the top right corner of the diagram, which kills harmful bacteria. The water then flows out over a waterfall, which adds oxygen to it, and into the swimming area once again. Meanwhile, surface leaves and debris are removed by a machine called a skimmer, which is on the left of the diagram. This basically clears the unwanted material by sucking it out. And there you have it – the natural swimming pool. I'm sure you'll agree, it sounds a lot more pleasant than swimming pools you're used to. Of course, the idea of using nature to purify and clean is nothing new, but natural pools are only now becoming popular …

🔊 2.3 page 71 exercise 8

hillside   cliff edge   ice storm
windbreak   pothole   sea eagle

🔊 2.5 page 71 Exam tip

In Listening Section 4, you have to label diagrams and you'll hear a lot of technical words. Quite often you'll hear words that you haven't heard before. If this happens, don't panic! Many of the words will be compound nouns – words made from two (or more) other words. Even if you don't understand the meaning of a particular compound noun, you should know the individual words that make it up. Listen carefully to the whole word and try to recognise smaller, individual words, using the context to help you to guess. The words in less common compound nouns are usually written separately.

🔊 2.6 page 71 exercise 10

Part 3

Something new and exciting is now happening in biotechnology – and this is the idea of taking ideas from nature and copying them, a process called biomimicry. So, why copy nature? Surely we've advanced beyond what nature can do? Well, let's consider this for a moment. Nature has existed for millions and millions of years, and over this time it's evolved and adapted to survive and be successful in extreme environments. In short, we have around us millions of solutions to survival problems. One good example is the termite mound.

You can see a diagram on this slide here. Termites – these tiny creatures – have learnt to create a comfortable home in some of the world's toughest climates. Outside, in the African savannah the temperatures vary from forty degrees in the day to one degree at night. Yet, inside the mound, the temperature stays constant. How? Well, let's have a closer look. To the left of the diagram, the arrows represent wind pressure that forces air into the mound and makes currents of air flow around the radial channel. Meanwhile at various points of the mound there are small vents through which water evaporates, cooling the structure.

Let's look at the middle section now, and we'll see a large space, which is the nest. Inside, at the top of this area, the termites look after their fungus gardens, which are their main food source. Below the nest area, and connected to the radial channels, is the cellar. Interestingly, the termites carry nothing out of their nest so they have found a way of recycling or removing all the waste that must be produced here. Above the nest is a long structure, a central chimney through which warm air currents rise up and leave the nest.

Throughout the whole mound you can see a network of lateral tunnels that give the mound a strong structure and also channel air. The termites constantly work to open and close off these tunnels and modify the airflow and keep the temperature of the nest constant. Already architects have tried to copy the structures identified in the mound to create tall buildings that require no additional energy to heat or cool. Perhaps one day all buildings will have a similar structure …

🔊 2.7 page 71 exercise 11

Part 4

But of course there are millions of other species that we could learn from, too. Water will be one of the biggest challenges in the future. There are organisms that pull water out of the air such as the Namibian beetle, which manages to extract water from fog. Wouldn't it be amazing if we could create artificial beetles with the same properties? Research is currently under way to do just that. While we're on the subject, another fascinating insect is the locust. There can be 80 million of them in a single square kilometre, but they don't crash into each other. We have a similar number of cars in the whole world yet we have 3.6 million car collisions a year! Scientists are trying to copy the neurons that help the locusts to navigate. Copying shapes is interesting, too. Scientists have noticed that whales have small bumps on their fins. By putting similar bumps on the wings of airplanes, they've been able to increase efficiency by about 32%, which saves a lot of fuel. There are also bumps on the underside of lotus leaves that help keep them clean. Paint manufacturers have already invented a paint that uses this design to help keep walls clean every time it rains. The list is endless and there's almost limitless potential. I hope you're beginning to appreciate what an exciting area applied biology can be …

🔊 2.8 page 73 Exam tip

Make sure your paragraphs are well structured. What this means is that the sentences are all connected logically. A main idea is given first in the topic sentence, and then other sentences in the paragraph support the idea of the topic sentence, providing explanation or examples. Your examples might include causes and effects, depending on the essay question. Make sure everything is directly related to the topic sentence and doesn't go too far from the main point of the paragraph.

🔊 2.9 page 74 Exam tip

In *True / False / Not Given* questions, you have to compare several statements with information in the reading passage. The *Not Given* option can make this type of question confusing. This is because *Not Given* doesn't mean *Not True* – instead, it means that a statement could be *True* or *False*. Also, *Not Given* doesn't always mean that the information is not mentioned. Information related to *Not Given* options may sometimes be in the passage but it won't be similar enough to decide if the answer is *True* or *False*.

🔊 2.10 page 79 Exam tip

In Speaking Part 3, you can be asked a wide range of question types related to the topic in Part 2. For example, you may be asked to predict, evaluate, speculate, or compare. Other questions may require you to talk about change, give opinions, explain, or hypothesize. The different questions will give you the opportunity to show you can use different grammar structures, vocabulary, and phrases. This is why you need to practise listening for certain types of question and prepare phrases that you could use for each type.

2.11, 2.12 page 79 exercises 9 and 10

1 How are town centres likely to change in the next ten years?
2 Which products make us the happiest?
3 Is it better to save money or spend it? Why?
4 Why do people buy things they don't need?
5 How are shopping habits of men different from those of women?
6 What products are the most difficult to buy?
7 What will happen if levels of consumption continue to rise?
8 Some people say we should give children fewer gifts. Why is that?

2.13 page 81 Exam tip

In addition to basic multiple-choice questions, you may have to choose more than one option from a list. This can be difficult because sometimes the answers may not be mentioned in order. For this reason, you should consider all the options on the list as you listen. As usual, preparation is important. Make sure you read all the options before the recording starts and underline key words that you should listen for.

2.14 page 81 exercise 8

Part 1

Tutor: So, how did the preparation go? I think I asked you to do the materialism survey.
Julie: Yes, it was fine.
Ben: Yes, OK.
Tutor: Perhaps you're both wondering why I gave you the survey to do. Well, similar questions have been used in research to find out how materialistic we are. Later we'll look at the survey in more detail but first we need to discuss some related themes. Now, can one of you explain what we mean by 'materialism'?
Julie: Yes, er, it's about how much stuff we buy.
Tutor: Partly, Julie, yes, it's about how we value our ownership of things. Now, why do you think sociologists are interested in this?
Julie: They want to find out what motivates us.
Tutor: OK, but individual motivation is more a question for psychologists who study how our brains work. How could materialism affect society generally?
Ben: Maybe it's related to happiness.
Tutor: OK, go on, Ben.
Ben: Er, well, I think materialism is a social thing – it's everywhere and it probably affects our happiness generally and our social relationships.
Tutor: That's right, and sociologists have studied the connection between the objects we possess and happiness ever since we started building large shopping centres in the 1980s. Erm, I'll give you the findings of the research in a minute. In the meantime, let's hear your views. Julie, do you think materialism makes us unhappy?
Julie: No, I don't. According to that survey we did, I'm quite materialistic, but I feel happy when I buy things. People might not be happy if they don't have nice things.
Ben: But how long are you happy for? You get one thing and you just want more.
Tutor: OK, that idea has a name. It's called 'adaptation theory'. The theory basically suggests that we adapt quickly to what we have and we start wanting more.
Julie: But it's important to have some things. We can easily say possessions are not important because, basically, we're wealthy, but possessions seem a lot more valuable when you don't have any. We all need houses, a phone, a family car … and the nicer the house, the better! Who wants to live in a bad area?
Tutor: That's all true. But perhaps it's not so much about the house itself as about our basic need for security or freedom. We all have basic needs, but that's not the same as wanting more and more possessions.
Julie: OK, so what does make us happy, then?

2.15 page 81 exercise 9

Part 2

Ben: I think happiness is about people.
Julie: Yes, I agree but that's my point. People want to know you when you have nice stuff. If I had a pool in my garden, an outdoor bar, I'd have crowds of people coming round every night to dance and have fun. It'd be great!
Ben: Right. But then they'd go away so you'd only have a relationship with them as long as you have stuff. I think lasting relationships depend on other things.
Tutor: Such as?
Ben: Well, close relationships like you have with your family depend on the time you spend together. People work so much to get money to buy things that they sometimes never see their family.
Julie: But you want to provide your family with a nice life, don't you? Children always want toys and games.
Ben: Maybe, but I think there's a balance. When I was growing up, I had a wonderful house, nice clothes, a new phone – all that stuff – but I hardly ever saw my dad. I only saw him when he was giving me things. I think I would've preferred it if he'd worked less – you know, if we'd spent more time together, doing things.
Julie: You say that now, but I bet if I'd taken away your phone when you were younger, you would've been upset!
Ben: Yes, but only for a while whereas I still think about my dad. Memories of people stay with you forever. If you think about a holiday you went on with your parents or your latest smartphone – which one creates more important memories?
Julie: The holiday, I suppose. But are you saying happiness is about memories?

2.16 page 81 exercise 10

Part 3

Tutor: OK, well, I think it's time to look at some of the research about what makes us happy. Do you remember the research that we looked at in the last tutorial?
Ben: Yes, hang on, I think I've got something about that in my notes. Er, yes, here we are. It said that people were happiest when they're in control … and when they have good relationships with others.
Tutor: Yes, it was a little more complicated, Ben, but that's certainly a key part of it.
Julie: OK, but you can shop with other people and talk about what you bought. That's a kind of relationship.
Tutor: Er, I agree, Julie, but how do we feel when we talk about our possessions?
Ben: I think people feel bad sometimes. I mean, they don't say it, of course, but they're going to compare their things with what their friends bought.
Tutor: Mmm, yes. Research has in fact shown that people who have materialistic values often have bad relationships.
Julie: So how do researchers know who is materialistic?
Tutor: Well, think about that survey you did. In fact, look at questions 3–5. Question 3 is about being generous – that's the opposite of materialism – and question 4 is about being envious, a characteristic of materialistic people, and question 5?
Ben: That must be about how much you value your possessions.
Tutor: That's right. These researchers also did a happiness survey with the same people and the results showed that there's a strong negative correlation, or connection, between materialism and being happy. Why might that be?
Ben: Perhaps people who value possessions are worried that people will take them away from them, or they'll lose them or they won't be able to afford them in the future. Perhaps they stop trusting people.
Tutor: Yes, that could be part of it.
Julie: So are we saying that we can't buy things any more? Would it be better if we didn't have money?
Ben: No, I think you could spend it on other things, like experiences.
Tutor: All right, so why might it be better to spend your money on a holiday, for example?
Ben: Well, life experiences can be enjoyed together and shared. You aren't comparing each other, so it brings you closer together.
Julie: OK, I think I see your point. I shouldn't spend all my money on things …

2.17 page 82 Exam tip

If a Task 2 essay question asks about opinions, check whether you have to write a discussion essay or personal opinion essay. This is important because they require different approaches. In a discussion essay, you should give a balanced response, by giving one view and then the opposite view. You can give your own personal opinion in the conclusion, but it's not required by the task. In a personal opinion essay, on the other hand, you must make your own opinion clear, right from the introduction. Then, in the body section, you focus on giving reasons for your opinion and, perhaps, reasons why the opposite view is wrong.

2.18 page 84 Exam tip

In order to understand the main idea of a passage, you don't always need to read the complete passage. Often, you need to read just the topic sentences of each paragraph. This strategy is particularly useful for questions where you choose the best heading or questions where you complete a summary. But it can also help you to predict the missing word for a gap or help you to find the paragraph of a passage that contains the most useful information.

2.19 page 89 Exam tip

In Speaking Part 2, you may be asked to describe a series of events or, in other words, to 'narrate'. For example, you may be asked to describe something that happened to you or something that you saw. This provides a good opportunity to use a range of regular and irregular past tenses. A good way to give background to your narrative is by using the past continuous tense, as in I was walking down the street near my home when … . You can then continue with the past simple tense to describe what happened.

2.20 page 89 exercise 11

discovered, reported, crashed, arrived, screamed, visited, attacked, survived, worked, rescued, posted, photographed

2.21 page 90 exercise 7

1 The main square's got a lovely fountain.
2 Does the gallery open at nine?
3 Let's look around that new mall.
4 You can take a photo of the harbour.

2.22 page 90 Exam tip

In the Listening test, you often have to write down individual words that you hear. This is difficult because, in natural spoken English, the words in a sentence often seem 'connected' together. You can't easily hear where one word ends and another begins! Also, the sound of the individual words sometimes changes when they're spoken with others. This means you might not recognize them. With practice, however, you can improve your ability to recognize individual words and work out which are important.

2.23 page 90 exercise 8

1 It's a really great town.
2 You'll soon see history's everywhere.
3 Is that the war monument?

2.24 page 91 exercise 9

Hi, I'm Aimee and this is my audio diary. I'm in Mexico City now. From where I'm standing, I can see the grand Monument to the Revolution, in Plaza de la República. Anyway, I think it's really worth coming here. I just love the life in the streets – everyone's so busy. There are lots of street vendors, families and young people walking around. I adore the many bright colours of the buildings, as well – they're pretty. The churches are beautiful, too, and have some really nice statues inside. There are some interesting things I've learnt about the city. One of the most fascinating facts is that it's sinking! If you look up at the skyline, you'll see the many towers are not completely straight. It looks really strange but apparently it's because Mexico City was constructed on a salt lake. Builders and conservationists are constantly trying to limit the effects. Anyway, there are many good ways to get around the city. Today, I'm travelling on a tour bus. I really recommend it and it stops at all the best tourist sights. And when you're tired of the city, which won't be soon, there are many options for further travel. Tomorrow, I'm going on a two-hour flight to Cancún. I'm really looking forward to dancing in the great clubs and spending time on the fantastic golden beaches!

2.25 page 91 exercise 10

Thank you for downloading this audio guide. We hope you'll enjoy your visit to Dubrovnik. First of all, if you're travelling by plane, don't miss out on the wonderful views as you fly past Dubrovnik to land. Try to book a seat on the left-hand side of the plane because then you'll get the best views of Dubrovnik itself as you head along the coast towards the airport. You will also get great views of all the islands along the coast. When you arrive at the airport a bus should be waiting to take you to the city. You can enjoy a coffee in the airport café while you're waiting. When you reach Dubrovnik, get off the bus at the stone pillar gate, a big archway at the western end of the city walls. Once through that, you'll be in the old city. Now, you can walk along the plaza, a walkway that takes you through the old town, which is lined on each side with two-storey mansions with Venetian-style shutters. You'll see the 16th-century church of St Saviour on the left and then you'll soon come to the ancient Onofrio's fountain where they say you can drink the clean water. At the end of the street you will find Luza Square. If you need accommodation, there are plenty of private apartments in this area. As you'll see, there are no cars at all along the streets, and it's worth spending an hour or two enjoying the chatter of voices, the live jazz, and the noise of the swallows as they sing and fly between the old buildings. The place has quite a sleepy feel to it and, in fact, there aren't many lively cafés but, later, the place does come to life a little bit …

2.26 page 91 exercise 11

In this section of the guide, we'll suggest some places to visit. First, we recommend going to a lovely little gallery called War Photo Limited. This small gallery is ranked the third most popular tourist attraction in Dubrovnik. Go inside and you'll see a small exhibition that tells you much about the city's recent history. Opposite the gallery, there's a coffee bar that remained open during the war at the end of the twentieth century and also shows interesting photos of the period. After that, we recommend going to the old city walls. Climb the steps and you can enjoy the view out across to the green islands and the sailing boats. The walk along the walls is about 2 kilometres. One of the first things you'll see standing tall over the city is the beautiful clock tower. Next, for a little trip, why not go to the harbour and enjoy a 10-minute ferry boat ride to the quiet island of Lokrum? There, you can sit in the public gardens and enjoy the view of the beautiful old harbour. Later in the evening, if you like to party, there's a popular club on the beach where you can dance until the early hours of the morning …

2.27 page 93 Exam tip

In a conclusion, you should include a summary of your main points and a sentence that directly answers the question – even if you've already stated this in the thesis statement. You may also wish to include a personal comment that's not connected to the essay question but which is relevant to the essay topic. This could be a prediction about the future – in an essay about energy use, for example, you could predict how people's lives might change.

2.28 page 94 Exam tip

Yes / No / Not Given questions are different to True / False / Not Given questions. Yes / No / Not Given questions test your ability to identify opinions rather than facts. You can often find the author's main opinion in the final paragraph. Understanding this can help you to predict or guess whether they agree with the statements in Yes / No / Not Given questions.

2.29 page 99 exercise 8

In the past, the population was much smaller than today and I think people used to have larger homes. However, the standard of accommodation didn't use to be so high. Lots of people shared bathrooms and many people didn't have electricity …

Our country didn't use to export much and now it sells things to the whole world. This has meant that workers earn more money than they used to and the standard of living has generally gone up …

2.30 page 99 exercise 10

In the past, people didn't use to use cars and they used to walk more.

2.31 page 99 exercise 12

A: How have people's lives changed in your country?
B: My family are richer. My father made some good investments and we have a much nicer house now. It also means I can go to private school and have a lot of holidays.
A: Do you think people are more or less satisfied with their life?
B: More, probably. Yes, more.

A: Is pollution more of a problem today than in the past?

B: Definitely. As a result, lots of people look to leave our country now. They study abroad or, as soon as they can, they get a job in another country. People didn't use to emigrate so much.

🔊 **2.32 page 99 Exam tip**

In Speaking Part 3, the questions are sometimes complicated so it's important you listen carefully and answer the question you're actually asked. Unlike in Part 1, you can ask the examiner for clarification if you don't understand. Try to remember some phrases to help you, and begin your question with *Sorry* or *Sorry, but* to sound more natural.

🔊 **2.33 page 99 exercise 13**

1 Sorry, but what do you mean by *community*?
2 Please could you rephrase the question?
3 Sorry, I'm not sure what you mean.

🔊 **2.34 page 100 exercise 2**

It's amazing how readily the public accept some things as facts. Take, for example, the commonly held idea that a coin dropped from a great height might kill someone. While people may think a coin dropped from a tall building would pick up enough speed to kill a person on the ground, this just isn't true. The non-aerodynamic nature of a coin, as well as its relatively small size and weight, would keep this from happening. A person on the ground would most certainly feel the impact, but the coin wouldn't kill anyone ... Not so long ago, an interesting study looked at the correlation between a country's consumption of chocolate and how many Nobel prizes a country had won. It seems that in countries that have won a lot of Nobel prizes, people eat a lot of chocolate. In other words there is a strong correlation between chocolate-eating and prize-winning. However, this simple observation would need a lot more testing before a causal connection could be proved ... Finally, an idea that's been around for centuries is that a full moon can make people go mad. In fact, the English words 'lunacy' and 'lunatic' come from the word 'lunar' – connected to the moon. But despite the general consent of mythology and numerous studies, this notion has no scientific support.

🔊 **2.35 page 101 Exam tip**

A few simple steps can help you to avoid common errors in the Listening test. First, it's important to read the instructions carefully so that you answer in the correct way. Make sure you know how many answers will be given in each recording as sometimes you'll hear the answers to more than one set or you may have to turn the page to find some of the questions. At the end of the test, you'll have time to transfer your answers to the answer sheet. Use this time to make sure that your answers fit the gaps grammatically and to check that they are spelt correctly. You can also guess any answers you weren't sure about!

🔊 **2.36 page 101 exercise 10**

Over one hundred years ago the science fiction writer H G Wells said that he believed that statistical thinking would be as important as the ability to read and write in the modern scientific and technological society. This is arguably true, but have we become good at interpreting statistics? The answer is almost certainly not.

In today's lecture, I'd like to look at some of the most common mistakes you find when people use and interpret data and we'll see why so many scientific myths are reported to us. The most common error is the confusion between 'correlation' and 'cause'. In the media, you see this a lot in reports on health studies. Typically, a scientific study indicates that whenever X happens, Y happens, too. This is called 'correlation'. But by the time it's reported in the media the story has become that X is the cause of Y. But just because two things occur together, it doesn't mean that one caused the other, even if a cause and effect relationship seems to make sense.

Let's take an example. People have often held the belief that there's a connection with success in elementary school and eating breakfast. We are perhaps therefore led to believe that eating a healthy breakfast causes students to be more successful. However, other factors are coming into play here, as students not eating breakfast also often missed classes or were late. So arguably, it could be the lateness or the absence that affects performance rather than missing breakfast. On retesting the idea, it was found that, when other factors were left out, eating breakfast only helped those who were not eating enough in the first place.

How, then, do scientists establish cause when they do experiments? Let's say we want to prove that eating five portions of fruit and vegetables a day lowers the risk of cancer. We have to make sure that other factors such as physical activity, hours of sleep, and genetic make-up play no part. Researchers do this through a controlled study, a method of research in which two similar groups of people are exposed to two different conditions. Once we do this, we can then compare the outcome for differences. Any significant difference could be related to the conditions as the groups were relatively similar.

Unfortunately, controlled studies still have a number of limitations. The first is ethics. It would be problematic to make one group of people smoke and to force someone addicted to smoking not to smoke, and in fact laws stop scientists from doing such studies. There's also the issue of paying enough people to take part in the study for a long enough time to make the study meaningful. The sample size has to be large and the experimental condition has to last a long time, creating great expense. Plus, of course, there may not be enough people who are genetically similar to create a large enough group to study.

There are many other sources of error and these are listed on your handouts, but there's one further problem I'd like to discuss now and that's a lack of critical thinking on the part of the people reporting the data. This issue is becoming more and more serious as journalists with poor statistical training increasingly attempt to deal with data. Furthermore, journalists are under ever-growing pressure to write interesting articles, and so they may take a number or a set of data and make their own interpretation quickly without thinking carefully.

One recent example of poor critical thinking comes from a statistic related to depression in England. Two leading newspapers reported that the number of prescriptions for anti-depressant drugs had gone up significantly and concluded that this also meant that the number of depressed people must have risen as well. In fact, the number of depressed people could be exactly the same. It's probably true that doctors are simply writing more frequent prescriptions to the same people but that each prescription is for a lower quantity of medication. And of course, when journalists make mistakes, the effects can be far-reaching. Take, for example, fish oil tablets. These are now the best-selling food supplement and sales have increased to around $2.5 billion after parents around the world were told by journalists that they increased academic performance.

However, what the original study actually showed was that brain activity increased when people took the tablets. Basically, they saw that parts of the brain had become more active when they looked at it in a scanner. But scientists did not confirm that this part of the brain was connected to school results. In fact, results of the academic tests showed that concentration and test results did not improve at all and later tests have proved that the connection isn't significant. The problem is that it takes time for scientists to disprove such claims and when they do their evidence is often not reported in the media because it's less interesting than the myth. And this of course means that the myth continues to persist.

🔊 **2.37 page 103 Exam tip**

When you describe a process, try to include an 'overview statement'. This is difficult because it requires a different approach to how you write an overview statement for describing data. With a process, there's no mention of trends, numbers, or possibly no comparisons. Instead, try to comment on a feature of the process as a whole that makes it interesting. For example, it may be particularly complex or have a surprisingly large number of stages.

🔊 **2.38 page 105 Exam tip**

You may be given a series of two or more graphics and be asked to complete labels for them or to choose the correct graphic. The first thing you should do in these cases is consider how they're different. For example, one may point to a square object and another to a round object, or one will refer to a certain century and another to a different century. If you have to complete labels, first study the visual information to help you to predict answers. The missing labels will quickly tell you the type of information you need – often a number or a name. You can then scan the passage and underline sentences which contain possible answers.

OXFORD
UNIVERSITY PRESS

Great Clarendon Street, Oxford, OX2 6DP, United Kingdom

Oxford University Press is a department of the University of Oxford.
It furthers the University's objective of excellence in research, scholarship,
and education by publishing worldwide. Oxford is a registered trade
mark of Oxford University Press in the UK and in certain other countries

ISBN: 978 0 19 470530 1

Printed in China

This book is printed on paper from certified and well-managed sources

ACKNOWLEDGEMENTS

*The authors and publisher are grateful to those who have given permission to reproduce
the following extracts and adaptations of copyright material*: p.7 Literacy rates
(2 stats) from Figure 2, "What is the global distribution of adult and youth
literacy, Literacy rate by region", in *UIS Fact Sheet September 2013, No. 26*, p.3,
© UNESCO-UIS 2013. Used by permission of UNESCO. p.7 Enrolment in higher
education (1 stat), from the UNESCO Institute for Statistics website about the
Global level of tertiary students, http://www.uis.unesco.org/Education/Pages/
international-student-flow-viz.aspx, © UNESCO-UIS 2014. Used by permission
of UNESCO. p.7 Average student to teacher ratio in primary school (1 stat)
from Table 11: "Indicators on teaching staff at ISCED levels 0 to 3", from the
UNESCO Institute for Statistics website, http://data.uis.unesco.org/(Education,
Human Resources, Pupil-teacher ratio), © UNESCO-UIS. Used by permission
of UNESCO. p.7 Number of educators (4 stats) from Section 2, "Secondary
school teachers, the learning environment and education quality" in the
Global Education Digest 2011. Comparing Education Statistics Across the World, p.56,
© UNESCO-UIS 2011. Used by permission of UNESCO. p.10 Adapted extract
from "Private Tutoring: how prevalent and effective is it?" by Judith Ireson,
London Review of Education, Vol. 2 (2), July 2004.Reproduced by permission of
Taylor and Francis Ltd and Judy Ireson. p.12 Figure A, "Number of students (in
millions) worldwide enrolled in school from the primary to tertiary education,
1970, 2000 and 2009" in the *World Atlas of Gender Equality in Education*. p.9,
© UNESCO-UIS 2009. Used by permission of UNESCO. p.22 Extract from Table:
"Sleep" by The Schools Health Education Unit, Exeter. http://sheu.org.uk,
accessed 9 April 2014. Reproduced by permission of SHEU, The Schools and
Student Health Education Unit. p.87 "TripBarometer Reveals Travel, Green
and Mobile Trends", www.tripadvisor.co.uk. Reproduced by permission of
TripAdvisor. *p.107 Figure 1 from "Sleep Problems*: An Emerging Global Epidemic?
Findings From the INDEPTH WHO-SAGE Study Among More Than 40,000
Older Adults From 8 Countries Across Africa and Asia" by Saverio Stranges,
William Tigbe, Francesc Xavier Gómez-Olivé, Margaret Thorogood and
Ngianga-Bakwin Kandala, *Sleep*, Vol. 35 (8), 2012. Reproduced by permission of
the American Academy of Sleep Medicine. p.107 Adapted by Oxford University
Press with permission, from *Life expectancy: Life expectancy, Data by Country*,
Table "Life expectancy at birth (years), for "Both sexes", http://apps.who.int/
gho/data/node.main.688?lang=en, accessed 13 May 2014. Reproduced by
permission of World Health Organization. p.112 Figure 6.1.2, "Gains in school-
life expectancy reflected in all regions" in the *World Atlas of Gender Equality in
Education*, p.88, © UNESCO-UIS 2009. Used by permission of UNESCO. p.137
Figure 8.1.1, "Proportion of female teachers on the rise since 1990, Percentage
of Female Teachers in Primary Education 1990–2009" in the *World Atlas of
Gender Equality in Education*, p.98, © UNESCO-UIS 2009. Used by permission
of UNESCO. p.153 Adapted extract from "Emil and the Detectives: why it
is a children's classic" by Michael Rosen, *The Telegraph*, 16 November 2013.
© Telegraph Media Group Limited 2013. Reproduced by permission. p.155
Adapted extract from "Jack Lynn – obituary", *The Telegraph*, 21 November 2013.

© Telegraph Media Group Limited 2013. Reproduced by permission. p.158
Adapted extract from "Robots, the 'uncanny valley' and learning to love the
alien" by George Zarkadakis, *The Telegraph*, 25 November 2013. © Telegraph
Media Group Limited 2013. Reproduced by permission. p.167 Adapted
extract from "What's the Earth's biggest threat to biodiversity?" by Jonathan
Atteberry, HowStuffWorks.com, 25 August 2010. Reproduced by permission
of Discovery Access. p.173 Adapted extract from "Causation vs. Correlation",
www.stats.org. Reproduced by permission of Statistical Assessment Service
(STATS) at George Mason University.

Sources: p.7 www.oecd.org; p.15 www.bcf.usc.edu; p.20 www.uky.edu; p.23
www.uswitch.com; p.25 www.varsity.co.uk; p.27 http://epp.eurostat.ec.europa.
eu; p.27 www.churchill.com; p.27 www.unicef.org; p.27 2011 American
Community Survey, U.S. Census Bureau; p.35 www.theguardian.com;
p.35 http://articles.chicagotribune.com; p.35 www.about.com; p.37
www.lafoundation.org;p.44,p.68www.wikipedia.org;p.47www.prnewswire.com;
p.47 www.thephantomoftheopera.com; p.47 www.theartnewspaper.com;
p.47 http://newsdesk.si.edu p.51 www.theproducersperspective.com; p.51
www.goethe.de; p.51 www.nielsen.com; p.51 http://music.uk.msn.com;
p.57 www.careertest.com; p.64 www.dailymail.co.uk; p.77
http://comtrade.un.org;p.77http://pacinst.org;p.87www.thinkwithgoogle.com;
p.99 www.oecdbetterlifeindex.org; p.104 www.usnews.com; p.105
http://ec.europa.eu; p.105 http://www.culturalcognition.net; p.107
www.universitiesuk.ac.uk; p.108 www.harvard.edu; p.109 www.columbia.edu;
p.138 http://nccam.nih.gov; p.170 http://news.nationalgeographic.com; p.170
www.pratt.duke.edu; p.173 www.badscience.net.

The authors would like to thank:
Nick Thorner: I'd like to thank all my colleagues at Kings Education for their
ideas and expertise. In particular, thanks to Louis Rogers for his invaluable
knowledge and experience, Andrew Dilger for his patient guidance, and
Jeanette Lindsey-Clark for her support and advice. Thanks also to my dear
family, Deyaneyra, Jacob and Dora, for allowing me so much time off.
Louis Rogers: I would like to thank my co-author Nick for all his ideas and
inspiration along the way. I am grateful to Andrew Dilger for his valuable
thoughts and advice in shaping the book. As always the patience and support
of my family, Cathy, Ruby and Lenny, is much needed and appreciated.

Although every effort has been made to trace and contact copyright holders
before publication, this has not been possible in some cases. We apologize for
any apparent infringement of copyright and if notified, the publisher will be
pleased to rectify any errors or omissions at the earliest opportunity.

*The publisher would like to thank the following for their kind permission to reproduce
photographs*: Advertising Archives p.94; Alamy pp.8 (Universal Images Group/
DeAgostini), 10 (MBI), 18 (balance board/Arthur Turner), 20 (motorbike/Bailey-
Cooper Photography), 32 (tourists/imagebroker, job centre/UK Stock Images
Ltd, subway/dbimages), 38 (sewer/Des Willie, man with inhaler/Science Photo
Library, rubbish dump/Andrew Aitchison), 40 (flood/Dorset Media Service,
skilled Amazonian/Mike Goldwater), 43 social worker/Photofusion Picture
Library, environmental march/B Christopher), 52 (actors/Keith Morris, art
class/Mike Booth, orchestra/Olaf Doering), 54 (Juice Images), 68 (Buddy Mays),
69 (GFC Collection), 70 (ice axe/Steve Allen Travel Photography), 74 (red crab/
FLPA, trout/Mark Conlin), 76 (Arco Images GmbH), 78 (designer bag/Marc
Tielemans, smartphone/Marian Stanca, crisps/razorpix), 83 (Bloomington
Mall); 84 (3D printer/Richard Levine), 88 (business man/Kathy deWitt, shark/
Michael Patrick O'Neill, Mars/Universal Images Group Limited), 89 (walking/
Andrew Watson), 90 (Marble Arch/AA World Travel Library), 98 (man in car/
Aurora Photos, school children/Janine Wiedel Photolibrary), 100 (MBI);
Corbis pp.32 (man on laptop/Caterina Bernardi), 35 (Hiya Images), 50 (Chen
dsb/Imaginechina), 58 (Joma), 59 (Lynn Goldsmith), 64 (Christopher
Morris), 72 (harvesting water hyacinth/Qin Qing), 75 (Frans Lanting),
92 (Billy Ray Harris/James Breeden), 104 (HANDOUT/Reuters/Corbis); Getty
pp.25 (Goldmund Lukic), 41 (Matt Meadows), 63 (Kristian Sekulic), 97 (Hulton
Archive/woman at typewriter, Hulton Archive/RCA computer, Hulton Archive/
early TV, Hulton Archive/Trevithick's Locomotive of 1840, Lee Celano/
Wireimage/satellite radio, William Vanderson/Fox Photos/Hulton Archive/
transmission mast, OFF/AFT/world's first artificial satellite, SSPL/ballpoint
pen, SSPL/penicillin, SSPL/The Wright Brothers, Justin Sullican/vaccine,
SisterSarah/patient being given anaesthesia, Universal History Archive/
UIG/Talbot's camera, Paul McKeown/antique telephone); Chris Madden
p.12 (Statistics cartoon); Oxford University Press pp.13, 15, 19, 20 (drumming,
swimming), 23, 29, 31, 33, 40 (desert), 43 (GP), 46, 48, 55, 74 (butterfly,
elephants), 79, 86, 93, 96; Shutterstock pp.18 (watch, man, exercise bike),
20 (walking dog, chopping wood, karate, running, scuba diving), 28, 38 (obese
woman), 40 (scientist, orang-utan), 42, 43 (businessman, artist), 45, 60, 65,
70 (flippers, staircase), 72 (dam), 74 (arctic tern), 78 (chocolates, boarding pass,
washing machine), 80, 89 (solution), 90 (all except Marble Arch), 92 (ring),
98 (exercising), 103.

Illustrations by: Clear as Mud/Folio: pp.7, 57, 87; Peter Bull pp.44, 50, 51, 71,
72 (all), 88, 91, 102, 109, 111, 140, 152, 157; Richard Ponsford: pp.27, 51, 67,
98, 103, 150; Paul Weston: pp.17, 37, 47, 67, 77